evolving
dharma

Other books by Jay Michaelson

God vs. Gay? The Religious Case for Equality

Everything Is God: The Radical Path of Nondual Judaism

Another Word for Sky: Poems

*God in Your Body: Kabbalah, Mindfulness
and Embodied Spiritual Practice*

Az Yashir Moshe: A Book of Songs and Blessings

evolving
dharma

Meditation, Buddhism, and
the Next Generation of Enlightenment

JAY MICHAELSON

Berkeley, California

Published by Evolver Editions, an imprint of North Atlantic Books
P.O. Box 12327
Berkeley, California 94712

Cover art by Cryptik Movement
Book design by Mary Ann Casler
Cover design by Mary Ann Casler and Michael Robinson
Printed in the United States of America

Portions of Chapter 4: Beyond Bliss previously appeared in *Exploring the Edge Realms of Consciousness,* edited by Daniel Pinchbeck and Ken Jordan. North Atlantic Books: 2012.

Evolving Dharma: Meditation, Buddhism, and the Next Generation of Enlightenment is sponsored by the Society for the Study of Native Arts and Sciences, a nonprofit educational corporation whose goals are to develop an educational and cross-cultural perspective linking various scientific, social, and artistic fields; to nurture a holistic view of arts, sciences, humanities, and healing; and to publish and distribute literature on the relationship of mind, body, and nature.

North Atlantic Books' publications are available through most bookstores. For further information, visit our website at www.northatlanticbooks.com or call 800-733-3000.

Library of Congress Cataloging-in-Publication Data
Michaelson, Jay, 1971–
    Evolving dharma : meditation, Buddhism, and the next generation of enlightenment / Jay Michaelson.
        pages cm
Summary: "*Evolving Dharma* is a next-generation book about the contemporary meditation revolution. The work shows how meditation and mindfulness have moved from ashrams and Buddhist monasteries to boardrooms and schools, and how neuroscience is changing how we understand the human mind and how to improve it"
—Provided by publisher.
    Includes bibliographical references and index.
    ISBN 978-1-58394-714-2 (pbk.)
1. Meditation—Buddhism. I. Title.
    BQ5612.M52 2013
    294.3'444—dc23
                                2013012662

1 2 3 4 5 6 7 8 9 United 17 16 15 14 13

Printed on recycled paper

It's always the same:
once you are free,
you are forced to ask who you are.

—JEAN BAUDRILLARD

There would still remain the never-resting mind,
So that one would want to escape, come back
To what had been so long composed.
The imperfect is our paradise.
Note that, in this bitterness, delight,
Since the imperfect is so hot in us,
Lies in flawed words and stubborn sounds.

—WALLACE STEVENS,
"THE POEMS OF OUR CLIMATE"

CONTENTS

Part Three: Fruition

INTRODUCTION

The Western world is on the cusp of a major transformation around how we understand the mind, the brain, and what to
do about them. Meditation and other forms of contemplative practice, once the provenance of religion, then later of "spirituality," are
now in the American mainstream, in corporate retreats and public
schools, as a rational, proven technology to upgrade the mind and
optimize the brain, buttressed by hard scientific data and the reports of millions of practitioners.[1]

And this revolution has just begun. In 1983, there had been
only three peer-reviewed scientific studies of meditation; by 2013,
there had been more than 1,300.[2] We have the data; this technology
works. It improves memory, immune response, self control, attention, recovery from addiction, and emotional resilience.[3] And when
the data about meditation and mindfulness becomes widely known;
when it is put into practice by corporations, the health care industry,

the military, and educational institutions; and when what my friend Kenneth Folk calls "contemplative fitness" is understood to be as essential to well-being as physical fitness, this moment will be remembered as a truly transformative one.[4]

Think about it: In 1983 meditation and mindfulness were fringe phenomena among Westerners, practiced (let's face it) mostly by ex-hippies on spiritual searches. As of 2013, ten million Americans meditate regularly.[5] Yet there are one million new meditators every year, mostly in healthcare contexts. A 2007 NIH study estimated that 20 million Americans had meditated within the last twelve months, up from 15 million in 2002.[6] Meditation is taught in therapeutic contexts, to patients with chronic pain; in churches, synagogues, and community centers; and in new, alternative communities of maverick teachers, independent brainhackers, and dot-com billionaires. We truly are at a turning point.

The original source of these cognitive technologies is the *dharma,* an ancient word meaning the way, the path, or the teaching. In the most general sense, it can simply refer to the truth of how things are: the laws of the universe, and of the mind. More specifically, it is used in Pali and Sanskrit to refer to the sacred teachings of Indian sages whose traditions eventually became known as Hinduism and Buddhism. Even more specifically, "the Dharma" is the set of teachings, ideas, and practices taught by Gautama Buddha from 586–546 BCE, and by thousands of subsequent teachers and scribes.[7]

Seen from a distance, that these quite ancient traditions are on the cusp of becoming a secular mass phenomenon is really quite bizarre. What was once a monastic tradition of meditation, virtuous action, and wisdom teachings (*samadhi, sila,* and *panna*) is now, depending on where you encounter it, a technology of brainhacking; a way to build insular thickness in the brain; a way to lower stress; a mystical path filled with unusual peak experiences; a way to grow more loving, compassionate, and generous; a method to get ahead and gain an edge on your competition; or any number of other things. Love it or hate it, the dharma has evolved.

I want to tell the story of this evolution not simply because it is interesting, but because it changed my life, and it might just change the world. I've written books about religion, sexuality, and politics; I've published poetry and prose. But my own story is incomplete without the practices of meditation and mindfulness; indeed, it would have been impossible without them. Thus, this book combines third-person storytelling—interviews with some key players, scientific data, a bit of history, and a fair amount of critical analysis— and first-person testimony of a decade or so in the dharma. I want to tell you about the most glorious experiences of my life, and how I outgrew them. I want to talk about what "enlightenment" can look like, and how meditation is understood neuroscientifically, culturally, even politically. This is a story of monks and soldiers; a history as well as a tale told from my own cultural position, conditioned by my age, gender, class, race, sexual orientation, and all the rest; a narrative of maverick teachers, online communities, Occupy, self-loathing, stress reduction, religion, sex, power, and Google.

Some of these stories are heretical in much of the meditation world today. For traditionalists, the dharma does not evolve; it is perfect, it is complete, it is timeless wisdom whose application may vary but whose essence does not. And for many Westerners, it may be equally heretical to recall that meditation did indeed start out in highly nonsecular contexts, that the practitioners of it were meant to evolve themselves, and that some of those evolutions might be the exact opposite of the cliché of the tranquil bliss promised in magazine ads. Well, these dogmas are wrong. The dharma has evolved for 2,500 years, at no time faster than in the last thirty, and it's either quaint or fundamentalist to pretend otherwise. And while attaining merit badges is not the purpose of meditation practice, it is also the case that this is a path, and paths lead to places, some of which are beautiful, and some of which are dark.

I hope that the greatest heresy of this book, though, is not substantive as much as stylistic. In the last fifty years, as meditation has become widely practiced in the United States, many if not most books about mindfulness and meditation practice come from a specific socio-cultural-economic background: the Boomers, usually those folks pushing sixty who lived through Woodstock and Watergate, and who, yes, changed the world, and thanks for that, but also, well, come from a set of socio-cultural-economic backgrounds that often don't resonate with those of us who don't share them. There's often a fear of irony in this literature, an affected gentleness that can be soothing or irritating, depending on your point of view. I'm not here to bash my teachers; if it weren't for their pioneering efforts in adapting the dharma to American life, I and millions of other people would never have encountered it. But we are all of our time and place, and I want to proceed authentically from a rather different context, style, and position.

Several years ago, when I was hiking in the Jordanian desert basin known as Wadi Rum, there was a mountain that seemed to be perched right on the horizon—a mountain at the edge of the Earth. Of course I knew that was only an appearance, but I was drawn to it anyway, and walked far out into the desert to approach it. By the time I reached the mountain, I saw that it was not perched at the edge of the world, but that beyond it lay still more mountains, stretched out under empty sky. What I thought was the end of the path was, in fact, more of the path. The scenery had changed. But after a couple of hours of desert hiking, my perspective had changed also. I had set off looking for the One Big Mountain, but as the path evolved, the goals evolved; I evolved.

When I started out in contemplative practice, I was searching for the mountain on the edge of the world: enlightenment, the big joy, *sat-chit-ananda,* mystical union, the whole spiritual enchilada of love, wisdom, happiness, perfection. With that aspiration, and with varying degrees of clarity and confusion, I've sat in silence for months at a time, grown long beards, and overcome a fair number of personal demons. I've traveled to Nepal, Peru, Mount Sinai, and far less exotic places in Massachusetts and California. And while I am hardly fully enlightened, I've made a bit of progress, according to my quite traditional monastic teachers, and according to the way

I seem to myself, my family, and my friends. And, surprise surprise, this particular mountain isn't at the edge of the world either; it's right in the middle of it, just like the sages, hippies, and pop songs have promised. The only difference is that my amygdala no longer drowns out my left prefrontal cortex. In other words, I am happy.

So, then, this is a story with many shapes: historical, conceptual, cultural, and personal. It's structured according to the three-part framework found in some schools of Tibetan Buddhism: Ground, Path, and Fruition.[8] Ground refers to the way things are, Path to the way they develop in practice, and Fruition to the way things are after realization—which, of course, is really the way they've always been the whole time.

In this book, I've adapted this structure to tell the story of the evolving dharma. The first three chapters tell the story of the dharma in the West, not to give a history lesson (others have done that quite well) but to contextualize and focus on the last twenty or thirty years of innovation, change, and revolution. There has never been a better time to upgrade your mental infrastructure than today—not least because we now have more clarity about how meditation does exactly that. Thanks to advances in cognitive neuroscience, computer science, and the behavioral sciences, empirical data supports some of the claims that an Indian prince made 2,600 years ago about the benefits of focusing the mind. At the same time, how and where people meditate has changed, so that what was once an elite practice of a few monks is now taught in strip malls and mass-market magazines. Of course, there are downsides to these trends: vulgarization, confusion, commodification, and more than a few profiteers. To my mind, however, the benefits far outweigh the costs: The dharma is more accessible now, to more kinds of people in different cultural and economic contexts than at any other time in history. And so in the first three chapters of this book we'll meet maverick teachers, eccentric iconoclasts, mainstream popularizers, scientists, geeks, traditionalists, monastics, and even a few normal people whose lives have been impacted by meditation in one of its many forms. I'll try to persuade you that meditation is best understood not as spirituality but as technology, as a set of tools for upgrading the mind, no more mysterious than barbells, and I'll introduce you to people who have benefited from seeing things this way.

The three chapters of Part Two, about the Path, focus on how the mind and heart evolve as meditation practice unfolds. Here we shift from the mass phenomenon of mindfulness to a more focused community of hardcore practitioners, in all of the major Buddhist traditions, who set liberation as their goal and do the intense work to pursue it. Oddly, there remains in many corners of the meditation world a taboo against frank talk about enlightenment. I intend to break that taboo, and you'll hear from voices far more enlightened than mine about what awakening is, and what it isn't. I'll tell you some of my own experiences of confronting personal shadows in the "dark night of the soul," of having incredible mystical experiences that dwarf anything else I've ever experienced, and of moving through all of that en route to loosening the knots in the mind.

Finally, the three chapters of Part Three explore Fruition: what awakening looks like in the contemporary world. I'll begin by questioning some of the convenient assumptions one often hears about such integration and try to demystify liberation as much as I can. Part Three also focuses in on non-self, which for me has been the most liberating of the Buddha's teachings, and situates it in contemporary contexts of postmodernity, gender, and identity politics, with which I've been closely involved for much of my career. And at the end of Part Three, I want to fill out and back up some of the more expansive claims I've made about dharma having the capacity to change the world for the better, looking not just at "engaged Buddhism" specifically, but at the nexus between contemplative practice and social justice—as well as where the American Buddhist community has notably fallen short of its ideals. So as not to end on a down note, I will then offer a few short prognostications about where the dharma may be heading in the future.

A few words about the boundaries of this project. First and most important, the practices of meditation and mindfulness are only a part of the overall Buddhadharma, even though they will be the primary focus of this book. In the Theravadan tradition in which I was trained, meditation *(bhavana)* is central, but so is virtuous conduct *(sila)* and the learning of the dharma itself, whether the four noble truths, or the doctrine of dependent origination, or other topics. When Buddhist purists object to contemporary Buddhism or secular mindfulness, often it's because it extracts meditation from its context. These complaints are fair, if we're trying to accurately represent (or practice) Buddhism as a religious/cultural path. The subject of this book, though, is how the contemporary dharma is evolving—and that is primarily along the axes of meditation and mindfulness. We'll return to these issues later on.

What do those terms—"mindfulness" and "meditation"—mean? For the moment, I will deliberately not be original, and instead cobble together the definitions others have used. Mindfulness, as it is understood today, is "paying attention in a particular way, on purpose, in the present moment and nonjudgmentally" (Jon Kabat-Zinn).[9] It is when "the mind is fully attending to what is at hand" (Barry Boyce).[10] It is "deliberately paying attention, being fully aware of what is happening both inside yourself—in your body, heart, and mind—and outside yourself in your environment. Mindfulness is awareness without judgment or criticism" (Jan Chozen Bays).[11] "Mindfulness is attention. It is nonjudgmental, receptive awareness, respectful awareness" (Jack Kornfield).[12] "Mindfulness is the quality and power of mind that is deeply aware of what's happening—without commentary and without interference" (Joseph Goldstein).[13] It is marked by "nonreactivity, observing/noticing, acting with awareness rather than automatically, concentration, labeling, and a nonjudgmental attitude" (Daniel Siegel).[14]

You get the picture. (As it happens, these definitions are somewhat different from the original meaning of the word *sati* in the earliest Buddhist texts, the records of the Buddha's teachings now known as the Pali Canon.[15] In those texts, *sati* often includes recollection and reflection, not simply present moment–focused attention. However, the current understanding is so widespread that I will not challenge it here.) To put it another way, Eckhart Tolle, on *Oprah,* was once asked to summarize the essence of his teaching. He is said to have replied, "What's going on right now? And can I be with it?" This, too, is a good approximation of mindfulness.

Meditation, in a sense, is a more specific, more focused kind of mindfulness. It narrows the attention and awareness to a particular focus, such as one's posture, the sensations of breath, a visualization, or the nature of the mind itself. In narrowing attention in this way, meditation can lead to deeply concentrated, relaxed, blissful states of mind, or to intuitive insights about the nature of reality, or, conversely, to lots of frustration, uncertainty, and doubt. As this range of effects suggests, there are many different kinds of meditation, with different purposes and techniques attached. Some of them—Tibetan Dzogchen and Zen Shikantaza, for example—even define themselves as a kind of "anti-meditation," since they lack concentration on a single focus and are instead "just sitting" or "non-distracted, non-meditation." But there's no need to get bogged down in paradox. Meditation is the focusing of the mind, a clear observation of a chosen object of attention, often with concentration, often with mindfulness, but in a more sustained and focused way than ordinary, and with more potential and power.

Meditation and mindfulness are, importantly, practices. This book does not include basic meditation instructions—these are readily available online,[16] as well as in several excellent books.[17] Yet what is essential about practices is that they are meant to be *done*, not simply read or learned about. Map is not territory, the recipe is not the meal, and talking about exercise won't shed you any pounds. There is no substitute for the experiential knowledge of meditation—indeed, the gap between conceptual knowledge and intuitive knowledge is one of the main reasons serious practitioners spend months on meditation retreat. After all, you can Google "the four noble truths" right now. But for the mind to intuitively "get it," for the brain to habituate to them—that takes work. This is why I've shared so many of my stories and those of other practitioners, and why they will necessarily differ from yours. Every mind is different, every brain is different, and the core of the contemplative path is indeed empirical and experiential.

Which points to the final, and most important, limitation on this book—which is me. If I'm going to speak credibly about how meditation practice unfolds, I need to speak in first person as well as second and third. Of course, as a scholar—I have a PhD in religious studies, specifically, Jewish Thought—I know that doing so risks contaminating the data. I have an experience in 2013, I read a text written in 1648, and since the two descriptions appear to correlate, I take an ahistorical leap and say we're talking about the same thing. It's a problem. But the alternative is mere description; spiritual journalism, really, which I find uninteresting and so should you. I want to talk not just about sociological trends or phenomenological characteristics of the contemplative path, but about technologies that transform lives—including my own. In Greil Marcus's *Secret History of the Twentieth Century,* there's a moment when he exclaims, in amazement, "This is actually happening." This is for real—not just theory, but practice; this is actually happening. Likewise here.

Having said that, in comparison with the senior teachers who generally write dharma books, I am just a beginner; eleven years of practice, several multi-month silent retreats, and a handful of "attainments" as understood in my tradition. Still, that is something, after all. And in addition to these traditional "attainments," this decade of practice, together with another twenty years spent studying mystical and contemplative traditions, has yielded some fruit that I think is worth sharing. Moreover, my relative youth is part of the point; as I've already suggested, much Western dharma discourse has been shaded by the very specific experiential and conceptual frameworks of the Boomer generation. That's fine, but it does also tend to laminate the dharma in a coating of post-Sixties spiritual plastic. I've got my own plastic too, of course, but at least it's different plastic.

I also approach this wisdom from a whole set of gendered, cultural, socioeconomic, and even religious frameworks. As readers of my other books know, I am heavily involved in the progressive American Jewish community, in the LGBT community, and in various contemporary subcultures and countercultures as well. A whole array of my personal experiences and circumstances (karma) influence how I approach contemplative wisdom—maleness, (off-) whiteness, Jewishness, queerness, and many others. Would my two-month *jhana* retreat with the Venerable Pa Auk Sayadaw have been different had I not also gone to Burning Man just a few weeks prior? Of course—for better and for worse, I'm sure. Likewise, my Western karma makes it unlikely that I'll ever become a monk, while my queer karma makes it unlikely that I'll ever be a wholly conventional householder either. As will become clear in the pages that follow, my experiences studying and to some extent practicing Jewish mysticism have given me a series of lenses through which to view my Buddhist practice, and vice versa. I've experienced a decent share of ordinary human suffering—living ten years in the "closet," for example, and lying to everyone I knew about my sexual and emotional life. But I've also experienced a tremendous amount of privilege, as an upper-middle-class, highly educated white male in the United States of America. All of that, and more, is in the mix.

Fortunately, I am hardly alone in bringing these overlapping identities to the table. There are other gen-Xers, -Yers, and millennials blogging and networking online. There are queers in organizations like Queer Dharma (and in anthologies of the same name). There are geeks in Buddhist Geeks, punks in Noah Levine's Dharma Punx community, hard-core progressive-path meditators in the Dharma Overground. And of course there are BuJus—Buddhist Jews—who have transplanted vipassana and Zen into Jewish containers, and published a small shelfful of books. I have been very fortunate to have these teachers and fellow travelers in my life, and their influences will be apparent in the pages to come.

When I refer to meditation as a technology, I mean that it is a set of tools and practices that, while ancient, is being refined every day. These techniques used to be for enlightenment, for awakening —now they're also for healing post-traumatic stress, and increasing productivity. Much has been lost in translation—but perhaps something has been gained as well. Some of the brightest Buddhists aren't even Buddhist anymore; this set of tools has been extracted from its cultural and religious containers (and also thrives within them, to be sure) and successfully adapted for use in prisons, hospitals, churches, family counseling sessions, hospices, schools, corporations, basketball teams, and online multi-player games. We are smarter about the mind today than at any time in human history—which is a good thing, since we are also stronger and more capable of destroying the world in fire, or drowning it in rising tides. Sometimes we seem doomed by the tendencies of the mind toward acquisitive greed and destructive violence. But there are contrary movements as well: yielding, witnessing, resting in the nature of the mind itself. Six thousand years ago an Indian prince developed new ways to develop these faculties, and while we are only now beginning to understand their neurology, we are also beginning to understand why they once were referred to as sacred.

part one

Ground

CHAPTER 1

NEW FORMS

The Dharma Evolves by Disappearing

You Can't Always Get What You Want

In the beginning of this story, life began on Earth four billion years ago. As the aeons passed, life evolved, usually according to the Darwinian principle of "survival of the fittest." This process ensured that only the strongest, fastest, best adapted, wiliest, smartest creatures survived and reproduced. Unimaginable millennia of evolution subsequently yielded a dazzling array of life forms, all struggling to survive, competing and cooperating, each with instincts embedded within them, driving them, in Tennyson's words, "to strive, to seek, and not to yield."

And yet, this situation sucks. Human beings are impelled, by these billions of years of evolution, to be dissatisfied with what they have, to want more, to over-perceive threats and act on them, to ignore what we mistakenly think is unimportant, to build and make love and achieve and flee danger—only to recognize, sooner or later, that we can never win the battle. On the grand scale, we will all die, and lose much of what we love along the way. Yet even in our mundane lives, we lose the battle every day—often in ways less tragic than comic. The damn webpage won't load, the mortgage has to be paid, the boss is a jerk, *I'm* a jerk—every day, the God-or-evolution-given instinct to "want it all" butts up against a reality that rarely provides it. From the paramecium recoiling from the scientist's pinprick to the existentialist bewailing the emptiness of the human condition, life on earth is hard-wired for kvetching. All life forms want more of the pleasant and less of the unpleasant, more of the good and less of the crap. But you can't always get what you want.

This is the core of the dharma: the completely natural state of affairs is one in which human beings cause suffering for themselves and others. It's not because we're evil, or because Eve ate an apple in God's garden; it's because we are animals living on this planet, and we have evolved to want what we can't get, and to run away from things we don't like.[1]

Fortunately, the instincts to fight, flee, and have sex are not the only faculties in the mind. And so, for thousands of years, people in various religious, philosophical, artistic, and other traditions have cultivated other qualities, among them capacities for wisdom, empathy, letting go, relaxation, concentration, compassion, awareness—not to mention justice, gratitude, love, and a sense of wonder. In some religious traditions, such capacities are labeled "good," whereas the tendencies toward greed, hatred, and delusion are labeled "evil." Some traditions even posit a whole cosmology in which the two are at war with each other, or in which some are accretions atop a pure layer beneath. But I prefer the simpler approach. Human beings have the inclination to be selfish and greedy because that inclination serves organisms well. Luckily for the planet, we have other inclinations, too.

Some 2,500 years ago, a renegade Indian prince proposed that it is possible to unlearn the basic human tendencies toward wanting the pleasant, hating the unpleasant, and ignoring the neutral, and in so doing to suffer less, grow wiser, and act more compassionately. Unlike most of his peers, he did not say that bad behavior will be punished by God or other supernatural forces (although he did have a cosmology that included a variety of supernatural beings), or claim any revelation from a supernal realm. Indeed, his view is almost mechanistic in its outlook. Water the garden of greed, and you get greedier; nourish the saplings of compassion, and eventually they grow instead. Such is the core of the Buddha's "four noble truths": that suffering exists; that clinging, craving desire is its cause; that it is possible to end suffering; and that there is a systematic, step-by-step, empirically verifiable process for doing so, known as the Eightfold Path.

From that root, as we've already noted, a thousand branches have spread. Quickly, this dharma, this teaching, this way, became what its founder claimed it wasn't: an ideology, even a religion. Indeed, quite quickly, entire sects of Buddhism arose based on rejecting the eightfold path itself; it's too difficult, these schools said, so we must appeal to the grace of semi-divine beings instead and hope that they will help us. Or it's only for some people and not for the rest of us. Or it really was supernatural after all. As the teachings spread throughout Asia, they merged with the religious and cultural contexts, developing beautiful art and fighting unfortunate battles. Different sects arose emphasizing one or another of the eight practices: focusing on emptiness, transcending logic, perfecting virtue, developing concentration, or even recognizing that the "end of suffering"—liberation, nirvana, the whole grand prize—is actually available right now, in your original, perfect mind.

And yet even in these different iterations of Buddhism, much of the core teaching remained: cultivating the mind with the goal of liberation from suffering. So while we'll get into the sectarian distinctions soon enough, let's stay for a moment with that basic evolutionary problem: that we are hard-wired for attitudes and behaviors that make us unhappy. What is to be done? Many answers are possible: We could distract ourselves with as much fun and stuff and intoxication as possible, so that we avoid as much unpleasantness as we can. Or we could believe some stories about why suffering is justified, or how it's temporary, or how it will be rewarded in some way after we die. We could draw consolation from philosophy, or relationships, or creativity—all of these have been tried by hundreds of millions of people, and if they work for you, that's great. Really.

The Buddhist notion that we're going to explore here, however, is to change the wiring. I've called the human propensities toward greed and aversion "hard-wired," but it turns out that's not quite an accurate metaphor. Actually, the mind can change. The *brain* can change. By installing new software—new habits, new ways of thinking—you can change the hardware. This isn't magic, or even mysticism. It's exercise.

Although the Buddha did not understand the brain scientifically, he did understand the mind experientially. It is possible, he found, to upgrade your mind through the practice of meditation, just as today you might upgrade your biceps by doing curls at the gym. For example, by focusing the attention on a fixed object, the mind is gathered together—"concentrated"—and calmed. It builds greater capacity to control itself, to not wander off or chase the impulses that naturally arise. Today, as we'll see in the next chapter, we have some hard scientific data to buttress these empirical claims. This has enormous potential.

There are many practices in the Buddhist tradition oriented toward this optimizing of the mental faculties.[2] The ones we will focus on here are meditation *(bhavana)* and mindfulness *(sati)*, both of which were defined, provisionally at least, in the introduction. If you like, you can think of meditation as a focused form of mindfulness, or of mindfulness as an expanded form of meditation. Both have in common the steady, regular cultivation of a kind of noticing or witnessing mind that, in its nonreactivity, exists in opposition to the usual fight-or-flight tendencies we all have. Tellingly, *bhavana* actually means "development"—not spirituality or mysticism, but the development of mental faculties, which we now understand neurologically as well.

Now, in the Theravadan Buddhist context, the aim is not merely to build large mental muscles but to exercise them in a particular way. This is where Buddhism diverges from the evolving secular dharma of the West. In traditional contexts, *bhavana* is not meant to reduce stress or improve immune function but to generate insight; specifically, in this tradition, intuitive understandings that transitory phenomena are impermanent, not ultimately satisfactory, and interdependent with everything else. Trying to hold on to any one of those phenomena—my car, my spouse, my sense of self—may work for a while, but eventually it will lead to *dukkha*, suffering. (That's my tradition's set of emphases; other traditions focus elsewhere.) Yet despite these very different approaches—as others have noted, Buddhist insight may induce, rather than reduce, some kinds of stress—the essential movements of the mind are quite similar. Meditation, calm, focus, concentration, attention, a direction away from discursive thought, insight, and some kind of awakening to the truth of the mind. And through these actions, a contrary movement to five billion years of evolution.

You may have already noticed that developing these mental capacities does not require any particular beliefs, or suspension thereof; you can do these exercises if you're an evangelical Christian or a Scientific Atheist, and you can do them if you're a Zen monk or someone who's never heard of Buddhism. And while some of the forms in which they're contained are religious in nature, in the last quarter century the dharma has evolved by disappearing: it's been taken out of its religious context, abstracted, and now appears in any number of secular (and multi- religious) forms instead. So while the Buddhist technologies of meditation were developed with specific Buddhist aims in mind, they can also be transplanted into other contexts and put to other uses. This irks traditionalists to no end, but it is happening.

Nor is this development particularly unique. The extrapolation of dharma from ritual forms, cultic ceremonies, and temple practice is a long intra-Buddhist development; one thinks of the Zen reformers, for example, defining themselves in opposition to scriptural, ritual, and scholarly traditions.[3] More generally, the dharma, like all other intellectual, social, and religious movements, has always evolved. Only Orthodox believers insist that their religions never evolve—fundamentalist Christians, ultra-Orthodox Jews, and, yes, some very proper Buddhists who insist that the dharma is perfect (an article of the faith) and that nothing has been added to it, or needs to be. Of course, this is obviously untrue historically, as evinced by variations among forms of Theravada/Hinayana, Mahayana, Vajrayana, Ch'an, Shin, Zen, Pure Land, and national variations in Burma, Tibet, Thailand, Bhutan, Japan, Korea, China, and Sri Lanka, as well as sects from dozens of other schools and regional backgrounds. True, traditionalists in all these schools insist that theirs is somehow the original teaching, even going to absurd lengths—one tradition has the Buddha teaching tantra on another world while he was teaching meditation on this one; another has him teaching secret sutras to fish, who revealed the teachings centuries later. But from a historical-critical perspective, it is obvious that "Buddhism" has evolved, and is evolving, and will continue to evolve.

Indeed, the reason I've scare-quoted that term is that the very word "Buddhism" is, itself, a Western import.[4] The notion that Asian "religions" (another Western word, from the Latin *religio*) should answer the same questions as Christianity does, should be about beliefs (i.e., -isms), and should in any way conform to what a religion is supposed to be is, itself, part of the inevitable misunderstanding of non-Western cultures by Westerners. "Hinduism" and "Buddhism" are both foreign terms—and, worse, colonial ones. Moreover, and this is something many Western dharma practitioners like to point out, the Buddha was not a Buddhist. On the contrary, according to the Pali Canon, he requested that his image not be depicted, he worried that he might be worshiped as a god, he allowed people to continue to practice their existing religious rites, and he remained agnostic on such fundamental questions about the creation of the world and what happens after we die. "I teach suffering, and the end of suffering," he said several times.

None of this is to disparage religious Buddhism. Millions of people around the world derive meaning, build community, and sacralize the events in their lives according to Buddhist religion and Buddhist ritual. And many forms of Buddhism are absolutely religious in orientation, involving devotion to divine entities (including thousands of Buddhas and Bodhisattvas), hymns, authority, morals, myths, temples, priests, rituals, life cycle events, power struggles, sectarian debates, and every one of the trappings of religion familiar (and often abhorrent) to Westerners. As practitioners, it's not only inevitable but advisable that we cherry-pick traditions and practices that work for us. This is what traditionally religious people do, and it's what nontraditional, nonreligious people do: we find what works, and leave aside the rest. Yet at the same time, as individuals seeking to be self-aware about the traditions from which we're picking the cherries, it's helpful to remember that there is no one Buddhist essence, except as rendered by a selection of sources and teachers. Sure, at some level of generality, there are core Buddhist values and teachings. But how they play out in practice is completely different, depending on where you choose to look.

For the purposes of this book, I am mostly interested in the generally nonreligious, generally pragmatic aspects of Buddhist teaching. I'm not terribly interested in the mythological structures of Pure Land Buddhism, for example, even though, numerically speaking, they are far more influential than the Satipatthana Sutta, one of the core teachings on mindfulness in the Pali Canon and one of the sources for the secularized dharma practices of the West. I refuse to go along with the claim that other Buddhist forms are some foreign attachments to some true dharma, or that millions of Asian Buddhists are just confused about their own religion; presented in that way, it should be clear why such a perspective is offensive.[5] Even in Western dharma, there are many Western practitioners of Tibetan

Buddhism who place ritual, chanting, and prayer at the center of their practice. Some regard these as contemplative tools, but others regard them as little different from how a Catholic might count the rosary, or a Muslim might recite the *shehadah*. While these forms of practice are not my focus here, I also do not want to delegitimize them or say that they are somehow less Buddhist or less valuable than the ones in which I'm interested. As I and my teachers understand it (and others are free to disagree!), the dharma is not about a set of rules, or beliefs, or axioms of magical thinking. It's more like a technology, a set of tools that, if used diligently and properly, can bring about some positive results. Yet that is only one of its many expressions.

Coming to America

The dharma came to America just under two hundred years ago, and has grown largely in two parallel communities: Asian-American immigrant and subsequent-generation populations, and what Richard Seager calls "convert Buddhists," a mixed bag of Americans who have embraced the dharma as some kind of spiritual, contemplative, or personal developmental path.[6] There have been several excellent accounts of this fascinating development, including Seager's *Buddhism in America*; Charles Prebish's *Luminous Passage, American Buddhism,* and (edited with Kenneth Tanaka) *The Faces of Buddhism in America*; Rick Fields' *How the Swans Came to the Lake*; Thomas Tweed's *The American Encounter with Buddhism 1844–1912*; and several others.[7] Because these volumes (and others) are quite comprehensive, I will not attempt to reinvent the wheel here. Rather, what I want to do is narrow the story to the trends within that history that have led to the new evolutions of the last twenty years.

There are really two American Buddhist communities and histories: "convert" or "white" Buddhism and traditional, "ethnic," or

"Asian" Buddhism.[8] This dichotomy is imperfect: many practitioners of traditional "Asian" Buddhist sects such as Soko Gakkai[9] and Jodo Shinshu[10] are non-Asian, and many practitioners of contemporary Western Buddhism are Asian, API, or Asian-American.[11] Yet in understanding the evolving dharma of the West, it is still a useful one—with "convert" Buddhism playing a far more significant role in this story, though "ethnic" Buddhists have always been far more numerous (and more studied by scholars).

There are many reasons why drawing this distinction is helpful. First, culturally and linguistically, the Western innovators of the last fifty years are quite distant from the ethnically Asian and heavily immigrant communities that created, for example, the Buddhist Church of America[12] (an American version of Jodo Shinshu that has adopted Protestant trappings such as ministers and churches); more often than not, the two worlds exist independently from each other. Second, the fundamental orientations differ as well: "Asian" Buddhist communities are often centered around preserving the cultural traditions of immigrant populations and on the observance of Buddhism as a religion; for example, Japanese Zen temples in America are generally more focused on priests and rituals than on Zen masters and meditation—as they are in Japan. "Asian" Buddhist temples look and feel more like traditional places of worship, and often tell stories that strike Westerners as preposterous religious tales;[13] "convert" Buddhist spaces are more like meditation centers with Westerners who have taken up these practices, often for nonreligious and entirely rational reasons. Thus, although there are some overlap, these two communities function almost independently, with different ends, means, forms, and institutions—and of the two, we will focus almost entirely on the "convert" community.

Until the nineteenth century, European and American encounters with Buddhism were limited to a few scattered reports of oriental mystery, and severely biased reports from Christian missionaries, who blasted Buddhism as a form of idolatry, misunderstood its doctrines, and often (though not always) perpetrated atrocities against the people whose souls they were supposedly trying to save.[14] Though there had long been points of contact between Asia and the West (Marco Polo even reported on Buddhism[15]), these were largely unknown until the rise of the early Orientalists, beginning with William Jones (1736–1794) and his magazine the *Asiatic Researches,*[16] and even then, knowledge was spotty, and confined to the few.

In the nineteenth century, this began to change. In America, the transcendentalists, chiefly Emerson and Thoreau, took a keen interest in both Hinduism and Buddhism, Emerson reading the *Bhagavad Gita* regularly and Thoreau publishing the Heart Sutra in *Dial* magazine in 1844.[17] The first American Buddhist temple, meanwhile, was erected in 1853. In Europe, philologist Eugéne Burnouf translated key Sanskrit and Pali texts, publishing the first significant European study of Buddhism in 1844,[18] while in Asia, Westerners such as Thomas Rhys-Davids and Edwin Arnold set about connecting, syncretizing, and "reforming" the different sects of Asian Buddhism.[19] Suddenly, widely divergent new perceptions of Buddhism emerged, from idolatry to vaguely Christian moralism to world-renouncing pessimism, to mystery religion of Asia.[20] During this period, the study of Buddhism remained the provenance of intellectuals and a few contemplative enthusiasts. Yet despite their many limitations, we owe these privileged men a great debt; they planted the seeds that flourished not just into the "New Age" but also into the variety of contemplative practices taught today in hospitals, prisons, and schools.

The generally established birth-year of Buddhism in America is 1893. That year, the Parliament of World Religions in Chicago brought Buddhist teachers and traditions into direct contact with large American audiences (in person and through the media) for the first time.[21] There, the Theravadan Anagarika Dharmapala and Zen master Soyen Shaku each launched long careers as Buddhist Johnny Appleseeds, creating dharma centers throughout America and, indeed, throughout the world. (In a foreshadowing of the Western dharma scene, the first American to take the Buddhist refuges was a Jewish businessman, Charles Strauss.[22]) Soon after, in 1898, Edwin Arnold published *The Light of Asia,* popularizing Buddhism in America; as Rick Fields writes, "It was from *Light of Asia* more than any other book that Americans first learned the story and teachings of the Buddha."[23] Henry Steel Olcott of the Theosophical Society set out to unify Buddhist communities around the world, writing a "Buddhist Catechism" that became enormously influential and insisting that "Buddha Dharma" was not a religion but rather a philosophy.[24] Yet notwithstanding this new burst of activity, non-Asian Buddhism remained a relatively minor phenomenon, perhaps because it was seen as unduly pessimistic and quietistic in a Victorian and post-Victorian period that appreciated optimism and activism.[25]

That all changed in the middle of the twentieth century, thanks largely to Zen practitioners and teachers. D. T. Suzuki, Soyen Shaku's translator at the 1893 World Parliament, eventually became the foremost interpreter of Buddhism in the twentieth century,[26] while Soyen Shaku's students Nyogen Senzaki and Sokei-an established Zen centers and communities.[27] It is worth noting that these Japanese Zen teachers were, themselves, reformers; by the time Zen reached American shores, it was already "Zen for export," purged of many of its traditional authority structures and forms.[28] To his millions of readers, D. T. Suzuki may seem like the genuine article— and he is, but only because reforming, innovating, and adapting are themselves genuine activities. In large part thanks to Suzuki, the middle of the twentieth century witnessed an explosion of Western interest in Zen primarily, and Buddhism secondarily. Alan Watts fused Zen, Advaita, and even some forms of Christianity into his own unique and iconoclastic spiritual path, turning on millions in the process with incredibly well-written books and articles.[29] Allen Ginsberg first read D. T. Suzuki in 1953, Jack Kerouac produced a "Buddhist Bible," and Gary Snyder and Philip Whalen each pursued serious Zen practice.[30] At the first Be-In in San Francisco in 1966,

Snyder read, Ginsberg chanted, and Zen master Shunryu Suzuki (later to found the San Francisco Zen Center) meditated.[31]

It was the generation of the Sixties—they weren't called Boomers then—who would eventually transform Buddhist meditation techniques into a practice offered in nursing homes and schools. At first, meditation was a countercultural movement, associated with hippie heroes such as Timothy Leary and Ram Dass and New Age gurus such as the Maharishi Mahesh Yogi, who popularized Transcendental Meditation.[32] Its association with the Sixties—for better and for worse—endures today. But at the same time, within Buddhist traditions proper, all three of the major streams of contemporary Western dharma began to assume their current form during this period. Zen centers became established coast to coast, with Westerners beginning to take leadership roles in place of Asian teachers. Tibetan teachers began to become known in America, chiefly Chogyam Trungpa Rinpoche, who, dismayed by hippies seeking to jump to tantric practice with no foundation in meditation, in 1973 set up Vajradhatu and the Shambhala path as a way of systematizing dharma for the West.[33] And in the Theravadan world, Ruth Denison, Joseph Goldstein, and Jack Kornfield each spent time in Asia, meditating with the Indian lay teacher S. N. Goenka, the Thai master Ajahn Chah, and Anagarika Munindra (whose affiliation with the Mahabodhi society links him to Dharmapala, the Theravadan at the 1893 World Parliament); Goldstein and Kornfield would eventually meet at the Vajradhatu-founded Naropa Institute in 1974 and form the Insight Meditation Center (later Society) in 1975 with Sharon Salzberg.[34] Alongside these developments, Vietnamese monk Thich Nhat Hanh initiated what would later be known as "engaged Buddhism," joining meditation and mindfulness practices with peacemaking and social justice work;[35] the Dalai Lama gradually became a global celebrity, most importantly by winning the Nobel Peace Prize in 1989; and Buddhism became a kind of cool alternative religion, attracting celebrities like Richard Gere, Philip Glass, Leonard Cohen, and, not least, Lisa Simpson.

As this process evolved, it gradually became clear that a new, Western dharma was taking shape. Lama Surya Das, Jack Kornfield, Joseph Goldstein (particularly in *One Dharma: The Emerging Western Buddhism*), and Robert Thurman (whose *Inner Revolution* has been called "a manifesto for an exuberantly American Buddhism"[36]), among others, each drafted manifestos defining and articulating this new *yana,* new vehicle of the dharma. For the American-born Lama Surya Das, it is marked by ten characteristics, including a dharma without dogma, a lay-oriented sangha, egalitarianism (particularly with regard to gender), and an engaged, simplified, pragmatic, and experimental orientation.[37] For Kornfield, it is defined by democratization, feminization, and integration.[38] To scholar Rick Fields, convert or "white" Buddhism is a phenomenon of laypeople practicing monastic-style meditation, with emphases on gender egalitarianism and social engagement—all of which, he notes, are anathema to traditional Asian Buddhism.[39] Kornfield noted that a partial secularization was also crucial: "We wanted to offer the powerful practices of insight meditation, as many of our teachers did, as simply as possible without the complications of rituals, robes, chanting, and the whole religious tradition."[40]

These were significant transformations that led to the secularized dharma of today. As a nontheistic tradition, Buddhism had long been regarded as not-quite-a-religion by Westerners: Nietzsche called it a "hygiene,"[41] not unlike Kenneth Folk's metaphor of "contemplative fitness" today, and mindfulness had already been secularized by none other than William James, who said that "the faculty of voluntarily bringing back a wandering attention, over and over again, is the very root of judgment, character, and will."[42] But as these mostly secular Westerners divested Buddhism of its religious forms and its cultural particularity, they created something new: a practice of personal and communal transformation that owed much to Western psychotherapy, a fair amount to Sixties spirituality, and a great deal to a pragmatic, scientific Western worldview that found resonances in the empiricism of the Buddha, but owed much to the specific cultural contexts in which the Western dharma was created.[43] To be sure, extending Buddhism beyond Buddhists is, itself, a Buddhist value: as the Dalai Lama once said, "There are four billion people on this planet. One billion are Buddhists, but four billion are suffering."[44] And the Buddha himself extended his teachings to people of all backgrounds, religious affiliations, and genders, even allowing his followers to continue practicing their existing religious rites. According to the sutras, he even taught a villager to practice mindfulness by drawing water from a well,[45] a foreshadowing of adapted mindfulness practices today.

Let me narrow the focus for a moment, to my own Theravadan tradition, which is a useful example of how this evolution has unfolded in America. Kornfield, Goldstein, Salzberg, and a few others have become almost legendary figures in the vipassana world—yet they were practically kids when they started. I remember Joseph telling how they cobbled the money together to buy the former Catholic monastery that became the home of the Insight Meditation Society (IMS); they were like a few twentysomethings borrowing some cash to pursue a quixotic dream. No one could seriously have predicted the spread of vipassana to dozens of communities around the country, let alone the secularized and transformed versions of Buddhist meditation that we'll look at in a moment. And, to be sure, there were many mistakes and course corrections along the way. Larry Yang is a "second generation" teacher-in-training at Spirit Rock, the somewhat more "California" version of IMS. He told me that "our senior, Western, Theravadan teachers will fully admit that when they started teaching, which was in their mid-twenties, they didn't necessarily know what they were doing, in terms of the larger picture."

The result was a lot of experimentation and evolution. As Larry also noted:

> All practice is culturally determined. The practices that are
> coming into the West are just beginning to be formulated

in our Western psychology. This has happened hundreds if
not thousands of times as the dharma has moved from India
to Mongolia and Tibet and China and Japan and Southeast
Asia. It's the process in which the dharma permeates the culture, so we're in that very interesting and exciting place, and
also it's a little bit confusing.

At Spirit Rock, for example, vipassana is often taught with a psy-
choanalytic orientation—Jack Kornfield emphasizes that meditation and therapy are meant to be complements, not replacements
for each other—and integrated with a variety of other modalities.
(As we will see below, this is not without its perils; the dharma is
not self-help, and its insights may reduce one's level of adjustment
to our rather insane society, rather than increase it.) In the 1980s,
the American insight meditation community began to emphasize
metta, lovingkindness, in part following the tradition of S. N. Goenka, in part responding to the needs of meditators for a more heart-
centered approach, and in part because of other sects' cultivation
of compassion as part of the bodhisattva path.[46] And as Larry also
noted, communities are still wrestling with issues of diversity and
inclusion, with how to balance traditional forms and the desire to
respond to participants' needs and desires, with challenges in training qualified teachers, and many, many other concerns. Throughout
these evolutions, the insight meditation community has adapted,
combined (even its founding teachers came from two different
Theravadan traditions, Burmese and Thai Forest), and blended
Buddhist and other forms.

In fact, this evolution preceded the dharma's coming to the
West. As with Zen, the "authentic" Asian forms of Theravadan
practice were, in reality, products of modernizing and reforming
enterprises. Mahasi Sayadaw's method, for example, de-emphasized
rituals, chanting, devotional and merit-making activities, and doctrinal studies, in favor of meditation.[47] His focus on the *Satipatthana
Sutta*, today at the center of most Theravadan communities, was a

deliberate choice of emphasis.[48] In Gil Fronsdahl's words, "Mahasi was part of what is sometimes called a twentieth-century Theravada modernization movement and sometimes a revival of original and canonical Buddhist ideals." [49] Mahasi also focused on getting lay students to attain the first of the four levels of enlightenment (stream entry; more on this in Chapter Five), and changed the focus of meditation in order to lessen the ecstatic states of concentration (discussed in Chapter Four). His contemporary U Ba Khin pioneered the combination of *anapanasati* (mindfulness of breathing, noticed at the nostrils—unlike the chest, as in Mahasi's method) with "body scans" throughout the body.[50] These were all innovations.

Today, the innovations have multiplied, and there are at least seven strands of Theravadan practice in the United States—the variety is, itself, instructive. First, there are traditional, Asian-American Theravadan communities, maintaining traditional rituals such as bowing, chanting, offerings, and observance of holidays.[51] Second, there are "Goenka vipassana" centers, which teach the original form of Mahasi-like vipassana style created by S. N. Goenka; this form of practice tends to be more rigorous than the IMS-type vipassana, and the teachings are largely confined to videotapes of Goenka himself. Third, the insight meditation movement that we have described maintains its flagship centers in Massachusetts and California and smaller centers in cities around the country; it is probably the best-selling and best-known of the American Theravadan streams. Fourth, the last forty years have seen an interesting resurgence in monastic communities in America and Britain, with new monastic communities such as the Bhavana Society (West Virginia), Amravati (California), Cittaviveka/Chithurst (UK), and Wat Metta (California), and Western-born monastics integrating Western scholarship with traditional Buddhist monastic life and practice. And then there are the mavericks, whom we'll explore in Chapter Three; the secularizers, whom we'll discuss in a moment; and the many independent teachers of vipassana-like practice combined with religious, spiritual, or esoteric practices—more on that in Chapter Eight. Indeed, there is an interesting irony at the heart of American vipassana. Of all Buddhist streams, Theravada is among the most conservative and mundane, still focused on the problems of suffering and the end of suffering, and on meditation, virtuous conduct, and wisdom as the ways to go about it. It's a little dour, reflecting its monastic origins. And it is sometimes regarded as somewhat basic—it's the "lesser vehicle" *(hinayana)*, or, more charitably, the "way of the elders" *(Theravada)*. Yet it has become the source of some of our century's most worldly and adaptive mindfulness practices.[52]

This somewhat dizzying array of dharma practice, even within a single sect, gives a sense of the breadth of the American Buddhist phenomenon. There are more than a thousand Buddhist centers in America today,[53] and there are, it is said, 84,000 doors into the dharma.[54] Not only the three great vehicles, Hinayana, Mahayana, and Vajrayana;[55] not only the flowering of dharma in the West in innumerable forms; not only the different emphases, on emptiness or dependent arising or liberation or compassion; but also different aims, different intentions, and hopefully a recognition that this pluralism and diversity is a strength rather than a weakness. As Goldstein wrote in his book *One Dharma,* "the factors nourishing the emergence of one dharma at this time are the great wealth of teachings readily available and the dilemma of assessing diverse points of view, each true and verified from its own perspective. . . . Our challenge is to hold them all in wisdom rather than in confusion or conflict."[56]

Bodhi Tree to Basketball Court

In 1997, the Buddhist scholar and pioneer Robert Thurman said, "Buddhism will not actually be able to succeed in its mission here in America unless it is able to perform that mission without being Buddhism. Buddhism has to go beyond being Buddhism in order to do the work that Buddha wants to do."[57] In the subsequent sixteen years, this has come to pass. The newest doors to the dharma are beyond even the dharma itself, beyond Buddhism, in what might be called a secular contemplative technology. Today, secularized forms of Buddhist meditation are taught in hospitals, to relieve pain;[58] in schools, to improve concentration and learning;[59] on corporate retreats, to improve teamwork.[60] Meditation is used to relax, to have spiritual experiences, to reduce conflict and increase compassion, to aid in psychotherapy, to build focus, to lessen the pain of chronic or terminal illness, to teach hardened criminals new ways of working with anger and the challenges of confinement, to help students prepare for standardized tests, to be a better parent, and, of course, to soothe the worried minds of upper-middle-class Westerners.

In most of these new contexts, the entire history we've just recounted is obscured. Indeed, to succeed in schools and churches, teachers of secularized mindfulness had to purge anything "Buddhist" from it. And yet, while mere relaxation is clearly not the original intention of the dharma, many of these new applications are not so distant from the Buddha's original intention to reduce suffering; indeed, the Pali word for suffering, *dukkha*, also has connotations of stress, anxiety, and feeling "stuck," each of which has its modern analogues in the therapeutic application. Matthieu Ricard, the monk who was one of the first subjects of a study looking at the long-term effects of meditation on the brain—he was shown to have higher levels of gamma waves than most people, and to be able to suppress the "startle reflex"—put it this way: these techniques "don't have to be labeled Buddhist, even though they are the fruit of more than twenty centuries of Buddhist contemplatives' investigation of the mind."[61]

The leading advocate for these new applications of mindfulness is Dr. Jon Kabat-Zinn, whose many bestselling books (*Wherever You Go, There You Are*, 1994; *Full Catastrophe Living*, 1990) and high-profile media appearances have given mindfulness (and his own work) its highest-ever prominence in American popular culture. Kabat-Zinn started out relatively modestly in 1979, with the

Stress Reduction Clinic at the University of Massachusetts Medical Center.[62] However, he is now at the head of a growing industry. His regimen of Mindfulness-Based Stress Reduction (MBSR), integrating various forms of meditation and relaxation exercises, is "by far the largest source of secular mindfulness training today,"[63] with hundreds of teachers and centers around the country, and with a popular offshoot, Mindfulness-Based Cognitive Therapy (MBCT), focused on treating depression.[64] Kabat-Zinn has consulted with Google and the Dalai Lama, helped launch several careers, and is probably responsible for more non-Buddhists practicing Buddhist-style meditation than anyone else in history. And like Ricard, Kabat-Zinn sees his work as having evolved beyond "Buddhism" specifically: "There was a time that I considered myself to be a Buddhist," he said, "but I actually don't consider myself a Buddhist. Although I teach Buddhist meditation, it's not with the aim of people becoming Buddhists, but with the aim of them realizing that they're Buddhas."[65]

In the next chapter, we'll look at some of the mountain of evidence that has proven the effectiveness of MBSR and similar techniques. Yet for me, the proof in the MBSR pudding came not through the data, but when a close friend of my sister's did some MBSR-related work while recovering from an illness. This friend was not a "spiritual person" by any conventional definition; he was a regular guy who liked regular guy stuff, and had trouble keeping on his diet. And yet, after just a few MBSR group sessions, he was doing the practice on his own and reporting less stress and a stronger recovery. He was so convinced that he even started looking into meditation groups, not for any spiritual reason, but because this was the first thing that helped him relax. I was impressed. Obviously, this is just one anecdotal experience, in the face of reams of scientific and statistical data. But it convinced me that Kabat-Zinn and his colleagues were onto something. MBSR is not for spiritual weirdos and dharma explorers; it actually works for normal people.

Similarly, mindfulness and meditation are now found in any number of contexts, some quite unconventional. Google's "Search

Inside Yourself" program, pioneered by Chade-Meng Tan,[66] is one of a number of corporate programs using mindfulness to reduce stress, improve productivity, and increase happiness among workers. Legendary basketball coach Phil Jackson famously taught Zen Buddhist philosophy and meditative techniques to his world-champion teams.[67] Congressman Tim Ryan has secured government support for mindfulness-based "social/emotional learning" programs in schools, and recently authored the first dharma book written by a sitting politician.[68] The U.S. Marines train new soldiers in mindfulness as a form of mental discipline, part of the program called Mindfulness-based Mind Fitness Training, or M-Fit, and the Marines have reported lower stress levels as a result.[69] The Prison Mindfulness Institute, founded by Fleet Maull when he himself was incarcerated, now has over 175 affiliates around the country.[70] Daniel Siegel and UCLA's Mindful Awareness Research Center have taught mindfulness to football players and medical students, created certification standards for mindfulness teaching, developed secular mindfulness practices focused on "Recognition, Acceptance, Investigation, and Non-identification,"[71] and combined therapeutic work with scientific study to inculcate values of curiosity, openness, acceptance, and love ("COAL").[72] Filmmaker David Lynch has promoted Transcendental Meditation to a legion of unlikely meditators.[73] Mindfulness has been taught to teenagers as part of programs such as Stressed Teens, Noah Levine's street work interventions,[74] and the Mind-Body Awareness Project, which focuses on at-risk teens, often in juvenile detention centers.[75] (These programs' complement is perhaps the Garrison Institute's Cultivating Awareness and Resilience in Education program, which teaches mindfulness to teachers.[76]) Michael Carroll, author of *Awake at Work* and *Fearless at Work,* has taught mindfulness at Unilever, Proctor & Gamble, and Comcast.[77] The Center for Contemplative Mind in Society teaches meditation to bankers and businessmen, and there are mindfulness-for-lawyers classes and conferences around the country.[78] Bill Clinton's doing it.[79] It's everywhere.

But is it a good thing? Well, it certainly is unexpected. Mirabai Bush, who as director of the Center for Contemplative Mind in Society has been at the forefront of these developments, wrote in the *New York Times* that

> In 1972, I was a thirty-year-old American traveling in India, with the smell of incense in my hair and mantras repeating in my ears. Back then, if you had told me that I would someday be training employees of corporate America to apply contemplative practices to help them become more successful, I would have said you'd been standing too long in India's hot noonday sun.[80]

And to be sure, not everyone is happy with these new developments. Naturally, there are Buddhist purists who object to the extraction of Buddhist meditation from Buddhist belief, ritual, and form. There are scholars of Buddhism dismayed at the selective and ahistorical way in which "convert" Buddhists relate to Asian Buddhist traditions. And, as we'll explore in more detail in Chapter Three, there is a new generation of neo-Buddhists who are returning to precisely the forms and contexts set aside by Kabat-Zinn, Siegel, and company, refocusing on liberation as the goal, and appreciating how the traditional contexts support intensive practice.

To be sure, there is an occasional vulgarity to the high-capitalist way in which mindfulness is sometimes marketed—perhaps not by MBSR or Search Inside Yourself, but definitely by less elegant providers. As with psychopharmacology or the latest fitness fad, if there is interest the market rushes in where monks may fear to tread. Thus the rather silly commercial image of meditation: a calm-looking woman in white, hands in a mudra, radiating some sort of bliss. Which, of course, is precisely the opposite of Buddhism in traditional contexts, wherein meditation is highly *un*-relaxing, at least some of the time. Sure, in the end, a dedicated dharma path does lead to a very specific, and very wonderful, kind of "relaxation": a relinquishment of the most powerful ties to egoic existence, a letting go that is truly liberating and from which one does not turn back. But en route, it can be hell. Sitting for endless Zen *sesshins* or performing thousands of prostrations to Padmasambhava—no, dharma practice is not a day at the beach, or the spa. It's the opposite, really. If a vacation banishes all cares from the mind, a meditation retreat puts them right smack in front of you. Indeed, as we'll see in Chapters Five and Six, my own traditional Theravadan path entails a harrowing "dark night of the soul" in which everything seems to be disappearing, crumbling, falling apart, and there's nothing to hold onto, and you typically feel nauseous and disoriented, and even your teacher can't help, and so you just soldier on, somehow, diligently, ardently . . . does that sound relaxing to you?

It's also true that the contemporary uses of mindfulness are quite different from the traditional ones, which include (but are not limited to) training the mind, moment by moment, to reduce clinging to the evanescent and ultimately unsatisfactory formations we ordinarily look to for happiness; gaining an intuitive understanding of the four noble truths by carefully observing moment-to-moment experience; building concentration so that one may "cut off the head of delusion," especially regarding the (non-)existence of the self; building concentration to enjoy "jhanic pleasure" (see Chapter Six); developing an attunement to the always-present knowing quality of consciousness itself; experiencing the incomprehensible, paradoxical truth of emptiness and form being identical; developing insight into the three fundamental characteristics of everything, namely, impermanence, satisfactoriness, and non-self/emptiness; uncovering the inherent radiance in the natural mind; and "just sitting" and transcending notions of emptiness and form. Obviously, stress reduction—even in very noble contexts, like easing chronic pain—is different from these original ends. Yet this (incomplete) Buddhist list is meant to convey two different conclusions. The first is that, yes, relaxation and corporate success are not among the traditional aims of meditation. But the second is that those aims have, themselves, always varied and always evolved. There may be, as Joseph Goldstein puts it, one dharma, but even within that one dharma, the purposes of practice have varied and still vary today. And really, if the simplification of mindfulness into relaxation gets folks interested in something that can eventually bring themselves and the world more happiness and peace, I won't complain.

Finally, what's remarkable about the strange evolution of Western Buddhism is that it is remarkably faithful, in certain ways, to the pragmatic orientation of Gautama Buddha himself. As many Western teachers (Stephen Batchelor, Sharon Salzberg, Joseph Goldstein) have emphasized, the Buddha was not particularly interested in starting a new religion. There were plenty of religions already in his native India/Nepal, and according to the texts contained in the Pali Canon, he was content to let people believe whatever they wanted to believe. Rather, what Gautama Buddha was interested in—according to these texts—was a practice, a technology, a way of gaining liberation. In this regard, the evolving Western dharma traditions are a return to the priorities of the earliest stages of Buddhist history.

For these reasons, I think the pragmatic orientation of Western capitalist society has, on balance, been good for the dharma. All spiritual traditions include universalizable elements within particularist containers, and to see the dharma evolve beyond Buddhism is, in this regard, a positive development, at least if one thinks that the dharma brings good results to those who practice it. Of course, it's also an experiment. We don't really know how sustainable it is to fuse monastically contextualized meditation practices with a job, mortgage, and family life. The flood of dharma books that tell you how to do that are really just best guesses, based on the experiences of teachers and their students, and rarely based on long-term empirical study (indeed, in some cases, often despising the whole notion of empirical study). And along with all the neuroscientific studies reporting good news about meditation, there are some ants at the picnic, including studies that suggest that serious meditation practice can, well, get serious, opening up cans of psychological worms that might well have remain closed.

But there's no denying that mindfulness does work in these various new, quasi-therapeutic contexts—that's why it's spreading, of course. And there's nothing wrong with teaching people to relax—wasn't the Buddha interested in reducing suffering? Well, stress is suffering and relaxation is its release. So I think Orthodox Buddhists need to, well, relax. It is true: many if not most of the applications of meditation and mindfulness in the West are, at best, side-paths alongside the main road to liberation. And yet, most of the folks taking them are not interested in "liberation," and even if they were, they don't have the kinds of lives conducive to really pursuing it. Which is fine; there are lots of valid goals in life, enlightenment being only one of them. We hardcore dharma practitioners need to make peace with Western mindfulness practices. They are indeed adaptations of the dharma, and not the dharma itself—but the dharma is evolving into new forms and contexts quite remote from their Buddhist origins.

The Buddha who appears in the Pali Canon was nothing if not adaptable. *Upaya,* it's called—skillful means. It's notable that in the discourses, the Buddha generally addresses his teachings to individuals or to groups, and not to humanity in general. And indeed, the emphases of those teachings vary according to the audience. The Buddha tells a warrior prince one thing, his community of monks another. The different teachings don't contradict one another—a remarkable feat, if you consider the Pali Canon the work of hundreds of years of redaction and editing; the Hebrew Bible has far more contradictions in it—but they do contain different points of emphasis. Sometimes dependent origination is the heart of the teachings, other times it's the four foundations of mindfulness. Sometimes the law of karma seems central, other times it's dismissed as irrelevant and incomprehensible. Hence those 84,000 doors.

There's something deeply democratic about today's mindfulness teachers: what used to be the elite practice of monastics is now taught to househusbands and firefighters.[81] It's an experiment, and it's inspiring, to me anyway. For centuries, lay Buddhists were told that they should observe various rituals, chant to the right deities and/or bodhisattvas, and, of course, support the temples and monks, and hopefully, maybe, in the future they'd be reborn as monks or nuns themselves, and be able to attain liberation. I recognize the important social function this myth has held, and continues to hold, for millions of people around the world. But I also want to applaud the very different notion that some measure of liberation is available to everyone, regardless of social class, gender, and station in life. We may not be able to go all the way, if we're "encumbered" with careers, families, and property—but thanks to a remarkable series of developments over the last hundred years, we can all get a taste of the very subtle bliss of freedom.

CHAPTER 2

NEW EVIDENCE

The Science of Brainhacking

Brainhacking works. By following a few simple instructions, you can, over time, change the nature of your brain to make it more resilient, more resistant to aging, and more capable of happiness, compassion, and clarity. The data is in, and it matters.

It matters, in fact, in two distinct ways. First, as this hard data filters through the U.S. healthcare industry, the educational system, the military, and the corporate world, to name just a few examples, it will become clear that mindfulness is among the most cost-effective methods ever for reducing hospital stays, advancing educational opportunity, and improving the functioning of organizations. This will be a game-changer. Second, the science changes how the dharma is even to be understood. This hard data is the opposite of soft spirituality. Meditation and mindfulness are tools, not a set of spiritual exercises whose merit depends on faith or some unknown forces. This is why I've used the word "technology" in describing the work of meditation, why Kenneth Folk calls it a form of "contemplative fitness," and why I like the term "brainhacking." We're not referring here to actual, physical technologies like electrodes or vibrating implants or special sounds that put you into an altered state (although all of these exist). Rather, when I say "technology," I'm thinking of how meditation and mindfulness are tools—processes that lead to predictable results.

When people go to the gym, for example, they know pretty much what's going to happen, and how it's going to happen. Lifting weights causes muscles to stretch and even tear a little, causing lactic acid to build up, causing the muscles to rebuild themselves bigger and with more capacity than they had before. It's a physical process, and while trainers will debate the best methods until the end of time, the basic operation is clearly understood. Meditation is similar. If you do the work, predictable changes in the mind (experience) and the brain (neuroscience) tend to result, in a fairly reliable way. This, in a sense, is the very opposite of spirituality—and it's certainly not religion either. It's more like working out: Each time I come back to the breath, I'm strengthening very specific neural networks. This perspective has already informed how millions of people around the world are enhancing their mental and emotional capacities. And the revolution has only just begun.

The Monk in the Machine

"Contemplative neuroscience." The term, and the field, didn't exist twenty years ago, but now it is changing how we understand the brain and how to optimize its function.[1] In 1980, not a single article was published in a scientific journal on the effects of meditation and mindfulness. In 1990, there were five. In 2000, twenty-one. But in 2010, there were 353; in 2011, 397; and in 2012, there were 526.[2] Scientists have measured mindfulness's capacity to reduce stress, improve immune response, and so on; they have detected activation in different parts of the brain during meditation; and they've conducted long-term studies of experienced meditators, beginning meditators, and even children practicing mindfulness in hospital settings.[3]

In the last ten years, there's been a small raft of books explaining how meditation changes the brain and specifically increases its capacities for calm, compassion, generosity, and other virtues. Richard Davidson's *The Emotional Life of Your Brain,* Norman Doidge's popular *The Brain That Changes Itself,* Rick Hanson's books including *Buddha's Brain* and *Meditations to Change Your Brain,* Alan Wallace's *Buddhism and Science: Breaking New Ground,* Jeffrey Schwartz and Sharon Begley's *The Mind and the Brain: Neuroplasticity and the Power of Mental Force,* Daniel Siegel's *The Mindful Brain,* John Arden's *Rewire Your Brain,* and a dozen other such volumes describe, often in usefully meticulous detail, the ways in which neuroscientists have been able to measure the increases in brain activity and brain capacity in areas correlated with positive mental capabilities. Fortunately for both of us, we will not be reviewing all of these findings here. But I do want to focus on two general types: clinical/behavioral and neurological. The first data set tells us what meditation does clinically, as measured by changes in behavior and mental health, the second set tells us how this happens in the brain.

One way in which studies have obtained the first type of data is to measure the effects of MBSR, the meditation and relaxation regimen that we discussed in the last chapter. Its effects have been measured by hundreds of research papers, more than forty projects at the National Institutes of Health,[4] and by mainstream scientists at mainstream universities, including UCLA's Mindful Awareness Research Center, the University of Wisconsin's Center for the Investigation of Healthy Minds, and labs at Yale, Brown, Duke, and elsewhere. In one long-term study, for example, Jon Kabat-Zinn showed that 225 chronic pain patients who were taught MBSR reported improvements in symptoms and mood, as well as fewer hospital visits.[5] (Interestingly, the study showed no diminishment of pain intensity; in other words, the patients were experiencing the same degree of pain but coping with it better.) MBSR has been shown to reduce stress and anxiety by a number of measures: heart rate, cortisol levels, a shift in the left frontal activity of the brain, and of course people reporting that they're not as stressed out as they used to be.[6] More broadly, here are some of the things mindfulness has been shown to do:

- Cut the relapse rate in half for patients suffering from depression[7]
- Reduce loneliness among elderly people[8]
- Quadruple the speed of healing from psoriasis[9]
- Improve overall immune function[10]
- Lower the rate of relapse among recovering addicts[11]
- Improve attention, planning, and organizational skills among grade-school students[12]
- Lower stress among breast cancer survivors[13]
- Reduce the side effects of organ-transplant surgery[14]
- Reduce ADHD symptoms in children[15]
- Relieve anxiety and depression in people with social anxiety disorder[16]
- Help patients manage chronic pain[17]
- Improve memory in older adults, with attendant neural correlates (increased symmetry in the thalamus) measured by brain scans[18]
- Counter age-related declines in brain function and fluid intelligence (problem-solving, reasoning, and similar abilities)[19]

This really is just the tip of the iceberg. The entire remainder of this book could be taken up with findings of this nature, and the rate of study continues to increase. Perhaps most remarkably, many of these benefits begin accruing after short periods of time. In one study, just two weeks of meditating just a few minutes each day was shown to be more effective than simple relaxation at lowering stress responses.[20] Even beginning mindfulness practitioners reported subjective improvements in awareness and nonreactivity.[21] Such findings have potentially huge societal and financial impact; imagine the value of a corporation improving its aging executives' mental abilities, or the impact of arresting memory loss in older adults. It's no wonder some of the hype about this new science is so breathless, why Silicon Valley types gather at conferences like Wisdom 2.0 to talk about how to adapt mindfulness to the workplace and market it to consumers everywhere. (More on that in Chapter Seven.) Meditation may be the ultimate disruptive technology.

Until very recently, however, it was not known *how* these changes in resilience and behavior came about. That has begun to change with the advent of contemplative neuroscience, and, in particular, our (only) fifteen-year-old understanding of neuroplasticity.[22] Neuroplasticity is the brain's ability to change itself, to paraphrase Norman Doidge,[23] in response to learning, experience, and other stimuli. Scientists used to think that brain development more or less ended at adolescence. Now we know that isn't true, and that, just like building muscles, you can build capacity in various regions of the brain throughout your life. This is true when you meditate, when you learn a new skill, and when you habituate yourself to various stimuli. A favorite example of neuroscientists is the study done on the brains of London taxi drivers, which found that the regions of the brain associated with visual memory (essential for memorizing London's rabbit warren of streets) were significantly more developed among the taxi drivers than among the general public. Neuroplasticity can also have negative consequences: one example Doidge discusses is how the overuse of pornography rewires the brain's pleasure centers, causing it to need ever-more-exotic visual stimuli to generate the responses associated with arousal.[24] As the saying goes (possibly coined by Doidge himself), neurons that fire together, wire together—for better or for worse.[25]

The myriad details of how neuroplasticity works in different contexts are quite complicated; it's not as simple as building up one part of the brain when you meditate, since various regions of the brain are involved in most activities.[26] They are also exhaustively discussed in some of the volumes I listed above, and as a non-scientist I'm not inclined to reinvent that particular wheel here. Instead, I want to bullet-list out some of the neurological changes that have been found to result from extended meditation, to give a sense of what we are beginning to understand:

- While meditating, meditators show enhanced frontal brain activity, enhanced gamma power in the occipital cortex, and decreased frontal reactivity to distracting and unexpected stimuli.[27]
- When MBSR students focus on body parts, alpha waves increase in the areas of the brain corresponding to the areas of the body under attention.
- When Richard Davidson measured Tibetan monks doing compassion meditation, he measured gamma activity— "the high-frequency brain waves that underlie higher mental activity such as consciousness"—greater than ever recorded in scientific literature.[28]
- An fMRI scan on the same meditators showed heightened activity in the insula, also associated with emotion and consciousness.[29]
- When Davidson tested meditators after a three-month retreat in 2005, he found their "attentional blink"—the brief gap all of us experience when we try to pay attention—to be much less than that of ordinary people.[30]
- Long-term meditators were shown to require less brain activity to perform cognitive tasks than non-meditators.[31]
- Mindfulness revealed activation in the anterior cingulated cortex (ACC), a "crucial node in the attentional network."[32]
- Meditators practicing focused concentration showed increased activity in the dorsolateral prefrontal cortex, visual cortex, and other areas involved in vision and attention.[33]

- Dr. Eileen Luders, in a series of studies, measured regional volumes in different parts of the brain, gray matter concentration, white matter fiber integrity, callosal thickness, hippocampal distances, and cortical gyrification—and found that meditators exceeded control subjects in *every one* of these measures.[34]
- One example in Luders's study: long term meditators' fractional anistopy (FA)—basically, the degree of connectivity in the brain's white matter fibers—was higher than control groups' in twenty fiber tracks. This is important because FA decreases with age, causing (scientists think) many of the symptoms of senility. Yet Luders found that FA decreased much less for long-term meditators than for other people.[35]
- Long-term meditation increases cortical thickness in parts of the brain[36] and increases gray matter volume.[37] These long-term results Davidson analogizes to "measuring the strength of the biceps of a bodybuilder when he's not doing curls."[38]

As before, these neuroscientific data are but a sliver of a large and growing scientific literature. Let me try to put this into a layperson's terms, focusing on how one region of the brain, the amygdala, interacts with others. (Interestingly, this description of the amygdala has been taught to high-schoolers as part of the MindUP curriculum, funded by Goldie Hawn's charitable foundation.[39]) The amygdala is the part of the so-called "reptilian" brain, the brainstem, that reacts quickly to threats, that has saved your life dozens of times by instinctively getting you out of a dangerous situation, and by firing off quick "fight or flight" responses. We all depend on our amygdalas, but if we're controlled by them, we're apt to be their marionettes, jumping when they say jump, fearing whenever they perceive a threat. (Indeed, you can see how the amygdala can be manipulated during any political campaign.) Animalistic impulses to anger, desire, fear—this is what the amygdala produces. How does meditation affect the amygdala? Davidson found that after two weeks of training in lovingkindness practice, there was less activity in the amygdala when subjects were shown distressing images.[40] In other words, they didn't react as strongly. Meanwhile, other parts of the brain that moderate the impulses of the amygdala are strengthened by meditation, including the medial prefrontal cortex, adjacent precuneus, and other areas necessary for self-regulation. For example, the prefrontal cortex is associated with body regulation, communication, emotional balance, response flexibility, empathy, insight, self-knowing awareness, and fear modulation—the last of which it accomplishes by releasing an inhibitory neurotransmitter (GABA) that actually counters the impulses of the amygdala.[41] In a study of MBSR practitioners, left side prefrontal cortex activation tripled after only four months of practice.[42]

In other words, activity in the reactive mind—the impulsive, want-it-don't-want-it, have-sex-with-it-or-kill-it parts of the brain—decreases with meditation, while activity in the reflective, regulatory mind increases. (By way of comparison, it's generally understood that when limbic activity in the amygdala and hippocampus dominates prefrontal activity, the result is a psychopathology.) Anecdotally, this model does seem to correlate with the experiences many meditators, including this one, have had. A stimulus is present that normally causes aversion: a difficult family member, a perceived threat. Yet rather than immediately react, meditators sometimes report a "spaciousness" around the negative stimulus. I want to lash out, but—okay, I don't have to. It seems to me that the physical processes these neuroscientists are describing do correlate to the mental-experiential processes I experience. There's no way to know, as yet, exactly what physical processes accompany or cause these mental events, and certainly no way to know that through introspection. But "feeling fear but not acting on it" is a physical, chemical process, even if it is experienced subjectively as purely mental in nature. As Freud is reported to have said, "all our provisional ideas in psychology will presumably someday be based on organic substructure."[43]

Why does all this matter? First, as Richie (as everyone calls Professor Davidson) said to me,

> The neuroscientific work provides a foundation that has enabled the incorporation of these practices in a wider swath of our culture. I see the work as creating openings in certain segments of healthcare and education that might not otherwise have been as receptive, by providing mechanisms, in modern scientific language, through which these dharma practices may actually be producing various effects. I think this has been extraordinarily helpful in these domains.

The science legitimizes the expansion of the dharma. It supports an overall view of the dharma not as religion, not as spirituality, but as a technology for upgrading the mind to be more resilient—"brainhacking," if you like. Appearances notwithstanding, it is helpful to regard the zendo more like a gym than like a church or a synagogue. In addition to its efficacy in talking about the dharma with others, I have found this outlook to be profoundly liberating, and will discuss it in more detail in just a moment.

Now, as with all such findings, there remains a significant gap between the scientific data—couched, as it usually is, in cautious terms—and its inevitable oversimplifications. Davidson again:

> There's a lot we don't know. People often think that we know that meditation has certain kinds of health impacts, but I think we know preciously little about that, and even less about *how* it may have those impacts. We know very little about the most effective ways of teaching these practices in a secular way. . . . We know almost nothing about what the optimal dosage, if you will, might be, and how that may vary across different kinds of individuals . . . we know a lot less in those domains than we think we know.

Even within the bounds of contemplative neuroscience, several methodological challenges remain: finding adequate control and comparison groups (there aren't so many people with 10,000 hours of meditation experience out there—my own number is around 3,000—and controlling for diet, lifestyle, and other factors is very difficult); correlating different meditation techniques, different stages of practice, and different states while measurements are taking place; selecting measurement techniques (fMRI, EEG, MVPA, etc.) and comparing results between them; correcting for other individual variations (including genetics: perhaps experienced meditators have different brains because they were born that way, and became interested in meditation as a result of those structural differences); and so on.[44] It's also unclear what scientists, and practitioners, even mean by "mindfulness" and "meditation."[45] As we noted in the introduction, in its classical definition in the Pali Canon, mindfulness (sati) includes recollection of thoughts; in its usual contemporary definition, based on the work of Jon Kabat-Zinn, it is focused entirely on the present moment, without recollection or judgment.[46]

And already, a backlash has begun. In general, the overreliance on neuroscience as a reductive explanation of all human behavior has rightly come under attack,[47] and so too within the dharma world in particular. For example, in a recent article in *Tricycle* magazine, Buddhist scholar Bernard Faure complained that people interested in the convergences between neuroscience and Buddhism have been selective in which Buddhist practices they study (true—no one is, as yet, interested in traditional Buddhist chants and rituals), overzealous in characterizing Buddhism as empirical (true, although the teachings of the Pali Canon are strongly empirical in nature, even if others are not), and that all this data is too preliminary to be meaningful (not really true).[48] Likewise, Donald Lopez, in the book *The Scientific Buddha* and the *Tricycle* article that preceded it, sharply critiques the tendency to see the Buddha as some kind of pragmatic scientist devoted to reducing stress, and analogizes the recourse to neuroscience to a previous generation's embrace of phrenology.[49] He notes that Buddhism has a long history of being presented as (or reduced to) science, and that the Buddha came not to prop up the conventional world, but to destroy it.[50]

These are useful, if overstated, correctives; it is certainly true that what neuroscientists are studying are aspects of Buddhist teaching, not the totality of it, and that Western popularizers are consciously extracting aspects of Buddhist practice from their contexts; that is exactly the point. Not only is mindfulness not the whole of Buddhist practice, it's not even the whole of Buddhist meditation practice, which also includes Tibetan *sadhana* visualizations, *tonglen* contemplations, and *ngondro* prostrations and offerings; Zen *oryoki* and *gassho* practices, together with an array of priestly rites; Theravadan chants and merit-making; and so on. But surely Faure's and Lopez's imaginary opponents are more straw men than real ones. Neuroscience is not and should not be the sole yardstick of the dharma's efficacy; the dharma has its own standards for that. But in the process of translation and evolution of the dharma, Western scientific language can be an extremely helpful way to understand how it works on those who take it up.

Lama Surya Das, the American-born, Brooklyn-accented Tibetan lama, occupies a unique position in this debate. He is, after all, a lama within an often conservative tradition. And yet, he is not just a Westerner who wears Western clothes and has many Western values, he has been also outspoken in favor of an emerging Western Buddhism that, in his words, is "pragmatic, effective, and experiential, rather than theoretical or doctrinal. We are drawn to spirituality that is simple, direct, and demystified—a sane, nonsectarian, integrated path to wisdom, personal transformation, and enlightenment for modern men and women actively engaged with life."[51] His ten principles of the Western dharma may have seemed fairly straightforward in Chapter One—but when they were published twenty years ago, Buddhists of all stripes were outraged. I asked Lama Surya who could possibly be opposed to a psychologically astute, egalitarian dharma. He answered in rapid fire mode:

> Those who want to preserve the traditional ways, the monastics, the male patriarchy, the people who do dharma in foreign languages, the translators, the academics. . . . Do I have

to go on? Many people look askance at egalitarianism—what about the guru and authority? Or gender: even now, Theravadan monks are unwilling to be equal with Theravadan nuns. Or, do we really want to have a psychologically astute dharma? Of course, but some say you shouldn't mix psychology with the dharma. So each of these points was very radical in the 1980s and 90s. And there are many people interested in preserving the original rituals, and the languages, and the scholarship, and the esoteric secret teachings for initiates only. So of course this westernization, secularization, scientificization is all well and good . . . but there's a lot going on.

Ultimately, and perhaps unsurprisingly, Lama Surya ends up with a "middle way" between the traditionalists and the scientists. Of neuroscience and secular mindfulness, he says,

I feel good about that, but of course we want to be careful not to throw the Buddha out with the bathwater and not end up with mere mental floss, good for your mental health but nothing about enlightenment, transformation, or radical evolution. Let's not fall into that. . . . The neurodharma movement is very exciting and interesting . . . but we don't want to reject the tantric juice, the transformative, the creative imagination of it all—in favor of a left brain, over-rational, and scientistic neurodharma. That would be a loss.

This seems an appropriate embrace, and an appropriate caution. As we'll see in more detail in Part Two, my own path was focused on the kind of transformation Lama Surya speaks about. And yet, a scientifically informed (not scientistic), pragmatically oriented approach can go hand-in-hand with serious contemplative practice. Consider the work of Stephen Batchelor, author of *Buddhism Without Beliefs* and a frequent colleague of Lama Surya at emerging Buddhism events. Batchelor once wrote that "there is nothing particularly religious or spiritual about this path."[52] This is certainly true for secularized and applied mindfulness—but for Batchelor, one of the leading voices for agnostic or secular Buddhism, it is also true for those pursuing the dharma as part of a serious contemplative path. Moreover, Batchelor told me in our interview, "Speaking as a meditation teacher, I can't tell you the number of people who come because they were interested in mindfulness and then wanted a deeper engagement with the teachings."

So is meditation exercise, brainhacking, religion, or—what, exactly?

Fresh-Baked Bread

The Insight Meditation Society in Barre, Massachusetts, occupies the site of a former Catholic retreat center. The meditation hall was once a chapel, and although the founders of IMS removed most of the stained-glass windows long ago, they left two of the windows in the vestibule (now used for walking meditation) intact. One of the windows depicts Christ in the wilderness, crying as if in desperation for the Lord. The other, directly across the room, depicts a scene from the Last Supper, with Christ distributing the bread of the meal, and, as every Catholic would know, initiating the first communion rite. One of the disciples, probably John, is looking on with rapt attention and a subtle smile on his face as he prepares to receive the flesh of God. There is love in his eyes, and he is resting on Jesus's shoulder. It is an exquisitely tender scene that can be appreciated by Christians, Buddhists, and, I hope, Jews alike.

Toward the end of a retreat I was sitting at IMS, someone stuck a yellow Post-it note next to John's face, with the words "Fresh Baked Bread" written on it, and a small drawing of a heart. It was funny, if a bit impudent, and it underscored the gap between the ornate mythology of Jesus and the clean, no-bullshit air of vipassana. The bread, after all, was symbolically contentious: I thought of all those raging Christian debates about transubstantiation, consubstantiation, and the ultimate significance of communion; about whether soda crackers really did turn into meat (to use Kurt Vonnegut's paraphrase of the ritual); and about how the efficacy of communion was one of the ways some traditional Catholics had maintained that theirs was the only way to salvation.

The Post-it poked fun at all of that. All these stories in the air— what if John and Jesus were simply mindfully enjoying the taste of warm, fresh-baked bread?

Religious people love to imbue objects with symbolic and mythic meanings. This bread is the body of Christ. This bread is what our ancestors ate at the Exodus from Egypt. This bread has social, cultural, even theurgical meaning. This is the critical move of most Western religion: away from the thing itself, and toward a web of significance. (Of course, there are also plenty of ways to re-embody Western religious rituals and center them around attention and mindfulness; I wrote a book doing so myself, and will return to the subject in Chapter Eight. But I am speaking here of the predominant tendency in these traditions.)

In my own Jewish tradition, this tendency is epitomized by the masterpiece of Jewish legalism, Rabbi Joseph Soloveitchik's *Halakhic Man.* Here is how Rabbi Soloveitchik describes the importance of a sunset inhering in its status as a legal signifier:

> When halakhic man looks to the western horizon and sees the fading rays of the setting sun or to the eastern horizon and sees the fast light of dawn and the glowing rays of the rising sun, he knows that this sunset or sunrise imposes upon him anew obligations and commandments.

Sunset and sunrise are important here not because they are beautiful, or because they, like everything else, arise and pass away, but because of their context in a conceptual map of meaning and obligation. So too with morality (this act is important because it is forbidden, or permitted, or will be punished after death), sacred text (this text is important because God wrote it), and other religious

obsessions. And of course, since only one set of symbolic associations can be ultimately correct, different modes of signification
quickly become grounds for conflict—even war.

Spirituality takes a different view—but one still distinct from
that of meditation. Spirituality is (often) about experience, not
myth. The bread is important not because of some religious notion
but because it can be eaten and enjoyed—because it can lead to a
spiritual experience. Mindfulness is often regarded in exactly this
way. When I eat the bread mindfully, I can appreciate it more. Indeed, the appreciation can often be quite profound. On that same
IMS retreat, I remember mindfully eating a single string bean and
having a sublime spiritual experience. The string bean was so beautiful, and so alive—its structure was intricate and harmonious, its
freshness felt vital. Eating it was almost tragic, as I felt those structures collapse in my mouth, but also quite sensuous. I don't want to
minimize the transformative power of these experiences—I'll talk
about them more in Chapters Six and Seven.

But I do want to distinguish them from what meditation is
about. Meditation is less about having a certain kind of experience
than about seeing *any* experience clearly, richly, and honestly. It's
not the what—it's the how. It does not require a taste for the touchy-
feely, a belief in God, or a suspension of healthy skepticism. It's an
empirical, mechanistic, and scientific process: by using one or another technique, the mind is gradually trained in a new way. The
brain is trained in a new way.

When people report that meditation has made them more pa-
tient and more resilient, for example, it's not because of magical
thinking. It's not the grace of the Buddha or the magical resonances
of these ancient chants that did it. It's the work that did it. Just like
doing curls at the gym builds larger biceps, meditating on the cushion builds a stronger prefrontal cortex (more or less).

Now, of course it's also true that meditation can lead to very relaxed states of mind, and that many people do it for that reason. It's
also true that mindfulness enhances spiritual experiences, just as it

enhances many everyday ones: if you meditate and then pray, your prayers will probably be more intense and sincere. But the essence of contemplative fitness does not depend on any of these intentions or contexts. Indeed, if "the point" is to retrain the mind away from its natural tendencies toward greed and revulsion, the process of doing so can be the very opposite of relaxation and joy. As I'll describe in some detail in Chapter Six, it can bring out all kinds of skeletons from the closet. Even on my very first meditation retreat, I spent several days "noticing" recurring feelings of self-doubt, self-loathing, and other aspects of my "shadow" that my very busy mind ordinarily occludes. Those were days of tears, of hard work—and yet also of a clarity of insight that I'd never before experienced. This was hardly the "spiritual narcotic" that one rabbi scolded me about when he heard I'd started meditating.

Nor is it Buddhism, exactly. Dharma is already evolving into non-dharma: it's already transcended its origins, it's become mainstream. Shoshana Cooper, who teaches meditation with her husband, David Cooper, thinks that within a few decades, Buddhist-derived meditation will be as unremarkable as Hindu-derived yoga. "Thirty years ago, yoga was for the weirdos, the hippies, and the drug addicts," she says. "Now, we don't give it a second thought. Why? Because it works, and we are practical people." And just as no one thinks that they are practicing Hinduism when they take a yoga class, so too have the forms of secular mindfulness we explored in the last chapter separated themselves entirely from Buddhism.

Really, the last two decades of dharma in the West suggest a very different mode of practice is taking shape. New ways of understanding and articulating meditation practice have arisen; mindfulness is about delinking, disidentification, reperceiving, decentering, defusion, distancing, and increasing meta-cognitive awareness.[53] It is contemplative fitness, optimizing the mind, rewiring the brain. If the generation of the hippies saw meditation first as a way to get high, then as a way to get connected with spiritual experiences, and finally as a way to relax amidst their stressful, upper-middle-class

American lives, today the dharma exists more as a diverse set of technologies for upgrading the mind.

This computational metaphor occurred to me not while I was wired up to an EKG matrix at Yale University, and not while trying out various new dharma gadgets, but, of all places, while I was on a three-month retreat in Lumbini, Nepal. Lumbini is the traditional birthplace of the Buddha, and as such has been a Buddhist pilgrimage site for thousands of years. It is also a backwater, perched on the Nepalese side of the border with India, far from Kathmandu, and lacking the tourist infrastructure of other such sites, like Bodh Gaya or Varanasi (Sarnath) in India.

The center in Lumbini, named "Panditarama" after the Theravadan teacher U Pandita, is not the cushy dharma resort that many Westerners, myself included, have come to expect from retreat centers. It's almost opulent by the standards of rural Nepal, but still, the electricity goes out most days, and in the winter, when I did my retreat, it can get cold and damp for days at a time. Plus, the practice is austere: meditating from before sunrise to well after sunset, no food after 12 p.m., and, ideally, no distractions such as popular culture, or music, or books. It's a demanding practice, and while it's probably the best thing I've ever done in my entire life, it can get rough at times, particularly when you're cold, and lizards are crawling around, and you wonder why you've schlepped thousands of miles to endure this particular form of misery.

One evening, I remember shuffling—mindfully, slowly, in fact, painfully slowly—into the small dining room for evening tea. The power had gone out again, so there was no heat or light, apart from a few flickering candles lit by one of the two nuns who ran the retreat center. I was hungry, and tired, and I'd had a rough several hours of monkey mind. As I waited with the other yogis, each of us bundled up in layers of clothing, blankets, and anything else that might provide some warmth, the head monk and one of the nuns went about their business, unperturbed by the challenging conditions.

It occurred to me at that moment that meditation practice is really quite straightforward. Each of us has a given mental architecture, but it's possible to improve it—to upgrade it, really. These Buddhist monastics, happily going about their business while the rest of us moped, are like an upgraded form of the basic human model. Of course, it also helps that they were just used to the conditions in Lumbini. But it wasn't just that. I knew how much work they had done, how many years they had trained, and how many months they had spent on meditation retreat. And it had worked: they were less stuck than the rest of us, more resilient, more happy.

Of course, a cold and dark evening is no big deal. But one of those same monastics, I later learned, was also dealing with a planned development right there in Lumbini that would threaten the retreat center's viability. Another had a very sick parent back in Europe. And another came from an impoverished family in India, with all the *dukkha* that entails. These were not privileged American yuppies learning to cope with the stresses of having a house in the Berkshires; these were people who lived close to the bone, and had augmented the human capacity for happiness.

This, then, is the dharma evolving—but dharma evolving *us*. The brain on dharma, conditioned by meditation, mindfulness, and related practices, is more evolved than the brain without dharma, if "evolution" in this sense is measured in terms of capacity for positive emotional and intellectual dispositions. The nuns bustling around Lumbini, Phil Jackson pacing the basketball court, Thich Nhat Hanh working for peace in the world's most troubled regions—these are all examples of brains evolved through dharma.

Can you see why this technological model might be so appealing, and so powerful, today? Cause and effect: do the practice, obtain the results. No need to believe anything, or be a certain kind of person, or take anything on faith or authority. I've found it very helpful over the years. There are times when I don't seem to be getting anywhere, where each sit is as hard as the one before it. Yet I know that the practice is working, regardless of how I feel about it. It's a mechanistic process. And indeed, so is consciousness itself.

Prayer may or may not work. God may or may not exist. These are impossible assertions to prove or disprove. But if you follow these particular instructions, you can see for yourself whether they work. That's a spirituality I can get behind.

Ajahn Sucitto, a British-born Thai monk, once described our situation as being like that of a donkey, tethered to a cart, with a carrot dangling just in front of its face. The donkey strives for that carrot, pulling the cart along, convinced that if it can just get a bite, it will be happy. When really, of course, what would make the donkey happiest would be to set down the burden.

As simple as this analogy is, I've come back to it time and time again. There are many carrots we humans chase after, some profound and others quite ridiculous. New cars, love, success, fame, promotions, property, spiritual merit-badges; it doesn't matter, really, whether they are absurd or sublime, because no matter what they are, they pale in comparison to the mind that has relinquished the burden it carries. Setting down the burden takes some retraining, some serious brainhacking, which in this case changes not only the software but the hardware of the brain as well. But on small and large scales, it does work. It works for the child dealing with pain in the hospital, it works for the yogi liberating herself from primal forces of greed and fear, and, yes, it works for the privileged Westerner at a cozy retreat center. Sometimes this can seem like mysticism—the bliss of being, the knowing of the Unconditioned—and maybe it is. But sometimes, and this may be even more liberating, it's math.

CHAPTER 3

NEW COMMUNITIES

Post-Traditional, Post-Speculative, Post-Boomer Buddhism

Memes migrate, and as they do, they adapt. Christianity enters "pagan" Europe and adopts its festivals and rituals. McDonald's moves into Japan and offers seaweed-flavored fries. And as the dharma has entered new cultures, from China to California, it, too, has adapted itself to changing social and ideological conditions. We've already seen how this process has unfolded in the Westernization of dharma, the extraction of meditation and mindfulness from their traditional Buddhist contexts, and their adaptation to mental health, organizational efficiency, and a host of other Western (and Western-capitalist) purposes. But not just dharma has been Westernized; sangha, community, has as well.

As we saw in the first chapter, most dharma communities in the United States were initially organized in a roughly traditional model: a head teacher or teachers, a set form and school of teaching, and some kind of hierarchical arrangement wherein students progress, apprentices are initiated, and the dharma is transmitted in an orderly way. Whether headed by Asian teachers or by Western ones, these dharma centers grew, flourished, and branched out all over America.

By the 1970s and 1980s, this began to shift—part of the processes Jack Kornfield has identified as democratization, feminization, and integration.[1] New kinds of people began teaching (and writing about) the dharma: most important, women, whose voices have significantly shaped the contours and priorities of the Western Buddhist world.[2] These have included Vipassana teachers including Ruth Denison, Sharon Salzberg, Tara Brach, Christina Feldman, Jacqueline Mandell, Kamala Masters, and Ayya Khema; Zen teachers such as Joan Halifax, Toni Packer, Jan Chozen Bays, Joko Beck, and Yvonne Rand; teachers from Tibetan traditions including Pema Chodron, Ani Tendzin Palmo, Sandy Boucher, and Khandro Rinpoche; independents including Joanna Macy, the writer bell hooks; and many, many more. As a result, not just the faces of the dharma (which have only recently begun to grow less white and less affluent as well as less male) have changed, but the nature of the dharma has as well, expressing more of women's lives and perspectives.[3]

But the experiences of women in the sangha also pointed to some fundamental flaws in the model inherited from Asia.[4] It concentrated too much power in the hands of omnipotent, guru-like teachers, which led to abuses, which we'll discuss in Chapter Nine. It replicated models of hierarchy, patriarchy, and authority, which thwarted personal actualization as much as they promoted it. And it perpetuated the sectarian nature of the sangha, as centers naturally specialized in specific schools and sects. In response, what some have called the democratization and "feminization" of the Western Buddhist community is a gradual process, I think, of correction.[5] Kornfield, in a 1998 article, said, "I do not want to be too idealistic. There are many problems that Buddhist communities must face— unhealthy structures, unwise practices, misguided use of power, and so forth. Still, something new is happening on this continent.

Buddhism is being deeply affected by the spirit of democracy, by feminization, by shared practice, and by the integration of lay life. A North American vehicle is being created. Already this vehicle draws on the best of the roots, the trunks, the branches, the leaves, the blossoms, and the fruit—all the parts of Buddhism—and it is beginning to draw them together in a wise and supportive whole."[6]

These evolutions are welcome, and fascinating. Yet even progressive, egalitarian dharma communities are often very culturally specific. Personally, there were times sitting at some meditation centers when I felt like the only non-Baby-Boomer-psychotherapist in the meditation hall. And while many sanghas work hard to diversify their membership, offering special programs for people of color, LGBT folks, and younger people, the cultures of many dharma institutions, publishers, magazines, and institutions are still slow to catch up with the post-white, post-modern, post-conventional, and fully wired world of younger Buddhist (and post-Buddhist) practitioners. So, while I don't want to jump on the all-too-easy anti-Boomer bandwagon (after all, these are the people who built institutions out of almost nothing), I also really appreciate the styles of non-Boomers, like self-described punks Noah Levine, Brad Warner, and others. Part of why I love these angry, straight, white punks is that they are stripping the dharma of its bullshit, and applying it to contexts and styles that, even if they aren't mine, are at least different from the norm. They're not soothing, they're not hippies, and they're often not even that happy, in a conventional sense—all of which are a welcome change of pace, I think, from the looming orthodoxy of sweetness which pervades the New Age world. I like art, not kitsch; Leonard Cohen Dharma, not New Age Music. (Cohen's Dharma name when he was a Zen quasi-monastic was Ryokan—I named my computer after him.) Maybe this is just style, but I feel like it's more than that.

Now, I don't want to overstate the case; there are plenty of Boomer-age teachers who dispense with the soft tones of Boomer-style spirituality. Some of the ones I know include Christopher

Titmuss, Guy Armstrong, Jack Kornfield, Lama Surya Das, Jan Chozen Bays, Pema Chodron, Joan Halifax, Bernie Glassman, Tsoknyi Rinpoche, and many, many more (if you're a cool older teacher, I'm sorry if I didn't mention you—I'm sure you are awesome). I still remember on one six-week retreat, when Guy gave a talk describing his struggles with fear and said "Fuck it!" from the stage— I almost squealed. And for every authentic punk like Levine or Warner, there are plenty of poseurs, hipsters, and, worst of all, professional packagers trying to make meditation seem cool or edgy. The fact that there is an emerging dharma community, often led by younger folks, does not mean that the existing dharma community is uniformly lame, or the emerging one is uniformly awesome.

Still, there is now a dizzying variety of dharma centers, teachers, communities, and modes of access out there, and some very different ways in which the dharma is transmitted—including by maverick teachers who deny that they're transmitting anything at all. Many Zen-trained teachers, such as Adyashanti, have blended Buddhism with Hindu-derived Vedanta, though stripped of the specific language of either tradition. Some, like Eckhart Tolle, have become better known than the traditions their teachings resemble. Some of this is just a matter of style and packaging—but some is more significant than that. Here, I'm going to explore two of these major trends: online communities and post-traditional teachers. Both, I think, are evolving the dharma in really useful and interesting ways.

Open Source Dharma

Avenue Q notwithstanding, the Internet is not just for porn anymore. Thanks to information technology, many dharma teachers and even "centers" now exist online only, and entire sanghas are constituting themselves in online communities.[7] Established teachers now routinely offer classes online, while websites like Dharma Seed offer thousands of dharma talks available free of charge. There is an extremely lively and diverse Buddhist blogosphere, ranging from post-Buddhist mavericks to traditional monastics: Buddhanet, The Buddhist Blog, Elephant Journal, Meaningness, Sweeping Zen, Thousands of Buddhas . . . the list goes on and on. Although an older generation might cringe at the idea, it is now possible to pursue a quite serious Buddhist contemplative path without ever leaving your home. As Lama Surya Das put it to me, "You don't have to trek to the East, give up everything, and learn foreign languages. You don't even have to go to a three-month retreat or sign up to be a Zen monk. You can click on the Web in non-real time and listen to a dharma teacher in any tradition and language." Enlightenment is streaming.

Now, there have been Buddhist resources on the Internet for twenty years, and the Internet simply as a distribution channel is quantitatively important, though not necessarily that qualitatively interesting. Where things get interesting is where the nature of online communities changes how Buddha, dharma, and sangha are experienced. Let's explore all three—in reverse order.

First, it is clear that the possibility for sangha—for community—is radically increased in online communities, because they can perpetuate themselves without the need for geographic contiguity. Clearly, something is lost when the personal contact between *kalyana mitta* ("dharma friends") and between teacher and student is absent. And yet, consider what's gained. Contemporary dharma teacher Susan Piver has created a fairly rigorous program of meditation, mindfulness, and study that exists entirely online. While some of her Web resources are available for free, subscribers are able to pay for additional content and, most important, access to Susan herself. The result is a level of teacher-student contact that is higher than on most retreats, let alone in daily life. Does it work? Before leading her first online retreat, Susan told me she was skeptical: "Doesn't a retreat mean you leave your house and your worldly concerns? Would the retreat magic arrive?" But, she says, "The retreat magic was there. It was very interesting that the people who were participating seemed to find camaraderie with each other even though they weren't in the same room. We were communicating off and on throughout the whole weekend online, and people were exploring things with a kind of freshness." Meanwhile, Susan is able to support herself financially, and her students are able to do the kind of serious practice that is difficult to do without an expert guiding the way. Moreover, they are able to do this without devoting money and time to fly off to a retreat center in Nova Scotia or New Mexico—Susan told me that many of her students live in smaller towns where meditation groups are small and hard to maintain. Her online community has made meditation practice possible for people in square states and red states, as well as for anyone whose family or professional life makes long retreats difficult.

Along with the networked nature of new online communities have come the values of the twenty-first century, Web 2.0 Internet: participatory culture, user-generated content, peer interaction, and frequent feedback among them. This has led to new iterations of what a sangha looks like. Buddhist Geeks, for example, is a national community of about 25,000 Buddhist geeks who come together every year for a conference but who are tied together largely by podcasts, group chats, and various social media technologies. (Actually, Vince Horn, who co-founded BG with his wife, Emily, said that the term initially meant "bringing the passion that a geek culture has to Buddhism" but that it came to refer to bringing "the geek ethos and geek culture . . . in contact with the Buddhist world.") The Dharma Overground is a lively discussion board made up largely of followers of the developmental path to awakening, which is discussed in Chapter Five. Such groups generally are not headed by a single guiding teacher, which resonates with a new generation's suspicion of top-down hierarchies and "expert" content providers, and with the previous generation's validation of those suspicions, in the form of power and sex scandals marring the Western dharma community. Rather, these new communities are participatory, often committed to some kind of egalitarianism, and, as a result, less focused and more diverse than traditional sanghas.

The dharma has evolved as a result. First, new kinds of communities have brought new ways of seeing the dharma. For example, Vince at Buddhist Geeks brought up the notion of "tightening feedback loops, trying to improve the quality of one's practice through improving the iterative cycle, the rapidity of the iterations." This is a concept from software development, but it applies to refining one's meditation practice as well. "That's a very systems way to look at improving something, as opposed to the traditional model of the brute force method, where you sit as much as you possibly can, and try to just figure it out over a long period of time."

Let's stay with Vince's example, because just on this point alone, the potential is significant. About three careers ago, I was involved in an open source software company. Open source means that the software's source code is available to all, rather than kept as proprietary. If you want to customize your version of Windows, you can't really do it—not without either an expensive developer license or an ingenious hacker. But if you want to customize, improve, and tweak an open source software product, you can go right ahead, as long as you possess the requisite skills. Over the last thirty years, open source software communities have created some of the most successful software on the planet—the guts of the Mac operating system, for example, or some of the earliest Web browsers. These were (and are) communities of interested, talented programmers, and the cream tends to rise to the top. If you submit a hack that doesn't work well, you'll be scorned; if you meaningfully improve on the software, you'll be lauded. Eventually, the messy ecosystem of open source software can create far more vibrant and resilient work than the tidy gardens of traditional closed source development. (That's my metaphor—the classic one is that of the Cathedral and the Bazaar, coined in 1996 by Eric Raymond.)

Brainhacking ought to be similar. The dharma is a thousands-year-old tradition of expert brain-optimization. Some very smart thinking and experimentation has gone into it. But no pre-modern monk had access to the science, the variety of contemplative traditions, or the technology that we have today. Religious fundamentalists like to say that each generation is worse off than the preceding one, but that is not necessarily true. Within five seconds of browsing, you can access more information, and more wisdom, about the contemplative path than the most dedicated eighteenth-century abbot could in a lifetime. And if there's something you learn by combining vipassana with core energetics, or questioning the gender assumptions of an ancient meditative tradition—that is valuable stuff, and it ought to be contributed to the wider contemplative community, where it can be explored, evaluated, and critiqued. The feedback loops are far tighter when you can get responses from other brainhackers and integrate them back into your practice; you improve faster, and a greater diversity of approaches results. Online conversations about mindfulness, stress reduction, enlightenment, productivity, neuroscience, and so on are not just facilitated by information technology; their very natures are transformed by it. We are witnessing the birth of an open source dharma, in which innovations and mutations can be assimilated (or rejected) in a way never before possible. And that is just one example.

Relatedly, the conception of the Buddha—both the traditional Buddhas and Bodhisattvas and the whole notion of a spiritual teacher—has changed as well. Now's a good time to introduce you to my close friends Kenneth Folk and Beth Resnick. I've known them for years—I had a retreat crush on Beth back in 2002, and first met Kenneth when he was just some guy Beth was dating . . . who happened to be enlightened. They're a great, odd couple: Kenneth is fifty-something, white-haired and gregarious; Beth is much younger, and on the quiet side. They both have great smiles. And lately, they've begun teaching—Kenneth is now a celebrity in the hardcore dharma world, and Beth will soon be also. Importantly, they teach almost exclusively online, enabling them to reach students who don't have dharma centers anywhere near them, and who are interested in the particular forms of practice that Beth and Kenneth teach. And notice how, for Kenneth, the means of accessing the teaching has changed how the teacher is understood—in his words:

> [Technology] is allowing access to other people we wouldn't have had access to before. And because we yogis don't have great population density anywhere, meeting online is the only way to get critical mass as a community, so online is really about the only way we can do it. If I'm a brainhacker and I'm with fellow brainhackers, I'll tell them what I know. But I'm not handing out wisdom here. In my experience, some people have no patience for the handing down of wisdom. The important thing here is that I am replaceable. There's nothing special about me in this relationship. So I expect everybody to get to where I'm at, as it were, and beyond. There's not going to be this power structure where you pay homage to me. In some ways, I'm like a physical fitness trainer. Clearly my trainer is stronger and more fit than I am. That's why I go there and pay him money. But he's not pretending to be special in that way. And everybody knows he's strong because he works out more than I do.

This, to me, is an important transformation in how the teacher is understood. In some quarters, it's more evolution than revolution—but in others, it's downright radical. And this isn't just Kenneth's sense of himself. Vince Horn told me, "Kenneth doesn't present himself as a guru, but as someone who has mastered certain techniques and can teach them. And Dharma Overground is a culture of DIY meditators . . . with a lot more experimenting. More like a maker culture than a university culture."

Clearly, there are costs and benefits of a less centralized, less guru-centric approach. Obviously, if you're a newcomer, it can be a bit bewildering to have multiple voices and different approaches. Then again, if you're a newcomer who's used to following Twitter feeds and Tumblr blogs, it might not be so disorienting after all; on the contrary, it might feel more like what you're used to. And within these new sanghas, there are more inclusive and interesting models of interaction, well suited to a more participatory generation. Teachers are tested and talked back to. Cults of personality are called out for what they are. Models are readjusted, and alternatives proposed. And participant communities decide, by feedback and by clicks, which methods work and which do not. Online communities are not completely circular, of course; there are still experts and beginners, and an information gap between them. But they have more robust mechanisms of feedback and innovation than the occasional evaluation form.

It's not all sweetness and light, of course; Buddhist flame wars are as obnoxious as any others, all the more so because people get to demean one another's spirituality. ("You're supposed to be so enlightened, so why are you being such a narcissistic idiot!") There are also serious gender issues in some online communities, with a kind of neo-macho hacker ethos marginalizing voices deemed too "soft," which often means too female, feminine, or femme. But ultimately, the flamers and complainers are unlikely to be the best contributors. No one likes to feel bad (well, almost no one). And so one can expect the worst offenders to be voted off the island sooner or later. Meanwhile, these communities' spirit of experimentation and curiosity is abetted by technologies that enable sharing, comparing, and conversation.

I'm optimistic about the possibility of an open source dharma, where sectarian differences are understood clearly, respected where appropriate, and set aside where they aren't; where fideism and group-think is valued less than iconoclasm and individuality. And I think there are hearty Buddhist precedents (not that they're necessary) for such things. Think of the Buddha saying not to trust anything he hasn't verified for himself; or Tibetan monks arguing the fine points of psychology; or the Zen koan that if you see the

Buddha on the road, kill him. Of course, almost all of this rubs traditionalists the wrong way. But wait, it gets worse.

Post-Traditional Buddhism

Blogger David Chapman writes on the current front page of his blog: "The past couple of decades have been dominated by a 'Consensus Buddhism,' whose time has passed. I am cheerleading for emerging alternatives."[8] Right on! But—let's go back even farther. The Western "Consensus Buddhism" that Chapman decries (at length) is itself a hybrid of tradition and innovation. We've already seen how urban Zen Centers and rural vipassana communities consciously blended the old and the new, leavening the dharma with social justice work, or yoga, or psychotherapy, or whatever. But let's go back even more. Even the first Zen teachers in America came from a "reform Zen" movement in the nineteenth century. And even before that, some Zen schools in particular critiqued temple ritual and religious trappings, focusing on the "single practice" of meditation/zazen.[9] Whatever the contemporary American "Convert" Buddhist scene is— Chapman has a pretty good point when he inveighs against "Nice Buddhism"[10]—it is already a reform of a reform of a reform.

Well, that process is continuing today, albeit in more radical ways. For example, contemporary figures like Chapman, Stephen Batchelor, Ken McLeod, Brad Warner, Glenn Wallis, Kenneth Folk, Hokai Sobol, Ted Meisner, Daniel Ingram, and Stephen Schettini (the "Naked Monk") have each—despite significant differences among them in style, temperament, and emphasis—articulated various forms of secular Buddhism, agnostic Buddhism, non-traditional Buddhism, scientific Buddhism, non-speculative Buddhism, and even (in Wallis's case) speculative non-Buddhism. Although several of these approaches explicitly disagree with one another, the mere array of labels gives a good sense of what these writers are on about: purging Buddhism of the myth (gods! monsters!

hell-realms!) and focusing on the practical, verifiable aspects of meditation and mindfulness practice.

One of the ur-texts for these forms of post-traditional/secular Buddhism is the Cula Malunkya Sutta,[11] in which the Buddha distinguishes what is important—how to eliminate suffering—from a host of metaphysical questions, such as "whether the world is eternal or not eternal, finite or infinite; whether the soul is the same as or different from the body; whether or not an awakened one continues or ceases to exist after death."[12] The Buddha analogizes this situation to a person struck by an arrow who refuses treatment until he knows irrelevant things like whether he was shot by a longbow or a crossbow; while he dithers with these questions, he bleeds to death. The message is clear: the metaphysical questions with which religion often concerns itself are probably not resolvable, and definitely not the point. Who knows whether the soul exists after death? And who cares? What difference does it really make, in terms of the suffering (or joy) you experience? I'm reminded of something Eckhart Tolle is reported to have said, that it doesn't matter who you were in your past life if you don't know who you are right now.

I find secular Buddhism deeply appealing, no doubt because I, like many secular Buddhists, was raised in a religious background that seemed to require belief in all sorts of preposterous statements. (Schettini, the Naked Monk, for example, was Catholic, and was later a Tibetan monk. Today, his outlook seems vaguely Theravadan but without the orthodoxy or the affiliation.) But I would like to part company with some of its less reflective evangelists and decline any claim that secular Buddhism is somehow closer to the "original" or "authentic" teachings of the Buddha, or Hui-Neng, than all the smells and bells are. Those claims are problematic for several reasons. First, they're often Eurocentric. Oh, those "ethnic Buddhists" with their primitive "folk religion." Good thing we Westerners have helped them understand their tradition better. (Of course, it's also true that however Eurocentric some reformers may be, the whole notion of "Buddhism" as a "religion" is a Western, Eurocentric one, first used in the nineteenth century and full of imported concepts about what a religion is supposed to be.[13] So it's possible that post-traditional Buddhism is an important corrective to other Western distortions.) Second, claims of authenticity are claims of power: I'm real, you're not, listen to me. Third, they're more than a little absurd coming from practitioners of a neo-Buddhism that clearly is of recent coinage and, as we just pointed out, is descended from a series of reforms.[14] What's the point of this rhetoric? Let's just appreciate post-traditional Buddhism for what it is, rather than claim it's more true or real or authentic than something else.

Now, it's true that the dharma I practice personally is post-traditional in nature, and that that is, in fact, part of its liberating power. One of the insights that has really "stuck" over the years has been the claim of the Buddha that rites and rituals do not lead to liberation. Matthew O'Connell, in an essay entitled "Post-Traditional Buddhism: The Quiet Revolution?" makes the bold claim that "the exotic"—the exotic symbolism of religious Buddhism, in this case— "provides us with a back door exit from our mundane existence, and further, from the pain and suffocation of modernity. The problem is that such an exit can lead us not to freedom but to escapism and the adoption of a new identity, a newly fabricated self that reflects its new environment, both ideologically and behaviorally."[15] This seems right to me, not just in the Buddhist case but in those of other religious communities as well. For O'Connell's part, he was enmeshed in the comforting, "exotic" rituals of Tibetan Buddhist practice for some time, only to experience "delusion, disappointment, and immense dissatisfaction that came about as a result."[16] Amid all the new jargon, clothes, and rituals, he found that "I was simply exchanging one internal structure that surrounded my core with another." Eventually, O'Connell went through a purgative period of undermining all the myths of Buddhism: its hagiographic tendencies, its ahistoricism, its tendency to whitewash the misdeeds of the past (and present). He even went on to question the post-speculative Buddhism he adopted as a result, catching himself preaching "that what I believe is best [and] must be best for you too."[17]

Having spent twenty years in multiple faith communities, and having worked as a progressive activist within them, I wish that every believer of every religious tradition would go through this process of questioning. From an evolving dharma perspective, this kind of refining of the dharma holds considerable potential. Stephen Batchelor, probably the foremost Western philosophical interpreter of Buddhism, made this point when I spoke with him:

> The West is the first encounter with Buddhism that brings a sense of historical consciousness. In China, there was a meeting of two high cultures, but there was not a sense that "this has happened before." One of the things the West can bring to Buddhism is a sense of historical consciousness. I think our practice in the West is necessarily a bit more ironic as a result. We're not going to practice on the assumption that this is what the Buddha taught and it's been passed down to what this lama is saying today.

This strikes me as an essential corrective to the tendency all of us have to make idols of our teachers and traditions—a tendency that, as we'll see in Chapter Nine, can often have disastrous consequences. Irony does not equal cynicism or alienation; it is simply the understanding that these are complex traditions, and that appropriations of them (together with statements that this is what Buddhism "is") are potentially Eurocentric, often misguided, and all the time selective in nature.

If post-traditional Buddhism is an experiment, what is the data? Liberation. Kenneth Folk said that in his maverick teaching:

> I'm not doing anything new, except being willing to talk about this any way that works, even if it means leaving Buddhism completely out of the conversation, which I'm more than happy to do. I happen to have training in Buddhism,

I can use those ideas, and I think you have to give people some sort of conceptual framework, but I don't care what that is. I am ruthlessly unsentimental and pragmatic about this. I'll talk about it any way that gets the job done. And the job, I'll reiterate, is this particular kind of mental development. So what's new is that when you don't feel married to any particular schema or any particular tradition, you can get really efficient.

In his conversation with me, Kenneth used the analogy of mixed martial arts, which began as an attempt to find out which martial art—karate, or kung fu, or whatever—was the best. Yet as Kenneth relates,

> it turned out, over time, it wasn't what any particular school or technique was consistently going to beat all the others. It turned out that you had to synthesize everything and plug the holes in your game. . . . This is what's happened in pragmatic dharma: all of us have gotten together online, and we talk about this very openly, and we see what works. If it doesn't work in the ring, it immediately gets tossed out. If we come up with some way to foster this kind of development without any kind of meditation and without any talk of the Buddha, great! I'll get another job.

This is radical stuff, of course, and it enrages traditionalists who regard "talk about Buddha" as sacred. But Kenneth and his friends at Dharma Overground are not simply making stuff up to suit their preferences; they are also highly traditional in their use of Theravadan Buddhist practices and maps, and highly dedicated ("hardcore" in Daniel Ingram's words) when it comes to diligent practice. They, like Jon Kabat-Zinn, are pragmatic rather than religious in their approach. But unlike Kabat-Zinn, their aim is not stress reduction but the big E: enlightenment. This is actually a very traditional goal, is it not?

Perhaps the most radical post-traditional Buddhist movement is that of "speculative non-Buddhism," centered around the work of Glenn Wallis, a scholar-practitioner who seeks to transcend both the "soft" Western Buddhism of stress reduction and the "hard" Asian Buddhism of ritual, tradition, and text. Wallis is an iconoclast, equally critical of the mavericks we've just discussed as of (in his surely exhaustive typology) accommodationists, apologists, comparativists, conservatives, constructionists, critics, fundamentalists, interpreters, post-traditionalists, secularists, traditionalists, and true believers.[18] Wallis denies that the mavericks O'Connell discusses are doing anything new, and argues against the creation of "Buddhist" discourse of any kind, which inevitably involves claims of authority, problems of ahistoricity, recourses to dyadic thinking, and elisions of the distinctions between rhetoric and reality.[19]

Interestingly, although Wallis's work is marked by academic sophistication and self-reflexivity, the actual practice of his sangha is not substantially different from the post-Zen Zen practices of independent teachers such as Adyashanti. Adyashanti and similar teachers also decline the label of "Buddhist," even though they, like Wallis, were trained in Buddhist traditions. It is surprising that Wallis, perhaps the most theoretically and academically rigorous of the post-post-traditional mavericks, converges with those who dispense with theory entirely. Perhaps the apophatic mystics are right after all.

Post-Post-Traditional Buddhism

Well, the backlash has set in. Not just fuddy-duddy scholars or orthodox Buddhist fundamentalists, but many dedicated practitioners are finding their way back toward some of the very traditional forms and models that the last three chapters' worth of maverick teachers, secularizers, therapists, and scientists had set aside. This, too, has taken many forms.

For example, Vince Horn told me that "the really difficult part of Buddhist Geeks has been holding the Buddhist part and not just rejecting it. I think there's value in working with the tradition as it is. We can't reject it wholesale, because there are actually things that have been figured out and worked out really well. If we reject them, we're just going to have to figure it all out again and go through the same learning process." It makes sense, of course, that Jon Kabat-Zinn and his colleagues stripped the Buddhism out of mindfulness—but it also makes sense that if one is pursuing mindfulness seriously, it might be worth learning from two thousand years of experience. Horn said that "holding the conservative and the innovative elements at the same time" is the current edge in his own practice.

A second way in which this return to traditional forms manifests is in the increasing numbers of students interested in the Tibetan, Zen, or Theravadan developmental models of enlightenment, which we'll look at in the next chapter. Indeed, simply embracing the goal of liberation more generally might be termed a return to a traditional form. Yet as we'll see in the next chapter, today's developmental meditators are embracing not just the goal but the means as well.

A third return to the traditional is occurring within the scientific community. I want to introduce you to Joe Wielgosz, a student of Richie Davidson's at the University of Wisconsin's Center for Investigating Healthy Minds. Joe and I have been friends and fellow travelers for over a decade now, sharing enthusiasms, beers, and plenty of misadventures along the way. Now, he is part of a younger generation of scientists—the students of the pioneers—that is questioning many of the core assumptions of contemplative neuroscience, and the mindfulness world in general. When I asked him about whether he loves or loathes the secular mindfulness phenomenon, he said:

> There are good and bad things about that, benefits and risks. One benefit is that it implants this idea in our culture of mental training being super-important: the idea that you

can train your mind, and the idea of non-doing and slow-
ing down. Those are super-healthy. The risk is that there's a
fundamental misunderstanding and betrayal of what mindfulness practice is for. It's marketed as being like jogging: it'll
make your heart work better! But that's not what these practices were for, and not what they're designed to do. Maybe
they *do* help your heart-rate, but that's a side effect. What
they are designed to do is undermine and dissolve your
sense of reality. As we get deeper into this, someone is going to have to confront the fact that Buddhism is not about
better health outcomes. . . . The parts that Jon Kabat-Zinn
emphasizes are the content-free parts. But, for example, the
preliminaries in Tibetan Buddhism? This is about the fact
that you're going to die and you have to come to terms with
it, not how to be relaxed and less stressed. It may be that
you'll become more stressed.

Surely that's an important point—as well as fighting words. Indeed,
the sometimes unhappy marriage between the dharma and psy-
choanalytic modalities can lead to a distortion of what the dharma
is trying to do. As Donald Lopez has pointed out, it's often more
about stress induction than stress reduction,[20] and as Ryo Imamura
once observed, you can be well-adjusted and dharmically deluded.[21]
Moreover, as we'll discuss in more detail in Chapter Five, not everyone who chants a mantra once a day wants to have their sense of
reality dissolved, yet such things do tend to happen if one stays with
meditation in a serious way. As Joe further pointed out, "We're navi-
gating five different worlds at once: Traditional Buddhism, traditional Western Buddhism, secular mindfulness, hardcore empiricist
neuroscientists, and neuroscientists who are into Buddhism," each
of whom may have different worldviews and operating assumptions. Today's younger neuroscientists, if the ones I've met at Mind
& Life and similar conferences are any indication, are at once more
radical and more traditionally minded than their teachers.

Perhaps the most radical mavericks today, though, are the most traditional of all. Their numbers are small, but many dharma practitioners have begun turning, again, to monastic forms. In the Theravadan tradition, several monasteries now exist in the United States, including Northern California's Abhayagiri Buddhist Monastery, established by followers of Thai master Ajahn Chah in 1996; the Bhavana Society, founded by Bhante Henepola Gunaratana in 1985 and hosting numerous Western and Asian monastics; and the nonsectarian Bodhi Monastery in New Jersey.

One friend of mine, for example, recently took on the practice of being an *anagarika,* a homeless dharma practitioner who acts a bit like a monk (specific precepts, shaved head, special clothing) but lives in the world rather than in a monastery. Now known as Ñaniko ("One of insight"), he says he chose the path of renunciation in part because his primary teachers were monastics, and he was inspired by their "teachings and their way of being." It's clear that his teachers, past and present, are the primary inspiration for Ñaniko's own decision to put on the white costume of the *anagarika;* he describes his current primary teacher as:

> very, very in himself, and spacious. There's a palpable presence and a depth to his presence that I feel. And an embodiment of wisdom and a warmth in his heart that I see again and again in different situations . . . he's living his dharma, he's living his practice. There's a peacefulness that's very tangible and very "this-worldly" in his way of being. And I say to myself, "Wow, this is possible."

Ñaniko did not take on this path out of disgust for the world, but rather because it was "a very useful form to deepen my practice and understand what the dharma is more directly." He doesn't even like the word "renunciation," preferring terms like simplicity, contentment, and release. In a way, his practice is the polar opposite of the secularized dharma taught in prisons and schools; it is monastic, even austere. It does not accommodate the dharma to daily life but requires daily life be accommodated to the dharma. And yet, maybe the distance isn't so great. First, Ñaniko himself teaches "applied dharma" in educational contexts, and in the context of "wise speech" and nonviolent communication. More to the point, his own life choices reflect a consummately Western search for meaning, and an embrace of Asian monastic forms that would have been unthinkable a century ago. Living in the city while renouncing a variety of material pleasures is, itself, an evolution in the dharma, and expresses the same spirit of innovation and pragmatism that animates the dharma punks, Buddhist geeks, and even, I would submit, the psychotherapeutically informed mindfulness crowd. After all, what did Ñaniko say? Not that his teacher was saintly, or exalted—but that "this is possible."

It is with this question—what is possible—that we transition to the second part of this book. So far we have seen how the ground of dharma has shifted, particularly in the last thirty years in America. And while not discounting the religious and spiritual aspects of Buddhism, we have seen how meditation and mindfulness have also been extracted from it to become a kind of contemplative technology, a way of upgrading the mind and building a kind of mental fitness that is as useful, mechanical, and measurable as physical fitness. Now, I want to explore how it unfolds in practice. How does dharma evolve over the course of the contemplative path? How have new generations of practitioners learned from (and not learned from) the wisdom of our distant elders, and that of our immediate predecessors? And for those who take seriously the aspiration of liberation, what is possible?

part two

Path

CHAPTER 4

BEYOND BLISS

When Every Mystical State You've Ever Wanted Isn't Enough

In the first part of this book, we've explored how meditation and mindfulness have been extrapolated from their Buddhist contexts and adapted to a dazzling variety of Western purposes, from relaxation at the spa to productivity in the workplace. We've seen how contemplative neuroscience has backed up some of the most enthusiastic claims of meditation's cheerleaders, and how it has brought us to a true turning point, a moment at which contemplative practice seems poised to enter the mainstream as it never has before. And just as this has happened, we've also seen how new communities and new forms of teaching have evolved as well, as if ready to take up the challenge.

In the Tibetan model of ground, path, and fruition, these evolutions constitute changes in the "ground," in how things are, in how the dharma is and is presented. Now, however, I want to shift the focus to the "path," which refers to how the dharma evolves in one's own practice, and how the practitioner evolves as a result. This necessitates a turn from these new contexts and new applications of mindfulness to a very traditional one: the pursuit of *nibbana,* nirvana, awakening, enlightenment. As we'll see, this, too, has been a site of enormous change over the last twenty years, with some very startling consequences: maverick teachers who talk openly of their own enlightenment, new warnings about the perils of the contemplative path, and, not least, the total inversion of everything many of us thought enlightenment was about to begin with. Let's start with the last point first.

In the Beginning,
There Was the Veridical Mystical Experience

I first got involved in contemplative practice because I was interested in mysticism. Mystics from around the world report remarkable experiences of body and mind that are highly unusual. They report a certainty of knowing, deeper and more sure than any ordinary perception, that they are at one with the entire universe, or with God. They claim to receive insights into the truth of reality. And, to my collegiate and young-adult mind, they seemed to bring together all that was worthwhile in the human condition: a powerful, self-splitting experience that was at once supra-orgasmic and completely enlightening. What could be more worthwhile, I thought, than getting It—the answer, the big E, the whole meaning of life?

For many people, these questions would lead immediately to experimentation: probably with entheogens (the more appropriate term for "psychedelics," the word means a substance which "brings the god inside") at first, then maybe with meditation, yoga, or shamanism. I dabbled in these in my twenties myself, and, as for many others, the experiences they provided were a gateway to the contemplative path.[1] But more than I dabbled, I read. In college and graduate school, I read testimonies, tracts, and accounts of mystic quests; accounts of visionary ascents, ecstatic unions, and divine theophanies. I was entranced by the possibility that "God," that be-ing or reality whose existence or nonexistence seemed to be such a critical issue—after all, some people made it the center of their lives, while others denied its very existence—could be directly perceived.

I also doubted. Scholars and philosophers have spent a fair amount of time trying to arrive at criteria for evaluating the mystics' subjective, hard-to-verify claims. On a superficial level, the details of mystical experience, naturally, vary from tradition to tradition: Catholic nuns have visions of Christ, Hindus of Krishna. Perhaps some of those experiences are false, or projection—or perhaps God manifests in a variety of forms, or certain ineffable core expe-riences are interpreted in religious language by the mystics. Even beyond the details of what is experienced, however, the subjective experience itself—the so-called "universal" experience of nearness of union, of knowledge that transcends verbal articulation—even this experience is difficult to verify. How do we know that what the mystic says happens, happens? And how do we know that it isn't all delusion?

Why I chose this intellectual path over a more experiential one is, itself, a long story. The short version is that I was living in the "closet" as a self-denying and repressed gay man, and the closet af-fects much more than just sexuality. When you're lying to everyone you know about something really important to you; when you're living a fake life, with a fake career and fake persona and fake identi-ty; when you're completely cut off from the sources of love and truth in your own life—well, it's hard to imagine that your dreams could actually be accessible. Other people would write books, have mysti-cal experiences, and have sex. I would do my best at masquerading.

And so I did, acquiring degrees and learning Kabbalah, practic-ing a kind of Orthodox Judaism, only occasionally nibbling at the edges of this self-constructed cage. Even studying mysticism was too "out there" to be respectable, so I went to law school, and pursued a serious career in environmentalism, ethics, and legal philosophy—which are subjects I am still involved with today. But throughout this decade of my life, I never lost the thirst for this supposed experience of ultimate truth—the Big One.

Just after I turned thirty, I was riding in a taxi with my then-girlfriend when the taxi was suddenly hit by a tow truck running a red light. She broke both her legs, I suffered a major concussion—I have very poor memory even to this day, which offends a lot of people whose names I forget—and both our lives changed forever. Within six months, she'd dumped me, I'd come out not as "bisexual" but as "mostly gay" (these days, I just say "queer"), and, for good measure, I quit my law job, grew my hair long, started writing and playing music, and finally made it to Burning Man.

A year after that, I started meditating.

I think it was helpful that, when I started, I really had no idea what to expect. My first retreat was billed as "Jewish meditation," and I actually thought that I would just show up, do some meditating, and probably have the huge mystical experiences that I'd read about for ten years. I thought that if the experience was powerful enough, well, that would be The Point, the mountain at the end of the world.

Little did I know that I'd be experiencing not God and all Her Angels but five days of knee pain, self-hatred, doubt, and restlessness. I couldn't sit still, I couldn't stay focused on my breath, and I definitely couldn't go without reading or writing for a week. What I went through was hard—really hard. I doubted what I was even doing there, feeling that religion was just a balm over deep, psychic wounds. I didn't want to be wounded—it seemed like other people on the retreat were, and would never get over it, and were doing all this work to just somehow convince themselves that the pain was worthwhile. I wondered if I wanted to dissolve my own ego in the All primarily because I didn't like myself, just as my favorite fun activities were those in which I "lose myself" in the music or visuals or sensual experience. And of course, I deeply suspected that the projection of God is only a projection of our great need to be held, cuddled, loved by our distant or dead parents. Bad enough, I thought, that I seek to overachieve and impress others so that I can earn their love, like my six-year-old self getting love for being clever. My perception that being radiates love, that all human interaction is just a clearer or more obscure exchange of yearnings for love—this awareness makes whole a void. Is it *only* that? Only a consolation?

And yet, a few days later, I had the mystical experience after all. From where I sit now, it was nothing special—which is to say, it was completely life-changing, and also completely the predictable effects of diligent practice for a few days. Indeed, what I experienced on that first retreat, and many more retreats since, is really just a side effect, if you can believe that. It's not even the *point*. It's like a delicious taste, which is beautiful and profound and sensual—but only a side benefit of nourishing the body with food. Can you believe that? What I'd wanted all my life—and then drank in, for years of meditation practice, perfecting the method, deepening the experiences, luxuriating in waves of joy and bliss and knowledge and oneness—all of it—I drank it in, I did more than my teachers said I should do, and I don't regret it—but all of it was a *side effect*.

What, exactly, took place, then and on many subsequent occasions? Well, that depends who you ask: the scientist, the contemplative, or the mystic.

Neuroscientifically, there have been only a handful of studies looking at different meditative states. One of the aims of Transcendental Meditation (TM), for example, is to cultivate a state of pure consciousness (*turya chetana* in the Vedic tradition) that has awareness but little to no cognitive content. And indeed, advanced TM meditators in this state have been shown to have high alpha coherence, showing consciousness but very little gamma activity, which would suggest discursive thought.[2] Other studies have looked at states of open presence, basic awareness, or nondual consciousness, with intriguing results.[3]

Experientially, of course, I had no access to any of that. I can only speak phenomenologically. In my first few years of practice, I learned that it is possible to slow down the mind so much that literally watching paint dry is fascinating, beautiful, and interesting.

Even if it's already dry. It's also possible to scramble the mind with letter permutations and free associations so much that the thinking mind seems to let go and a strong sense of unitary consciousness arises. And it is possible to refine awareness itself so much that the emptiness of things, and the role mental construction plays, becomes a directly apprehended reality. Moreover, there is a sense of presence in these experiences that is more than a sensation of having one's mind altered. A great love arises, and an obvious certainty that the love is not just arising within the self. Rather than the self containing the feeling of love, the love seems to contain the "self" and everything else within it. When the thinking mind and desiring mind are slowed down enough, this love and compassion arise naturally, without any prodding or effort from me. (I'm very bad at prodding myself to be nicer; for me, the only way that works is to actually become more loving, sincerely.)

In other words, in highly concentrated mental states, I have had experiences that conform almost exactly to mystical testimonies and descriptions—including many I had not yet read when I had the experience. A sense of union; a feeling of peace; a sense of proximity to the Divine or the Universal. It is all exquisitely beautiful. For many mystics and "spiritual people," this is enough. It's the answer. Trustworthy, experienced writers promise a glimpse of Ultimate Reality, and an upwelling of authentic love—and there it is. And for many religious people, it is painfully obvious that what is happening here is an encounter with God—it fits all the criteria, it leads to expressions of love; what more could one possibly want?

Well, I was educated to be a skeptic, and I've seen the danger of naive faith in spiritual experiences. When a New Ager concludes that "We're All One," that is, at worst, harmless. But what about when someone concludes that only his or her religious dogma is true? How different is the New Age leap from that of fundamentalists? So, back in those early years, I wrestled with the meaning of these peak experiences. Here is some of what I wrote on a meditation retreat in 2004:

The relaxation response critique says: when you're relaxed, your brain thinks all is one. But really that's just a feature of brain chemistry.

In that state now, I can hold the critique. However, the critique cannot hold the state I am in now.

If I were seeing pixies, the critique might be stronger. But I am just seeing a light, a bed, a computer, etc. It's true that my body and mind are relaxed. But that is neither adding to nor subtracting from theological speculation. What it is doing is letting me absorb the magnitude of the truth.

For example, every time you eat, you are eating the sun. All sources of energy on this planet, stored up in plants, long-dead plants, animals—all comes from the sun. This is true even of plastic soda bottles. And every atom in everything you see was once in a star. In busy, ordinary, "small" mind, these truths are just facts. We can evaluate whether they are artfully expressed or clichés, or whether we think they are mere diversions. We may have other things that we think are more important.

All relaxation does is allow the truth to be felt. The mind is cleared, like a dirty window wiped clean, and the magnitude of what we might ordinarily take for granted inspires tears. Moreover the mind is quieted so much that all that's left is its true nature: God. Awareness, radiating love. I have said this before, but what a miracle, that all we have to do to be beautifully loving creatures is just relax and allow.

As Hafiz says, you are God in drag.

Those were beautiful years—even if, as has to be the case, those great highs were unsustainable, and caused the inevitable lows to be more and more painful. When I work with students today, I'm often uncertain as to how to guide them when they report experiences like these. On the one hand, I would like to save them some of the suffering that I experienced by getting attached to mind-states and getting heartbroken when the most exquisite of them pass away. On the other hand, those first few years of practice were so lovely! The only analogies I can think of are sexual. Sure, today I have better technique, and I'm not so swept away by a single kiss, a single caress. But wasn't it wonderful to have been swept away for a while?

In my case, the novelty wore off due to repetition. Whether I was deluded or not (and of course, whether generations of mystics were as well), whether the sense of knowing was real or not, began to be less and less important. It became more relevant to understand even the most wonderful, rapturous mystical experiences as just a mind-state. Granted, it is a very pleasant mind-state, but it passes, and it's just a contingent phenomenon like everything else. Anyway, most traditions hold that mind-states *(devekut, samadhi, unio mystica)* are significant not because of a story about what they represent but because they can engender more compassion and more wisdom. The stories cannot be verified; but the effects can.

So, having cultivated these states for a while, and having watched them all ebb and flow, I began to be interested how they might help me along the path of insight (described in the next chapter). Luckily, at just the time I thought I'd plateaued in my various concentration states, I learned that much stronger concentrated states of mind were possible than anything I'd experienced so far—and that they could be put to use. That's where I turned my attention next.

And Then There Was *Jhana*

The *jhanas* are states of heightened consciousness, brought on by intense concentration, that have been cultivated by Hindus and Buddhists for three thousand years. They are altered states, full of bliss and a sense of the sublime/numinous/holy, and they play a central role in the Buddha's Eightfold Path ("right concentration"). Indeed, the way I now understand the wonderful mystical experiences I've just described is that they are simply products of a highly concentrated mind: the same states regarded as the *summum bonum* of some forms of mystical praxis are regarded in most Buddhist traditions as a potential dead end. As a means to acquiring insight, they are of instrumental value: dozens of times in the Pali Canon, the Buddha describes the *jhanic* mind as "purified, bright, unblemished, rid of imperfection, malleable, wieldy, steady, and attained to imperturbability," and thus ready to do the work of insight. But as an end in themselves, they get you nowhere.

Well, sort of. In my experience, they do get you somewhere—precisely by getting you nowhere, and showing you that wonderful, life-changing mind-states are not really "it" from the point of view of really changing the mind, evolving compassion and wisdom, and moving along the contemplative path. This came as a shock to me; I'd spent about fifteen years yearning for powerful, consciousness-altering experiences—only to find, having achieved them without the use of any external substances, that they were kind of beside the point. They're very, very nice, and that's about it.

Here, after a few introductory notes, I will describe my experiences of the *jhanic* states and describe what I believe to be their significance for spiritual practitioners. Readers interested in more detailed accounts of the *jhanas* might look at Ajahn Brahm's *Mindfulness, Bliss, and Beyond*; Shaila Catherine's *Focused and Fearless*; Richard Shankman's *The Experience of Samadhi* (featuring useful interviews with leading *jhana* teachers); and Leigh Brasington's encyclopedic website, LeighB.com. Here, I'll start with introductory notes about what I did, why I did it, and how it compared with other things I've done.

What I did was cultivate *jhana* states—there are eight of them in traditional Buddhist thought, though other systems have more—by cultivating *samadhi*, which in this context means focused, one-pointed concentration. This is done by laser-pointing the attention on a single object, and holding it there no matter what. You don't spend a lot of time processing your feelings in *jhana* practice, although you certainly learn a lot about the mind, its resistances, and how to work with them. Rather, the instruction is to zoom in on the object of concentration: perhaps the minute sensations of the breath at the nostrils, as described in the Anapanasati Sutta, or on colored discs called *kasinas*. In the practice I learned, taught by the Venerable Pa Auk Sayadaw, a Burmese meditation master (who looks, incidentally, like the stereotypical image of an enlightened Buddhist monk—robe, walking stick, Yoda-like appearance and speech patterns, etc.), one focuses on the sensations of the breath just below the nostrils until the mind creates a mental image of the breath called a *nimitta*. This image looks like a stable light on the inside of your eyelids, and during *jhana* practice, it grows and morphs in remarkable ways. (Some *jhana* teachers, I should note, don't teach in this way and even argue that doing so is based on a misunderstanding of the Buddhist sutras. Fair enough.) Eventually, the mind gets really, really quiet, and enters some very distinct and distinctive mind states—the *jhanas*. It is fascinating, really, that 2,500-year-old texts describe these states of mind, and some New York Jew sitting at a retreat center experienced them both as they are described in the texts, and as recounted by thousands of other practitioners.

Incidentally, there are different schools of thought among Buddhist teachers as to what constitutes a *jhana* and how to cultivate it.[4] Some hold that discursive thought and perception of the outside world must completely stop for a *jhana* to be truly taking place. In this model, a *jhana* is a totally absorbed, dissociated state of mind; the meditator is only aware of the object of meditation and nothing else. Even the passage of time is not noticed in such an absorbed state. Other teachers, however, will say that a *jhana* has commenced as soon as its factors are in place and an obviously altered state of mind has arisen. My own practice was a hybrid of these two approaches. Pa Auk Sayadaw holds the more strict view. Yet after a full month of rigorous concentration, I was unable to achieve the total absorption his practice demanded. I would enter clearly altered states, but would still be aware of strong bodily sensations and the sense of time. Therefore, after one month, I switched to the more moderate approach, which I had learned earlier from an American teacher named Leigh Brasington. (If Pa Auk Sayadaw is the quintessential Buddhist monk, Leigh is the opposite: a self-described computer geek, he is totally down to earth, funny, and Western.) I still cultivated *jhana* in the "strict" method: I created and concentrated on the *nimitta*.[5] But I proceeded through the first four *jhanas* even though the absorption was not total. My experiences, as profound and powerful as they are, should thus be understood as only partial in nature. I am a beginner, not an expert in these practices.

So: why did I do all this? I had three reasons initially, and discovered two additional ones along the way. First, insight depends on concentration; you've got to get the mind quiet enough to see these characteristics clearly. In one Buddhist metaphor, concentration sharpens the sword of the mind, which can then be used to cut through delusion.[6] So I went to practice concentration for two months as a kind of warm-up for a three-month insight retreat, which I subsequently completed in Nepal. In my estimation, the concentration I built up really helped move me along the path of insight. Second, I did *jhana* practice because the pleasure of *jhana* is an aid to hard meditation retreats, and is, let's face it, delightful. Distractions and hindrances are suppressed in *jhana*, and the experience is deeply purifying and refreshing; one emerges with an extremely sharp, clear, and quiet mind, which can be like a fresh drink during a long, dry meditation retreat. Finally, I admit, I was curious about *jhana* itself. On those earlier retreats that I've just described, I experienced what many meditators experience when their minds become concentrated: deep contentment, bliss, gratitude, love, and awe at the beauty and miraculousness of ordinary life. *Jhanas* are like those concentrated mind-states squared, amplified, distilled— and I wanted to see what they were like.

Along the way, I discovered two additional purposes to the practice. One is the deep "purification of mind" that is required to enter *jhana:* you really have to see and let go of all of your stuff, which in my case included a lot of grief, confusion, loneliness, ego, expectation, and just plain chatter. Every moment is an opportunity to let go of all this stuff, and I had a number of extremely powerful openings that I talk about in other chapters. In addition, the *jhanas* were themselves a powerful lesson in letting go. They are like everything I had dreamed about from the moment I became interested in spirituality as a young adult. Imagine your greatest dreams fulfilled, in oceans of light, bliss, love, and mystical union. Now imagine that you have to let them go. This is the lesson: that even the greatest of states arise and pass. You can't hold on to anything conditioned, even the dearest and most precious experiences imaginable. This insight alone was surely worth the price of admission.

I will now describe my experiences of each of the four basic *jhanas.*[7] (The "upper" four are less essential to insight practice and the points I'd like to make here. They are described well in the books I mentioned earlier.) While the descriptions that follow may seem hyperbolic and overblown, I assure you that I am deliberately understating and underdescribing the experiences. By way of comparison, when I described some of my experiences to a friend, she remarked that they sounded similar to what Elizabeth Gilbert describes in her book *Eat, Pray, Love.* Well, as it happens, the experiences I described earlier in this chapter were quite similar to those Gilbert describes. They were world-shattering, mind-altering, and profound. But the *jhanas* were far, far more powerful and more profound—perhaps an order of magnitude more.

The first *jhana* is like the "big wow," an awesome peak experience that arises after the mind has finally settled on the object of concentration with focused, sustained, one-pointed attention. Bodily or emotional rapture called *piti* may arise, suffusing the body with bliss or filling the mind with awe—sometimes the feeling is more "gross" and embodied, other times more subtle and purely mental. In my experience, the *nimitta* would become radiant, awesome, and beautiful, and grow to fill my entire field of vision and surround my body; the experience was like a glowing, energetic light surrounding and cocooning my whole being. It's quite captivating. There is also a sense of seclusion—of finally being safe from the chattering mind. From a spiritual perspective, this was like holiness as the big amazing awesomeness, full of *mysterium tremendum* and radical amazement. It's Niagara Falls, the Grand Canyon. Like many mystics, I'll use erotic analogies as well; the first *jhana* is like having sex, before orgasm: panting, arousing, *ah—ahh—ahh*—that sort of thing.

Eventually, though, the first *jhana* begins to feel like too much effort. You have to work to keep it up. And so, after anywhere from fifteen minutes to an hour or more (my longest was one hour), the mind gets tired of ecstasy, excitement, and bliss and moves naturally, without a lot of directed effort, onto the second *jhana*. The transition between *jhanas* is always from gross to subtle: the more gross factors drop off, revealing the more subtle ones underneath. In the case of first-to-second, the factors of applied and sustained thought drop, and the other factors—rapture, joy, and one-pointedness of mind—reveal themselves more. Usually this "drop" is conscious; after a few weeks of practice, I would feel a kind of mental itchiness when it was time to move on, and would consciously resolve to let these factors drop and the others predominate. A few times, though, the drop happened automatically; the mind would just bail out. Eventually, the four *jhanas* are kind of like four rooms in a house that you've come to know; you don't even have to make the resolve clearly, because you know the territory and can recognize it and adjust quite naturally.

In the second *jhana*, the feeling shifts to joy—"drenched in delight," in Shaila Catherine's words. Effort drops away, and the mind rests one-pointed on its focus. I experienced the second *jhana* as being like swimming in a *mikva* (the term means "ritual bath" but that doesn't quite get at the womblike sense of it) of light—in my journal I wrote that when the *nimitta* expands, it is a "waterfall of shimmering light that fills your body with joy." Again, sometimes this was partly a bodily sensation, other times purely mental. There

was often a bright light in my eyes as well—more on that below—
and sometimes a deep sense of healing. This is it, you're here, you
can trust and let go. The sexual analogy here is to the time of orgasm
itself—not the first moment, but the longer period of time if, like
me, you like really long and drawn-out orgasmic states. It's like that
gorgeous sexual feeling of letting go. Sometimes it really felt as if
the light were kissing me, penetrating me, filling me. In religious
terms, this felt like God as lover; the *fascinans,* the erotic partner
envisioned and embodied by mystics. It's really something—and all
this while sitting quietly in meditation.

Believe it or not, the mind eventually finds all this ecstasy, even
without effort, a little gross. *Piti* becomes too showy; it's almost ex-
hausting. When I was first learning the *jhanas,* I would spend several
days focusing on each one before moving on. Part of this was to really nail down the *jhana;* the Buddha said that someone who moves
on too fast is like a foolish cow wandering from pasture to pasture.
But another reason was that it took me a while to get disenchanted
with these states. For several days, I couldn't imagine anything more
wonderful than the second *jhana.* But eventually disenchantment
sets in—once again, an insight that is itself worth the price of admission: eventually, the mind gets disenchanted with anything. So
the grosser factor of rapture drops away, leaving behind only joy
and one-pointedness.

If the second *jhana* is like an orgasm with God, the third *jhana*
is like resting comfortably on the breast of the Goddess; its dominant sensation is contentment. Here, the love is less erotic and more
familial; it's like being cradled by your mother—that kind of *ahh.*
The light I experienced was golden, radiant, and warm. Many times
I cried and felt healed. Other times I was still and concentrated. And
sometimes I felt like a little boy sitting by the window, with sunshine
streaming in. In the third *jhana, piti* is relinquished, and *sukha,* joy,
becomes predominant. *Sukha* is quieter and more subtle than *piti,*
it's less embodied and more like an emotional, intellectual joy with
a honey-like component. Meditators know *sukha* from whenever

the mind in concentrated and everything just feels lovely. The mind is content. What could ever be wrong with the world? Of course, *sukha* is so lovely that we naturally cling to it, which means we suffer when it's gone—that's what's wrong. But in and of itself, *sukha* is like honey.

Unsurprisingly, for many people, including me, *sukha* was once the whole point of meditation. In the years I described in the first part of this chapter, I basically spent my time cultivating *sukha*, thinking it was enlightenment and being devastated when, a few days after retreat, it seemed to disappear. In all, I spent three years down this false path. Three years! Buddhists call it one of the "corruptions of insight." Others might call it a galactic waste of time.

Finally, there is the fourth *jhana*—the real point of it all, it sometimes seems. In the fourth *jhana*, even joy passes away. The experience is totally neutral: just *ah* as in "Ah, I see." And yet, it somehow—just *is*. I can't quite describe it; there's a powerful sense of equanimity, a closeness to the object, and not much else. Somehow, this state is the most beautiful at all, even though it is totally colorless, blissless. The erotic flavor is not even postorgasmic; it's post-post. The mind is clear, the restlessness is gone. It doesn't feel good anymore, but in some deep, profound way, it feels so extremely good and peaceful that it's not even necessary to feel good. This is not awe, not love; it's just *What Is*. It's a love beyond love; satisfaction without joy or even contentment.

For me, the fourth *jhana* is really the point because it leads to one of the deep insights of the *jhanas:* that God is not in the fire, or the earthquake, or the flood. There's a tendency that all of us have to deify and thus "idol-ize" certain states. Oh, that gorgeous warmth of lighting candles. Oh, we were so high during that drum circle/yoga session/whatever, that was really *it*. But that's not *it*. *It* is what's always here; even the fourth jhana isn't *it*—it's a state, with equanimity and focus that are conditioned and thus pass away after a time. You can't cling to it either.

Now, does that mean that these great altered states—including the *jhanas* themselves—are without value? Well, not quite.

Getting Beyond the Good Stuff

Most spirituality is, in large part, a state-change business. Before you pray, do yoga, meditate, et cetera, you're thinking about mortgages and to-do lists, but during your practice, something shifts and you feel opened to something that feels "greater." Afterward, you feel refreshed and reenergized. This is what state-change is: moving your mind from one way of being to another. And spiritual seekers have developed a wonderful array of tools to enable it to happen. These are good things, right? Sure they are.

States are also valuable in that they move you along the path, they give you some rewards along the way, and when they lower the walls of ego, they can open the heart and help people become kinder and wiser. If you've ever felt transformed after an experience of prayer, or yoga, or shamanic work, you know this yourself: the mind has far more capacity than we usually understand, and when its capacities are explored, we grow as human beings. Many people never even get to this stage—and if only they would! So, while I personally am interested in the further stages of the spiritual path, I am politically more interested in the initial stages. I believe that spirituality can bring more and more people over to the good side of the fence—the side with more concern about equality and justice, more respect for the environment, and more pluralism on global and local levels. All that work happens at the basic level of spiritual states: just helping people discover these deep truths for themselves.

But the limitations of spiritual states—and thus the path of concentration itself—are perhaps as important as their strengths. First, states can lead to their own kind of addiction: Wow, that was a great edge realm, now can I have another? How do I get high again? This is a spiritual dead end, a kind of masturbatory spirituality that's not so different from being addicted to drugs. You get high, you get withdrawal, you get high, you get withdrawal. It's kind of ironic, since, as I just mentioned, one of the many benefits of spiritual highs is that they tend to reduce clinging to getting high. But sometimes it doesn't work that way, and one addiction is simply substituted for another. I've met a lot of "spiritual" people who really are just looking for their next fix, and it's sad. Check out Jack Kornfield's *After the Ecstasy, the Laundry* for more on this phenomenon.

Second, and relatedly, state-withdrawal sucks. Wonderful spiritual experiences can lead to a whole huge pile of suffering when the effects pass, and you're left wondering what the hell went wrong. Believe me, I've spent many months in just that sense of bewilderment. The answer is actually pretty simple: I mistook something conditioned for the unconditioned. You just can't relive those peak experiences after a while. I've tried. I've tried really hard. It just leads to suffering. The only thing you can do, over and over again, is let go. Let go of everything. Every desire, every identification, every place where your ego is hiding out and saying "I'm this." Let go, let go, let go, and keep on falling—because there ain't no place to land. Yet this falling, I am here to tell you, is the same as flight.

Because, third, the states are not the point. As Joseph Goldstein put it, "one week [on retreat] gives the breakthrough to getting a little high and coming to the false conclusion that this is what meditation is all about. But two weeks, we've found, gives enough exposure to enough ups and downs so that you can see the balance between particular states—which is the whole message."[8] This is also true if the "point" is something more than balance between states but, you know, God, Liberation, the Unconditioned, Emptiness, Nirvana, call it what you will. If that is the point, it doesn't come and go; it is what's always here, totally colorless, totally omnipresent, and in fact, it's the only thing that *doesn't* come and go. There is no state that is it. Not feeling special about this, not feeling relaxed or wise or anything in particular—although sometimes those feelings may arise in the wake of letting go. It just *is*. States thus can be confusing as to the Really Big Stuff.

Finally, mistaking a state for It can have real political consequences. The reason is something I've elsewhere called "fetishizing
the trigger." Fetishizing the trigger happens when we find a trigger to amazing mystical states, and then mistake the trigger for the
state, the finger pointing at the moon for the moon itself. This is the
root of fundamentalism: this ritual is holy, that one is not; this religion is right, that one is not; this experience is real, that one is not.
States are powerful, and that means they can be dangerous.

Anagarika Ñaniko, whom we met in Chapter Three, told me
that today "mostly my practice is very mundane, very ordinary." He
says that he used to have "'bells and whistles' retreats where there
were a lot of those kinds of experiences opening up. That was great,
very useful at the time, and went a long way to strengthen faith and
to dispel certain doubts. But it also had its negative effects in terms
of the corruptions of insight. . . . There are transformative moments
on the path, and those moments are significant. But they don't come
about through craving or clinging."

This, to me, is wise advice. States are great, but they propel you
along the contemplative path—they're not the path itself, whether
that "path" is that of a serious meditator on a long silent retreat, or a
worldly mindfulness practitioner. The buzz is not the point.

Now, as it happens, I was told on one of my first retreats that
concentrated mind-states can become narcotic. But I wanted them
anyway—and I don't regret it. Those three years of concentration-
idolatry brought on all kinds of insight, compassion, and the other
benefits I've just described. They were also freaking amazingly awesome and beautiful. So if you're just starting out: Cultivate states!
Just try not to get too attached to them or think they're something
they're not. Love, learn, and let go.

The *jhanas* taught me that all I'd ever wanted—experiences of
mystical union, bliss, and beyond—weren't enough. Or rather, that
they weren't "it." But for those of us who have eaten the apple, tasted
the forbidden fruit, and been transformed by it—is there anything
beyond? Sure there is.

CHAPTER 5

BEYOND NOW

The Evolution of Enlightenment

"Enlightenment" is a supremely misleading term. The Buddha never said it; there's not even a Pali word for it. And while later Buddhist traditions described enlightenment in various ways, many of which seem to have to do with extraordinary experiences (and even extraordinary powers, in the traditional texts), the Buddha himself simply said, after his night under the Bodhi tree, that he was "awake." Awake to suffering, its causes, and how to end it; to the delusory nature of the separate self; to how things really are. He talked about liberation, and about the end of suffering—but "enlightenment" came later.

Obviously, enlightenment is not everyone's goal. Certainly, the world of therapeutic mindfulness has a different set of aspirations: healing illness, easing pain or stress, and so on. But as one's individual engagement with the dharma evolves, it's often the case that one's interests and goals do as well. On the surface, two Buddhists sitting on meditation cushions may look quite similar. But if one of them is sinking into a Zen *koan* to unstick certain patterns of mind, while another is following the breath to train the mind in nonattachment, while a third is cultivating concentration to enter into bliss states—well, those are different mental activities, even if they look the same from outside. Let alone the Christian Buddhist meditating to have an experience of the Holy Spirit, the therapeutic Buddhist trying to get some insight into her "stuff," and a post-Buddhist aiming to develop calm and clarity in the workplace.

Can we make sense of this mess? Sure we can.

What's It Going to Be Then, Eh?

Once upon a time, mysticism was thought to be everywhere the same. It was first articulated by William James in the early twentieth century (though it was also put forward by the Theosophists before him). At first, this view was adopted by many scholars of religion, who set about drawing correspondences among different religious and spiritual traditions. Then, just as it began to be seriously questioned by academics, who began to note difference after difference among mystical testimonies, it became picked up in the 1960s and the New Age as a maxim of spirituality. Of course we're all the same, all fingers pointing at the moon; of course a Kabbalist, a Buddhist, a Hindu, and a Christian are all basically talking about the same reality. Whatever differences occur in their testimonies are just details—societal constructs, the wrapping around the Gift.

Unfortunately, this well-meaning New Age view tends to be, well, colonialist in nature, setting up a uniform hierarchy of world mystical experiences and ranking as inferior those that do not accord with the "highest" form (usually identical with the form the ranker himself practices). Unitive mysticism is the best, some say. Others say personal, devotional, and theistic mysticism. Still others favor communion with plant and animal spirits. To me, rating and

ranking these different iterations of realization is a job for dogma-
tists, not contemplatives—and certainly not scholars.

I prefer the way Kenneth Folk's conception of "contemplative
fitness" put these debates in perspective. As Kenneth put it, "No one
would say that Michael Jordan is a bad athlete because he doesn't
play tennis as well as Serena Williams." Surely this makes sense.
Basketball players and tennis players do different things—but they
can both be star athletes. Likewise in contemplative practice. Some
grow the heart, others the mind; some stimulate more love, others
more wisdom; some stir up energy, others calm it down.

Even within the dharma, conceptions of the "goal" are at least as
varied as machines in a contemporary gym. For the Buddha of the
Pali Canon, the goal is liberation: the cessation of suffering, the end
of the endless hamster-wheel of dependent origination, of mental
formations leading to desire leading to clinging leading to suffering and so on. *Nibbana,* or nirvana, was not originally conceived as
some magical heavenly world, or even a permanent altered state of
consciousness. It is usually described, in the early texts, negatively: as
a candle being snuffed out, for example. Yet as the dharma evolved,
so did its ultimate goal. As Buddhism became a religion, personal
liberation was quickly seen to be too difficult for laypeople to actually attain. So, if you ask many Asian lay Buddhists about enlightenment, they will say that this is for monks only, not householders—or
that it can only be accomplished in a future incarnation (perhaps
into a Pure Land), which you attain by accruing merit, or by the
grace of a bodhisattva. This is one reason why Western Buddhism
looks so foreign to Asian practitioners: accountants and shipping
clerks behaving like monks, sitting on retreats, even taking some of
the monastic precepts for short periods of time.

Moreover, different sects vary in their conception of what enlightenment even is.[1] Mahayana Buddhism shifted from the ideal of
the *arahant,* the fully liberated being, to the *bodhisattva,* one who
voluntary postpones his (or, rarely, her) own enlightenment out of

compassion to liberate other beings. This means that laypeople have much more that they can do besides behave virtuously and support monastic communities; now they can petition bodhisattvas for help, pray to them, honor them, and treat them as semi-divine beings with the power to change lives. To some, this aspect of Mahayana can feel like a defeat. And indeed, it does represent a shift (back) to traditional religious attitudes: the belief in beings who have the power of salvation, the focus on prayer and petition and ritual, and the new prominence of a priestly clergy. But Mahayana also made the values of Buddhism comprehensible to a far wider audience than earlier forms did; there's a reason it became known as Mahayana, the Great Vehicle, while older forms (including Theravada) became disparaged as Hinayana, The Lesser Vehicle. Mahayana Buddhism also shifted the meaning of nirvana; if Theravada practitioners described nirvana as the extinguishing of a candle, Mahayana practitioners described it as seeing emptiness *(shunyata)* in everything, and being liberated within the phenomenal world, rather than "beyond" it. The candle need not be extinguished in order for you to understand its emptiness, and thus nirvana and samsara are really one and the same. Subsequent schools of Buddhism took this even further. In Tibetan Vajrayana practice, for example, the goal is to recognize that you have Buddha-nature in you right now, that your perfect mind is present right here and now, and that really, there is nothing you have to do, since your radiant, perfect mind, the crystal-clear, mirror-like quality of the mind, is present right here and now. [2]

If all this sounds paradoxical, then the Rinzai school of Zen emphasizes precisely that element. To really, intuitively understand that everything is empty, that nirvana is samsara, you need to short-circuit the mind's ordinary logical processing. In contrast with the Soto school's emphasis on gradual awakening, Rinzai teachers say that you need a radical break, a *kensho* or *satori,* an enlightenment moment. Yet there is development even here. In some Rinzai schools, one *satori* will do—but in most, there are many such moments,

integrated into a long and gradual path of mental training. Hakuin—
the seventeenth-century Zen master who first uttered the famous
koan "What is the sound of one hand clapping?"—had thirteen *ken-
shos* over the course of his practice.³ In one Zen parable, the evolution of enlightenment is likened to the arduous process of finding
and taming a wild ox.⁴ Even in those schools that hold that you're
perfectly enlightened already, there can still be a lot of furniture
cluttering up the mental room, so to speak. Many Tibetan teachers
speak of the *bhumis*, for example, which may be likened to stages of
awakening to awareness—although even those teachers point out
that you're already enlightened and just need to realize it.

Back in the American vipassana world, a funny thing happened on the way to the meditation hall: people stopped talking
about enlightenment. These days, only beginning meditators talk
about enlightenment at vipassana retreat centers. Teachers try to
gently guide them away from such things, and toward more attain-
able goals such as being more present on a moment-by-moment
basis, gradually increasing one's capacity for compassion, and so on.
Why has this happened? In the early years of the Insight Meditation
Society, we're told, American yogis, mostly freshly returned from
India, would indeed jockey for sublime states and lofty spiritual attainments. According to folks who were there (I was in diapers), the
whole scene devolved into spiritual materialism, with rumors about
who was an *anagami* and who a mere stream-enterer, who could
attain absorptive *jhana* and who could not. (It's funny—I wonder
how absurd that sentence must seem if you don't know these particular terms. Maybe it makes more sense, actually, since once a
practice becomes a sport, it really doesn't matter what the ostensible
goals are; the essence of it is the competition.) In response to this
trend, IMS and others in the American Theravada scene buried talk
of enlightenment, stages, attainments, and the rest, and focused on
what one might expect a psychotherapist-heavy group to focus on:
gradually improving practitioners' abilities to be happy, compassionate, and well-adjusted people. Liberation became a matter of

degree, and with an assumption that some days will be better than others. The whole notion of a path with goals became seen as part of the problem.

Now, this divestment of goals was not universal. Daniel Goleman's *The Meditative Mind* (originally published as *The Varieties of Meditative Experience*), published in 1977, charted quite clearly developmental models both for the path of insight (which I'll discuss in this chapter and the next one) and the path of concentration (discussed already). But Goleman's approach eventually became the exception, rather than the rule. "Be here now" won; "strive diligently to gain your liberation," at least in a developmental sense, lost.

Enter the Pragmatic Dharma movement. As studied by Jared Lindahl, Sean Pritchard (formerly a Theravadan monk), Jake Davis, Willoughby Britton, and others, there is today an emergent movement—part of the maverick trends we described in Chapter Three—interested in a return to a more developmental approach to meditation. These scholars have created the Contemplative Development Mapping Project, a fascinating new attempt to synthesize and understand developmental models of enlightenment, primarily from Buddhist traditions but across religions as well.

The most outspoken exponent of the Pragmatic Dharma movement is also the most unusual Western meditation teacher to ever be featured in a *New York Times* story,[5] "The Arahant Daniel Ingram." Daniel is one of those characters who make life endlessly enjoyable. He's not a professional dharma teacher—actually he works in an emergency room in a hospital, where he puts his full enlightenment to good use. He also has strong opinions, expressed in clear, strong words. When we first talked on the phone several years ago, for example, he accused me of representing "the absolute worst of the vipassana mushroom culture," which was about "keeping 'em in the dark and feeding 'em shit," the 'em in question being the naive yogis kept insulated from the details of the developmental path. Then again, as an *arahant*, a fully enlightened individual who has completed the Theravadan path—and a resident of Alabama—

he did so with a loud, cheerful twang, as if he were talking about whether the bottom was gonna drop out of that there thundercloud or not. That Daniel calls himself an *arahant* irks traditionalists to no end—and, I've noticed, causes my Facebook friends to disbelieve him as well. Which suggests that he might be on to something. Why don't we want to believe that some people may have actually achieved this goal? What belief are we holding onto that their success might violate? In Daniel's view, "you're totally disempowering people" when you don't talk about enlightenment. "You're not saying it's possible. It's closed, it's cryptic."

As I've already suggested, I tend to take a less harsh view of a previous generation of teachers. I both understand the reasons they chose to minimize the linear models of contemplative development, and I do not agree that there's been some sort of sinister plot to keep the yogis ignorant. At the same time, Daniel is correct that much is lost when the maps are set aside. It can be very helpful to have a sense of where one is, and where the pitfalls are likely to come next. And it can be life-changing to know that others have had the same experiences as their practice evolved. Consider the diagnosis Daniel gave me of one hypothetical meditator, to illustrate the degree of clarity his ever-evolving maps of practice can provide:

> Suppose they are able to see emptiness in real time, the vast majority of the time walking around without a sense of self or control or center point being relatively subtle, but it still flares on occasion, particularly when they cross into an arising or passing-away cycle. They have moderately good mastery of the formless realms in daily life. They're able to occasionally chance into *Norodha* in daily life, though it's easier for them on retreat. Their primary practice is now [Here Daniel whirled his head around on Skype] an open spacious awareness where they attempt to see everything just as it is, these luminous empty objects in space, and it's got a little bit of a Dzogchen influence. They've also got some influences

from some of the nondual traditions, so they're attempting to cultivate some happiness where they are, as much as
possible, and right now they're an independently wealthy
Trustafarian who can have as much retreat time as often as
they want and are in good physical health. . . . Oh, and by
the way, they're currently in a phase where they only need
five hours of sleep a night. They don't know why, but they're
feeling great. They don't appear to be manic. So now we're
starting to get a more sophisticated description of what the
practitioner is.

I should point out, this took Daniel about thirty seconds to say.
Yet to me, when I first encountered his way of thinking about the
dharma, it was revelatory, even if I did get called a mushroom. At
the time, I'd been meditating seriously for five years, going on one-,
two-, and three-week retreats, as well as a six-week retreat at the Insight Meditation Society one fall. Like many meditators at my stage
of practice, I had the zeal of the converted. I had begun teaching,
and writing, and I'd had those delicious altered states I described in
the last chapter. I was also more open, more loving, and obviously
happier than I had been. Other people noticed it, too—my family and friends remarked on how I'd changed. My spiritual life was
expanding as well, as reflected in my first two books, on Kabbalah,
mindfulness, and nondual philosophy.

But five years in, I had begun to stagnate. I felt like I'd plateaued:
I was good at the basics, but not improving anymore. I'd lost some of
the motivation to sit regularly, and felt less inspired by the spiritual
juiciness than I had been earlier. Life was intervening as well: the
relationship I was in at the time had started to disintegrate, and I
was working as a law professor, which was interesting enough, but
not very nurturing of my contemplative practice.

It was at this time that I heard about the developmental model of
awakening, from multiple sources: Daniel (and his book *Mastering
the Core Techniques of the Buddha*), but also Kenneth Folk, whom

we met earlier; plus a handful of books such as Jack Kornfield's *A Path with Heart* and Christopher Titmuss's *Light on Enlightenment*. I then went to earlier sources, especially Mahasi Sayadaw's *Practical Insight Meditation*.[6] I was hooked. Not only did these various sources describe experiences I'd had already, and contextualize them in a way that made sense, but they charted a way forward as well. Even more tantalizingly, they suggested that meaningful, lasting "progress" was possible: that there were "points of no return" along the way.

Kenneth's own story had been similar. As he told me,

> By the time I heard about developmental maps, I had already been casting about for years with some vague notion that there was something called "Enlightenment." I'd had some taste, and to me a very profound taste, about what people were talking about when they used that kind of language. I was reading a lot from about 1982, when I had my first big opening, until 1990, when I met my first teacher, Bill Hamilton. But a lot of it had this really vague notion of mystical enlightenment, and there wasn't a sense of developmental process. You either had it or you didn't, and not only could these books not say what it was, none of them seemed to be able to say how to get it.

Sound familiar? But then everything changed:

> When I met Bill Hamilton in 1990, and he laid out the Four Paths of Enlightenment model from Theravadan Buddhism, specifically from the Burmese Mahasi lineage as he understood it, this was a revolution for me. This was moving toward a type of concreteness that I intuitively craved. And the way Bill told the story, he knew people who had attained certainly the first or second paths of enlightenment, and could speculate about people who thought they had attained the third or fourth path of enlightenment. That's when maps got on the map for me.

So, in the next section, I'm going to lay out the path of insight that I followed, and tell you what I found.[7] I'm going to break the code about talking about one's own experience and "attainments," not because my attainments are so grand, but precisely because they aren't. In fact, every Theravadan teacher I've spoken to has told me privately that they've attained what I've attained, and most have gotten farther. My point is, I am not special. I'm a few steps ahead of being a novice, but only a few.

The Map Is Not the Territory
(But It Is Better Than No Map)

For fifteen years, I've had a hand-scrawled note taped to the wall of my bedroom: "Map is not territory." Since, as I've described, I used to study mysticism and meditation, and not actually experience them, this maxim is an important one for me. The maps are not the territory, and reading a recipe is not tasting a meal.

Yet maps can be useful. In probably the most important sutra for Western Theravadans, the Satipatthana ("cultivation of mindfulness") Sutta, the Buddha says that by cultivating mindfulness (of the body, mind, dharma, etc.), an earnest monk can become fully liberated in as little as one week! Really? For most of us, liberation takes a lot longer than that, and is a path with high ups and low downs, both over individual retreats, on a day by day basis, and over the course of time. The most famous Theravadan map of how this unfolds is found in a fifth-century text called the Visuddhimagga, the Path of Purification,[8] which has by now become semicanonical for traditional Theravadan Buddhists. The Visuddhimagga is not exactly a Buddhist bestseller competing with Jack Kornfield and the Dalai Lama; it's long, dense, doctrinal, and it contains a whole lot of weird stuff, like a proto-atomic physics that talks about the fundamental particles of matter, and how you're supposed to be able to see them in deep meditative states. But it is also the root text of the Mahasi tradition of Theravadan Buddhism, and the source of the developmental maps that inspired Bill, Kenneth, Daniel, and me.

In 2008, I had the opportunity to put this map into practice. I had just broken up with my then-partner, and was devastated. I was at a transition point in my career, about to move full-time to direct my nonprofit, but I needed time to myself first. The French theorist Jean Baudrillard once said, "Once you are free, you are forced to ask who you are." Well, I was certainly free, and when I reflected on who I really was, what I most wanted out of life, liberation was the answer. So, in 2008–09, I did two long retreats, back to back, a two-month retreat focused on building concentration and *jhana* (described in the last chapter), and then a three-month insight retreat, with a monastic teacher who uses the developmental model of the Visuddhimagga.

Basically, this model sets out a series of "purifications" that take place over the course of sustained meditation practice. This doesn't have the connotation it might have in Christian or Jewish contexts, as in purifying what is impure or dirty, but refers to refining or cleansing one's views, and conduct, in various ways. In the context of a retreat, there are eleven types of intuitive insight one develops, followed by six "awakening" insights, which often happen together quite quickly, and which are understood as "seeing the dharma" or knowing *nibbana* (nirvana).[9]

Done? Not quite. This whole process of the stages of insight is itself repeated many, many times, with four major milestones.[10] The first time it is completed, one is said to be a "stream-enterer," having entered the "stream" of the dharma and attained the path for the first time ("first path"). Second, third, and fourth paths may take many more years to attain, and one may cycle through the stages of insight many more times, without the "path moments" coming at the end. In most Theravadan models, fourth path is equivalent to *arahant*-ship, the state of being fully liberated from suffering.

To be sure, this is only one of many maps that are out there.

Tibetans, Zen practitioners, and even other Theravadins have their own. This is hardly "the" map. And of course, it's possible that one's experiences on a retreat are shaped by the guidance of the teacher. Look for a particular insight knowledge, and you'll find it; look for something else, you'll find something else. But my own practice did indeed evolve along the Visuddhimagga's lines, and so I will go a bit more into depth into them. (That said, my account here is much shorter than those in Daniel's book, Kornfield's, and others that are out there;[11] for more details, check them out.)

The first three insight knowledges—body and mind, cause and effect, and comprehension of the three characteristics—arise in most meditators when they commit to a week or so of practice. They are the garden-variety dharma insights that make up, oh, about 90 percent of Buddhist writing and teaching in the U.S., about clinging, impermanence, suffering, non-self, letting go, and the close obser-vation of bodily and mental phenomena. Most of the time, when people describe insights that they've had during meditation, they fall somewhere in these three initial stages. And if that's as far as they go, their practice will absolutely have been worth it.

The fourth insight knowledge, called the knowledge of arising and passing away (or "A&P" for short), is different. Generally, the A&P is a peak experience, a big-wow moment. Maybe it comes with flashes of light, perceptual or metaphorical, or with a sense of awe or understanding, or with bodily or mental rapture—goose bumps, en-ergetic currents, the works. (I doubted all this until they happened to me.) You feel like you've got it: this is it! You may even feel like you're enlightened, and get the urge to tell everyone how great med-itation is, or how grateful you are to the Buddha, or even (sigh) how great you are. I certainly experienced this exuberance, to my hardly unique misfortune. And indeed, this knowledge is a powerful one: an intuitive (notice how I keep repeating that word) sense of how things are radically impermanent, both on macro and micro scales. Nothing lasts, everything arises and passes away, from previous causes and toward future effects, and that's all there is. Not that that's a bad thing; like a Memento Mori, the knowledge of arising and passing away is a reminder to live deliberately, to front the es-' sential facts of life, and to do everything else Thoreau and Emerson (both influenced by the dharma) suggested.

But the A&P is not enlightenment. Not only that, but in this particular model (as in others[12]), it's followed by a series of really difficult challenges. First, there's the sheer disappointment that, alas, you're not liberated from suffering after all; not only do bad things still happen, but you react badly to them. You're human. Second, all the bells and whistles of the A&P can become a distraction—the "corruptions of insight," as they're known in the tradition. You get high on your own wisdom, or on the light, or the rapture; you get sidetracked. Third, and worst of all, in the Visuddhimagga's model, the A&P is followed by six further stages of insight that are often very difficult. Several writers have borrowed John of the Cross's term "the dark night of the soul" to describe these stages of insight, and indeed, they can seem like a long, dark night.[13] They even have dark names: knowledge of dissolution, of fear, of misery, disgust, desire for deliverance, and re-observation (in other words, seeing the same crap over and over again).

Unsurprisingly, these insight knowledges are not advertised in brochures for meditation. Moreover, many meditators, unaware of this predictable course of the development of insight, fall into the Dark Night and hang out there for a long, long time. Years, even. They fall into mild (or not so mild) forms of depression and despair, they stop meditating, they go back to cultivating the corruptions of insight, because at least those feel good. They plateau. So now I have to pause the progress of insight—as I did in my own practice for a couple of years—to discuss it.

The Dark Night has begun to be the subject of scientific study, led by Dr. Willoughby Britton at Brown.[14] Like many people, Willoughby started meditating because of *dukkha,* suffering: a friend had died and Willoughby was suffering from anxiety. As she described it to me, "My motivations for practice were very real-world—not enlightenment-based at all." Her intentions were clear:

> I really had a fairly predictable and somewhat naive view of what meditation was going to do. It was going to calm my mind, and calm my body, and the more I did it, the calmer I would get, and eventually I would reach some state of über-calm where I could have emotions and they wouldn't bother me, and maybe that's what the Buddha had. But it really wasn't that well-thought-out.

Moreover, since in her early years of practice Willoughby was mostly following books and tapes, she had few teachers to guide her when problems arose. As they inevitably do, when one practices diligently, especially on retreats. At one point, for example, Willoughby began "seeing a light in my visual field" and was afraid she was going blind. It was only years later that a teacher told her this was a common side effect of meditation known as a *nimitta*. Not only was nothing wrong; the *nimitta* was a sign that things were going well. And then there was the long retreat during which she experienced the dissolution and fear stages of the Dark Night. "It pretty much undid me," Willoughby said. "I had been teaching meditation for several years, but I didn't know how to get out of it." Willoughby had a teacher at that point, but not one familiar with the stages of insight, and so she struggled on, "feeling ashamed and demoralized and feeling meditation had betrayed me." Years went by before she learned that these stages were entirely to be expected with intense practice.

As a result of these experiences, Willoughby says,

> I've become a bit of a missionary about informing people what to expect. I run a kind of halfway house for yogis who have various difficulties, including insights they are having a hard time integrating. We're also doing research, scientifically documenting the full range of contemplative experience,

both positive and negative, so that we can really know what the train looks like and what to expect.

The result of this research is the "Varieties of Contemplative Experience" project, which has begun to uncover striking similarities in the experiences of advanced meditators. Willoughby's story also accords with my own, which I'll talk about in the next chapter, and with that of many other long-term practitioners. It also points to a sobering possibility: as Willoughby put it:

> Regular American people who went to a stress clinic thirty years ago, and have been diligently practicing, following their breath, and have no idea why, if they've been doing that for an hour a day, they just hit 10,000 hours in the last five years. That is when things get interesting. We're starting to see people who really had no particular interest in enlightenment or Buddhism, or any kind of particular insight into the nature of reality, people who were just trying to decrease their stress levels or control their blood pressure, now starting to have fairly radical shifts in the way they experience reality and themselves, and they're really unprepared.

This does make a certain amount of sense, if it's true that the mind finds its way to certain experiences and insights largely on its own. Mindfulness may have been extracted from its Buddhist container, but it remains a powerful practice that tends to lead in certain directions. As Willoughby points out, "This is not just benign—these are quite powerful practices. My research is about offering a high-level respect for just how powerful they are."

Daniel expressed a similar concern:

> It's people above the A&P that I worry about. For garden-variety householders, studies show and experiences show, basic mindfulness, basic meditation, tasting your food better, noticing what you say, trying to be less reactive . . . you

can't argue against that. That's totally awesome, that's completely amazing. Except some of them will cross the A&P and then they're fucked, because they have no support, nobody normalizing it for them, nobody telling them what happened, and it causes staggering chaos. . . . So what I want is for the breadth of society at the junior high school level to be educated on the basics stages of the human contemplative fitness development, to use Kenneth Folk's model, or something straightforward that they can handle. . . . People should know the A&P to Dark Night cycle and what gets you out of that and what helps you mitigate that, because the number of people who have crossed that is staggering and the number of people who do mindfulness training who have crossed that is much more staggering.

Now, how much of what Daniel and Willoughby describe is really about the Visuddhimagga's stages of insight, and how much is simply the vicissitudes of life? It's certainly possible to take the map *too* seriously. Maybe it's best to view it at arm's length, in which case what it's really saying is you'll work hard, you'll hit a breakthrough, and then—as Jack Kornfield's book perfectly describes it—after the ecstasy, the laundry. Or, as Gershon Winkler, a Kabbalistic-Shamanic teacher, once told me, "When you invite in the light, you invite in the shadow." I'm perfectly willing to let this be the truth of the developmental path: not its details, but its general contours. The rest may well be commentary, and I'm prepared to hold the entire thing lightly. If it's easier to simply understand this as an oscillation between ecstasy and laundry, between high and low, that's fine. Beth Resnick navigates the Dark Night with her students in this way:

I just tell them that the practice allows sort of a full potential of their human emotional experience. There are times that will be blissful and pleasant and there will be times that are gruesomely difficult. And we're not working on trying to hold on to the very pleasant and keep it. We're actually going to go through the whole cycle together.

Eventually, though, the cycle turns; the Dark Night yields to dawn. This may take days on a retreat, or months, or years. But eventually, one finds oneself in what the Visuddhimagga calls "high equanimity," or the knowledge of equanimity about formations. This, in my experience, is really quite profound, although it can sound a bit negative at first. You've seen through the unreliability of formations (i.e., everything, internal and external) and the mind has learned, intuitively again, to become disentangled from them. This is renunciation in the high, and I think quite beautiful, sense: not swearing off something out of disgust or fear, but settling out of it. The carrots dangle, and the donkey doesn't bite at them. Some are pleasant, some are unpleasant, but basically, they're all just a shadow-dance of evanescent and empty phenomena. Why get involved?

And if the conditions are right, this profound renunciation leads to a deep letting-go, a temporary relinquishment of the whole mind-body-world process, a cessation of consciousness itself, and a glimpse (sort of) of the great Nothing itself: *nibbana*, the snuffing out of the flames of life, perhaps just for a moment, perhaps for long periods of time—a brief extinguishment, the knowing of which is permanently transformative. This is the path and the fruition of the path, and it is very much territory, not map.[15]

If all this sounds a bit profound, it is. It is one rendition of the spiritual quest that has animated mystics and monks for thousands of years. Not the only rendition, not even within the tradition that birthed it. But it is profound, and seems to be real, and has changed the course of history. In Joseph Goldstein's words, it is one of the "transformative moments on the path" that occur and, having done so, leave their mark. Traditionally, it is said to remove certain kinds of doubt (since, after all, you've just seen that the practice works) as well as beliefs that things like rites and rituals will lead to liberation. More generally, there is a sense of having "been there" that does not get eradicated easily. Practice becomes more about remembering than discovering—at least until one goes on the next cycle of insight and things become new again. This is not a diminishment, however. On the contrary, it's like coming home every time, and since "home" is in the awareness itself, always present, always here, it becomes easier and easier to get to.

This is, indeed, the most profound transformation many of us can experience. And yet, at the same time, I love the Theravadan master Ajahn Brahm's insistence on demystifying *nibbana*. In his book *Mindfulness, Bliss, and Beyond,* a comprehensive rendering of the traditional Theravadan path, he describes fancy descriptions of it like "attuning to the ungraspable" as "foolishness dressed up as wisdom."[16] For him, *nibbana* is simply the "highest happiness, the complete ending of sense desire, ill will, and delusion, and the remainderless cessation of body/mind processes."[17] Again, this is only one perspective on nirvana, but I thoroughly agree with Ajahn Brahm's down-to-earth approach. As Stephen Batchelor told me in our interview, "the problem with religions is they make it seem that the goal is unattainable, that no one can do it. That is not what the Buddha taught." Or as Beth Resnick put it to me:

> For the most part, if people can get a sound technique, and understand the right approach to experience, which is just letting things be as they are and noticing what's happening, and really not just going for one experience over another, and then just applying the technique with the appropriate momentum, which is basically all the time, First and Second Path are really doable. I'm seeing people get there.

You Are Here

So what is the place of the developmental model in the evolution of the Western dharma, more broadly? On the fringes of the Buddhist community, it has clearly struck a chord. Yet it is clearly quite far from the mainstream meditation world, which is ostensibly focused on stress reduction, not enlightenment, and which might regard these advanced stages of the path as terrifying, nonsensical, or both. Perhaps the dharma is evolving in opposite directions:

mainstreaming for the masses, and more intense developmental practice for the few.

At the same time, the focus on development can become an impediment, ironically, to progress. Buddhist Geeks co-founder Vince Horn told me that the model

> was hugely influential for me for several years [and] a really important bridge to get to where I am now. But I started to feel like there's a problem with the developmental model in that it's very difficult to appreciate where one is, and drop into a more simple experience of "just this," when everything is oriented around development. . . . Some people get completely hung up on the theoretical framework, and don't figure out how to connect it to their own motivation for why they want to practice and just take it as an external authority—oh, I have to go experience these things, because Daniel wrote about it. And then as soon as they hit that stage of practice, in my experience I've seen people, their motivation completely disappears, because it's based on some ideas that they've read rather than something connected to their motivation for why they're doing it at all.

I can relate to Vince's ambivalence. In fact, as we talked, we realized we both had the same sense of confusion about stream entry, because in both of our cases, it didn't conform to what Daniel had written about in his book! It's probably best to take any particular model a bit lightly—really, if everyone acted that way about their own religious traditions, we might be in better shape. And in fact, Daniel himself agrees:

> It's still in its infantile stages. We still have very little idea what the hell we're doing and how it all connects. . . . Now, when the science can actually look three-dimensionally at specific structures of the brain and how they oscillate back and forth in terms of how they light up (this one, that one, this one,

that one), because it's a resonance problem that creates the sense that this side is in control and that side is not. . . .

Meanwhile, the trend from the last section has not yet intersected with the trend from this one: as of now, we lack good scientific data on the nature of the post-stream-entry brain specifically. Certainly, the advanced lamas who have had their brain activity measured are far beyond stream-enterers. But we do not yet have the data to be able to explain these difficult-to-convey changes in the mind in terms of Western science. Yet.

Still, the evolution of enlightenment—how the concept has evolved, and how enlightenment itself evolves in practice—is, in my view, one of the most important developments in the contemporary dharma world, even if it remains an emergent phenomenon that has not yet broken through to the mainstream. It offers a way forward for those seeking not just relief from or better adaptation to Western life (and no, there definitely is not anything wrong with that) but a deeper upgrade of the mind, a more thorough transformation. Obviously, the amount of time required to pursue such a path puts it beyond the reach of most householders. (Some teachers, like Beth and Kenneth, claim to have brought several students to stream entry based solely on intensive practice in non-retreat life, though it's still a very rigorous practice.) Yet even if it remains feasible only for a minority of practitioners, just knowing that the maps are there, that fellow travelers have followed them to successful outcomes and destinations, is, I think, a source of comfort and inspiration.

Sometimes, sitting there on the cushion failing to watch your breath, it can feel like you're the only weirdo weird enough to be wasting your time in this way. But you're not! There are generations of weirdos, monasteries full of them, and we have the benefit of their accumulated wisdom. We are not in this alone; we are supported by generous benefactors who have traveled this road before. The maps they have left us may not be perfect, but it at least means that we are not entering uncharted territory.

At the culmination of all of these developmental models, though, there is the paradox that what you're looking for is, indeed, what's already here. Really, all this talk of cultivation, meditation, and development can be quite misleading. In most traditions and in my own experience, what it is that's being looked for in these practices is actually already present. In fact, it's never not present, which is very helpful in discerning the path from not-path. Simply put, if it wasn't always here, it's a conditioned phenomenon, not "it." If you've cultivated a glorious state of bliss, such that all the world seems suffused with love, but that state was not and is not always present—that's not it. If you finally understand how things really are, but that understanding wasn't always present—that's not quite it either. I'm sure this all sounds quite mysterious, as if I've suddenly lapsed into a pop-Zen oracular mode, but I'm not trying to be mystical here. The "eternal peace," awakening, whatever it is, is not a conditioned phenomenon that comes and goes.

It's notable, in this regard, that even developmental paths tend to culminate in non-effort, non-doing, even non-meditation. As we saw, for example, in the Visuddhimagga, the final stage of insight before the mind turns toward the fruition of the path is known as "high equanimity." To inhabit this insight-knowledge, the mind really has to give up all preferences, all aspirations. Effort continues, sitting continues, but they continue seemingly of their own accord; you're doing this thing because you're doing it. I remember realizing at this point in my own practice that I had to become equanimous even toward enlightenment vs. non-enlightenment. I was already sitting for three hours at a clip, my mind moving very slowly, very subtly, but also very closely aware, since I was practicing the Mahasi method of noticing everything as closely and subtly as possible. I was super-concentrated. But there was still a bit of striving there, and a bit of "I" conceit as well. There was no faking it; I really did have to give up and just sit.

Practitioners of Zen, Dzogchen, Advaita, and the methods of

contemporary teachers such as Adyashanti might recognize those last two words. All these methods are "direct path" practices, in contrast to the developmental path of the Visuddhimagga. In a sense, they skip right to the end, with the final instruction—"just sit"— being the primary one. In practice, of course, it's not skipping at all, and there are stages of realization even along the direct path. But notice how these various paths converge in a seemingly paradoxical non-technique, even non-meditation. ("Non-distracted non-meditation" is a way some Dzogchen teachers describe it. "True meditation" is how Adyashanti does. *Shikantaza,* just sitting, is how it's known in Soto Zen.) There remain subtle differences in these different approaches, but the simplicity at their core is nonetheless remarkable. So let me not be understood to propose that the way forward is arduous striving with the eye always on the prize. In fact, at the last stages of the journey, there's no journey at all.

As Ramana Maharshi said, "Let come what comes, let go what goes. See what remains." That is the essence of enlightenment right there.

CHAPTER 6

BEYOND PEACE

What It's Like to Spend
Lots of Time in Silence,
and Get to Know Your Shadow

Okay, but what is it *really* like. The last chapter had
a lot of theory in it: maps, structures, paths. But what does the Dark
Night *feel* like? For that matter, what's it like to be silent for weeks at
a time, speaking only ten minutes a day to a teacher?

"I think we have a couple of notions about where meditation
goes, neither of which is accurate," Kenneth Folk once told me. He
continued:

> If you acknowledge that there are benefits to meditation,
> you probably think either that it's this soulless, gutless, ster-
> ilized, sanitized, medicalized version that happens in hospi-
> tals so you won't be stressed out, or you have this image of
> the beatifically smiling yogi in a cave, and if you don't have
> that experience, it's simply that you haven't gotten there yet.

That's complete nonsense, in my opinion. Enlightenment is much more analogous to evolution.

I think that is right on. And so, in this chapter, I'd like to continue the discussion of the developmental path of insight, but perhaps bring the conversation down to earth. If the previous chapter was theoretical, this one is practical. I want to talk a bit about how practice evolves, particularly on extended retreat, with a special focus on "working on your stuff," the bad stuff, the shadow, the dark night. This will require a bit more of my personal story, but I think it's an essential part of the picture. The evolution of the dharma is personal, first person as well as third person; and it's often, importantly, messy.

What's It Like to Spend Weeks in Silence?

I am not a natural dharma practitioner. I have been a law professor, magazine editor, queer activist, nonprofit director, dot-com entrepreneur, and have written five books and 200 articles. I have a JD, a PhD, plus an MFA, MA, and BA. In 2012–2013, as part of the LGBT advocacy work surrounding my book *God vs. Gay?* I gave more than eighty lectures, classes, and workshops to various audiences around the country. My childhood nickname was "Chatterduck." So in many ways, I am a rather poor candidate for spending months in silence and watching the minute processes of mind and body. On the other hand, maybe that makes me a good candidate for conveying some of what that process is actually like. If Chatterduck can do it, you can do it. So what is it like for someone like me to go on an extended silent retreat?

First of all, to get one thing out of the way: not talking is the easy part. You don't go crazy on long retreats, and you don't forget how to speak. (The silence is rarely absolute, either; on most retreats I've had daily or semi-daily interviews with my teacher.) There's just not that much to say anyway, when all you're doing is sitting and walking, and noticing the moment-to-moment sensations of whatever is going on. Eventually, the silence becomes second-nature—even for someone like me.

Much harder than not talking, though, is not thinking. In most forms of Buddhist meditation, the objective is not to ruminate, but to abstain from the indulgence in rumination. Thoughts arise, thoughts pass, and the job of the meditator is move on. Vipassana meditators might note "thinking," Zen meditators might purely sit without distraction, Tibetan Dzogchen meditators might zoom back from the thought to the View that surrounds the thought. Even contemplation practices like Tibetan visualizations, *chod*, or classical Theravadan contemplations on various principles of the dharma require focused attention rather than distracted meandering. Easier said than done, of course. In practice, it's just about impossible to stop thinking. This, itself, is an important lesson (we'll return to it in Chapter Eight): that your mind is not under your control. Nor, when it does think, does the mind naturally stay on lofty topics like the meaning of life, the universe in everything; no, usually it wallows in *papancha*, the needless proliferation of pointless thoughts. I often daydreamed of utterly meaningless drivel—I must've rehashed the plots of the *Star Wars* saga a hundred times over the course of one five-month stretch of retreat, for reasons that still escape me. (I think it had something to do with meditation training being a lot like Jedi training, but maybe it was just my childhood.)

It's at this point in the story that most of my friends usually roll their eyes and say that the whole thing sounds crazy. Other times, they reach the same conclusion when I talk about my traditional retreat in Nepal, where we didn't eat solid food after noon, and I slept on a mattress thinner than a grilled cheese sandwich. (Obviously, American retreat centers are much plusher and more nourishing; I can still taste the Insight Meditation Society's peanutty tofu *gado gado*.) However, I can safely say that my long retreats have been the sanest things I've ever done. Not the easiest, to be sure, but infinitely more balanced, awake, and instructive than the chatter-filled world

I live in most of the time. Eventually, the internal noise really did subside, and the mind started to relax. It took a lot of letting go, a balancing of diligence on the one hand, nonexpectation on the other. Once again, this is easier said than done, because for several billion years we've evolved the basic instinct to hold onto the pleasant and push away the unpleasant. If we didn't do this, we wouldn't eat, run away from predators, fight when necessary, or reproduce. Natural selection does not favor Buddhism. So while "letting go" may sound pleasant and relaxing, it runs, as we've seen already, against aeons of biological conditioning.

Let's focus on that for a moment. Often in extended practice there is an oscillation between effort and surrender, ardency and yielding. That's why I love a pair of enlightenment stories in the Theravadan Buddhist tradition that illustrate how what is needed for liberation is unique to each individual. The stories are of the Buddha himself, and his longtime aide and disciple, Ananda.

In the classic story of the Buddha's enlightenment, he sits under the Bodhi tree and resolves not to get up until he is fully liberated from suffering. Over the watches of a single night, he recalls all his past lives, goes through a series of trials, and finally is besieged by Mara, the embodiment of all obstacles seekers face along the spiritual path. Mara, in a role similar to that of Satan in the story of Christ, tempts the Buddha with wealth, sensual pleasures, and so on. Mara tries to terrify him. And finally, when all these tactics have failed, Mara assails the Buddha with his ultimate weapon: doubt.

Who are you, Mara says, that you deserve to be enlightened? Who do you think you are? In reply, the Buddha, in a gesture preserved in millions of images around the world, points to the Earth. The Earth has seen my efforts, in this life and previous ones, and can testify as my witness that I deserve to be enlightened. It's a beautiful moment of calm self-assurance (as well as a reminder of the importance of the natural world) and in the moment the Buddha points to the Earth, he becomes fully awakened. The "Yes" the Buddha silently utters is the key to his liberation.

Over forty years later, shortly after the Buddha dies, his closest disciples call a meeting to record and clarify the Buddha's teachings. All of these disciples are *arahants*, fully enlightened beings, except for Ananda, who had followed the Buddha since his enlightenment. This posed a problem. The disciples, in order to ensure an accurate transmission of the teachings, needed Ananda there—he had been present for more of the Buddha's discourses than anyone else. Yet the teachings also needed to be uncorrupted by selfish desire, and that meant everyone in the conference had to be an *arahant*.

The disciples turned to Ananda and told him to get to work. For decades, Ananda had been a stream-enterer, one who had attained the first stage of enlightenment, but this was not enough. Practice diligently, the disciples said, so that you can become an *arahant* and join us in this important meeting.

Ananda tried his best, meditating day and night. Yet the night before the meeting had come, and still he was only a stream-enterer. Undeterred, he kept practicing, entering deep states of concentration. But eventually, sleep overcame him, and Ananda realized he would not be able to attain *arahant*ship. He made his peace with this failure, and prepared to go to sleep. And as he lay down to bed, he became fully enlightened.

Ananda's awakening story is the opposite of the Buddha's. Where the Buddha said "Yes," Ananda, in a sense, said "No." No, this attainment will not be mine—and, we might add in our language, that's okay. Ananda's lying down is a moment of relinquishment, of admission. For forty years, he had followed the Buddha, and watched countless other women and men become enlightened, while he did not. Can any of us imagine what that must have been like? And then, under the pressure of his peers and with a council that would determine the shape of the Buddha's legacy, to be unable to attain the same goal? The tradition does not record that Ananda lay down in defeat or despair. He simply recognized what was true, and lay down to rest. He also lay down, we might say, the burden he had been carrying for decades. In this way, his "no" was really a "yes."

In relinquishing the goal that he and others had set, he affirmed his truth. His surrender was total, and thus liberating.

I suspect that all of us encounter moments of doubt such as those experienced by the Buddha and Ananda. What these two stories teach me is that there is no one surefire way to respond to them. Rather, diametrically opposed responses may each be appropriate. Perhaps, in the midst of a wave of doubt, what is called for is the Buddha's calm assertion. Yes, I do deserve this. I have done the work, and the Earth can testify to it. This is not arrogance or conceit—after all, the Buddha has called a witness. It is an authentic confidence that calmly refutes the doubting voice.

Or perhaps the moment calls for Ananda's surrender. No, I cannot do it—and that will have to be enough. In the Theravadan Buddhist tradition, the last stage of understanding prior to awakening is called "high equanimity." In this stage, one must become so equanimous that one is even equanimous as to attaining enlightenment or not attaining it. This is where Ananda found himself on that night before the council. And it is where many of us practitioners can find ourselves along the path. Maybe that goal is beyond our reach; so it is.

In my experience, this kind of equanimity cannot be faked. You can't outwardly relinquish something while inwardly still hoping it will come to pass. It just doesn't work that way. The equanimity, and thus the relinquishment of a preference for one outcome or another, has to be authentic. It's ironic, really; only by truly not wanting something can it be gained.

These days, thanks to the so-called "law of attraction," the Buddha's model of awakening may seem more attractive than Ananda's; if you will it, it is no dream. But in my experience, the contemplative life oscillates between both. Sometimes assertion, sometimes surrender; sometimes confidence, sometimes letting go. Personally, I am grateful for the multiplicity.

When it comes to insight, it's not the "what," it's the "how." There weren't many weird mystical fireworks that shot off during my months of silence—just a lot of time to see the ordinary very, very clearly. Sure, along the way, all kinds of delicious and terrifying experiences arise as well—more on them in the next chapter—although unlike insight, unlike rewiring the brain, none of them last very long. A few weeks of silence is long enough for the wheel to slow down, and real progress to be made along the path of insight. According to the tradition in which I practiced, the mind really does relearn some of those basic instincts, growing a little wiser and a little less obsessed with itself, and those new lessons don't disappear, even as noise and distraction return.

Doubt as Dharma: How I Learned from Shadow

Well, easier said than done. There's no getting around the reality that extended retreat brings up all kinds of difficult and painful experiences. In shamanic traditions, it's understood that in this kind of intensive work, you get what you need, not what you want (or what you think you want). This has been my experience on retreat as well. There's no way out but through; there's no path to liberation that doesn't pass through the shadow.

To speak about this more directly, I want to share the story of a "dark night" through which I passed on a forty-day retreat I sat in 2004. As you'll see, I am not offering this up as a story of how you should practice, or what will happen to you, or as anything other than one yogi's personal narrative that can hopefully be useful to fellow travelers. I didn't do everything right; indeed, a lot of the point is what I did wrong. Possibly you'll make similar mistakes. Then again, who knows.

When this difficult episode occurred, I had been sitting for about a month, and had long since acclimatized to the rhythms of a long meditation retreat. The first few days had come and gone—it was right after the 2004 presidential election, and I had volunteered for the Kerry campaign, convinced that we were going to win. The resultant loss had thrown me for a loop, and I spent much of that first week getting over the grief—as well as the physical exhaustion—not to mention letting go of a whole lot of anger, thinking, and distracting nonsense that was entirely useless for the work I was on retreat to do.

Fairly soon, however, I'd found my groove. At this point in my practice, I was still overly interested in *samadhi,* in cultivating states of bliss that were conducive both to dharma insights and to content insights—as I describe in Chapter Four. Sometimes, I'd spend these altered states noticing the three characteristics and doing other good dharma things, and other times I'd wander off the dharma path, indulging in the beauty of the retreat center's natural surroundings—there's really nothing like a snowfall on *samadhi*—or even sneaking off to enjoy some highly ecstatic iPod time. Bad Buddhist, I know.

Several weeks into the retreat, I'd had a powerful "peak experience"—later (much later; two years later) interpreted as the Knowledge of Arising and Passing Away, as I described in the previous chapter. There was a moment, during walking meditation, in which everything seemed to stop. It was incredibly profound, as if the universe were looking at me with the gaze of a close friend, in one crystalline instant that seemed to crack like thunder through the ordinary passage of time. All kinds of enthusiastic thoughts started popping: insights about this and that, inflated egoic thoughts about how awake I now was, plans to evangelize about the dharma because it is so great and awesome, plus a deep sense of having figured something out. Like a lot of people at this stage of insight, I got a little carried away. It sure felt good, though.

No one told me that it's typical, after this particular insight knowledge, to then fall into the "dark night" of difficult experiences and states of mind. My teachers guided me carefully, but consistent with the practices at this particular center, they didn't explicitly refer to the Visuddhimagga's maps, and I had never heard of them. I thought I'd had a life-changing peak experience, and then . . . maybe I'd have another.

Instead, about a week later, I experienced a wave of self-hatred so shocking, so intense, that it changed the way I relate to sexuality, guilt, homophobia, and healing, not to mention my own dharma path and the meaning of life itself.

It began innocently enough: during a dharma talk one evening, a teacher said that all of our habits, preferences, and opinions are conditions in and of the mind, and all of them can be changed. Though we may derive an identity from some of these dispositions and beliefs, it is incorrect to do so.

I recoiled. Having spent over ten years trying to change my sexuality, having despaired of it to the point of suicide, and having finally come out the other side, healthy, sane, and sexually whole, I felt as though I knew from experience both that sexuality cannot be changed and that to say it can be is enormously harmful. Even if sexuality is a phenomenon of the mind and not the body—i.e., even if it is a result of conditioning, childhood, and behavioral patterns, and not of genetics or biology—sexual orientation is effectively hardwired in. Trying to change it is as healthy as trying not to breathe.

I spent the next half-hour in walking meditation, furious at the ignorance of this teacher. I paced back and forth, noting a whole lot of anger. But then, literally mid-step, I realized how attached I was to my own belief that sexuality cannot be changed. It wasn't just an intellectual difference I had with the teacher—I was really attached to my "story" of how sexuality develops in the mind. And immediately, I realized that I was so attached to my story that "sexuality is unchangeable"—because I would change my sexuality if I could.

This came as a shock. At the time, I was directing a national LGBT organization, and celebrating the erotic and spiritual possibilities of being queer. But here I was, realizing that a part of me was still self-hating, still telling myself that the way God made me was wrong. I couldn't believe that, after all the work I've done on myself and with others, after all that—I would still change it if I could?

Over the next few hours, sitting with all this pain and self-hatred, I stayed with the practice on and off. About half the time, I kept doing the work: watching, noting, doing the sits and walks. The rest of the time, I stewed in this bouillabaisse of doubt and self-hatred and confusion. Of course, that latter stuff should all just have been noted and let go. But this was like being hit by a storm. So I allowed myself some divergences from proper form and technique.

At one point, noticing the different feeling-tones associated with the thoughts that were arising, and trying to feel them in my body, I came to another realization: that I hated the self-hatred much more than the sexuality. There were multiple layers, but the strongest hatred was not of being gay—but of the fact that still, after all this time, I had all this homophobia inside. More than anything else, I hated the hatred. By this point, my formal practice basically collapsed. I broke down in tears, crying and journaling. Later, I wrote:

> *I'm tired of hating myself.*
> *I'm tired of wanting myself to be straight, even a little.*
> *I'm tired of "well, all things being equal, I'd prefer. . . ."*
> *I hate the hatred.*
> *It makes me feel unlovable.*
> *It makes me feel like I don't deserve to be loved in any case.*
> *It makes me feel like a fraud.*
> *It makes me incredibly envious of undeserving straight people*
>   *who have it so easy.*
> *It makes me feel like I can never be enlightened, and definitely*
>   *have no business being a spiritual teacher.*

I spent a lot of time that night struggling to believe that I—"even I"—still had so much self-hatred. How could this be? Why was it so stuck in me? And what could I do about it? Today, I might encourage a student not to follow such thoughts; the best thing to do is practice, not believe your thoughts, and let them ebb away on their own. But that night, I lay restless. I saw that the self-hatred was made of many, many different component parts. Although it wasn't good vipassana practice to go into the "story"—we're supposed to explore the feeling itself, not its reasons; this is the difference between insight meditation and therapy—I did it anyway. I saw how strongly my sexuality made me feel rejected—by my parents, by my "internal parent," by authority figures, and by others. I saw that just the label of "gay" felt bad, in a stupid, nonrational way, because people have told me so for decades: I knew that faggots were the worst thing in the world before I even knew who or what they were. Intellectually, of course, I knew and know not to believe the bigots, that homosexuality is found everywhere, and so on—I did write a whole book about that. But on a gut level, I wanted to be loved, not unloved, unsuccessful, unappreciated. And so, regardless of the obvious falsity of what these people say, part of me believed them. I let all these absurd feelings flow: hearing voices say that sexuality cut me off from conventional family, conventional religious community, and from the easy, full acceptance that most people take for granted. And at the same time, I made lists about what I love about my sexuality; affirmed the freedom, joy, love, and intimacy that it brings me; and recited lines from the anthology *Gay Soul* by heart.

All the while, there was another voice, noting, watching, listening. Gradually, this voice grew stronger: the watcher grew more prominent than what it was watching. I thought of the story of Milarepa, the great Tibetan master, who finally had to invite his worst demon into his cave, surrender to it, completely let it take him over, rather than continue to fight. The first aspect of my dharma work was to make space even for the self-hatred. Can I be with it? Can I accept—not in the sense of saying the demon's okay, but in the sense of acknowledging its presence, and letting it in without pushing it away—even the demons that cause me pain? Doing so allows the mind to stop pushing, and also teaches the mind to know the demon when it sees it, to know it as such, not to believe it.

Then some insights began to pop. I saw the self-hatred for what it really is, a transitory mind state like any other, not what it is conventionally thought of as being, which is something more. At first, I interpreted the feelings I was having according to the conventional geology of the self. This is what I felt "deep down." This is was what

I "really" believed, despite all the rationale I'd proffered to myself and to others. But that entire geology is a fiction—deep down inside what? All that was actually present in my experience were different beliefs. One belief (gay is bad) had the character—the "feeling tone" in Buddhist language—of being long-held. Another belief (gay is good) didn't, even though I knew it made more sense, and had led me to more happiness and more spiritual capacity. But the former belief wasn't really "deeper" or truer. It was merely its character—its feeling—that was being interpreted as "deep."

This was such a critical turning point for me—and it was an evolution point that I've never crossed back over. Of *course* the guilt felt "deeper"—it's had thirty years of constant reinforcement, as compared with just a few years of acceptance and understanding. But the "self" in which it felt "deeper" within is itself just a label for a million conditioned phenomena, woven together by consciousness. The self is like a bundle of sticks taken from elsewhere—"we" are neither any individual stick, nor the string that ties them together. And what you discover in meditation is: There is never any time at which the bundle as a whole does anything. It's always one stick or another. A desire. A fear. A thought. Some will feel deep, some will feel shallow—but those are just sensations, nothing more. There's no truth to them. Here's another journal entry:

> If we are raised from a young age with a belief that red is better than blue, and so when we are 33 years old and on meditation retreat and seeing our feelings clearly we see that, wow, I really prefer red to blue, what are we seeing? It may be a strong, deep-feeling emotion because of its age, but it isn't deep in the sense of foundational. Because there is nothing to be a foundation of. . . . A strong desire, a feeling it in your guts, does not make it "what I really feel" or "more true."

This was my experience, anyway. So much of religious practice, ethics, even basic human decency is based on the conventional model of conscience, in which you "trust your heart" or in some other way access that "deep" part of the self. But that is bullshit. "Deeper" doesn't mean more reliable, or truer, or better—it's just a sensation that *feels* "deep down." The mind's "deep down" impulses are unreliable—"gay is wrong" felt just like "prayer is good," simply because both ideas were drummed into me from a young age.

At this point, I was ready to return to the cushion, but I wanted some time to sum up first. So I went for a walk in the woods, to rest, reflect, and maybe even rejoice. The day was clear and crisp—a late November morning, in a New England forest. There arose, as I walked in the cool air, some very un-Theravadan gratitude: that I am so lucky to be an erotic being, growing and learning and playing and occasionally performing magic. I sang, I danced, I took off my shoes. The movement of energy in my body was like a tonic. That's right, I remembered, I'm *alive*. Finally, that evening, I sat outside to watch the sun set. Where I was sitting, a line of telephone wires was blocking the view, so I thought I might move to a different spot. And then I saw it, what I'd been working with all along: that the wires weren't blocking the view, the wires were part of it. I might prefer a different view, of course, one that conforms to images from postcards or fairytales, but this is the one that is. The guilt, the self-hatred, the thousand demons I have yet to encounter—I sought that evening the courage to invite them in, rather than deny them or push them away. Only then, maybe, after I've stopped trying to make them go away, might they eventually begin to disappear. As when you're looking at a sunset, and you know the telephone wires are still there, but you've learned to accept them, and not be distracted by them quite as much.

I've told this story in some detail for several reasons. First, it's a crucial part of how the dharma evolves over the course of practice; although the particulars are specific to my "story," I'm sure that if you've done long retreats yourself you can relate to the general contours of it. Meditation may have a popular association with relaxation, and indeed, it can produce some very pleasant relaxed states, particularly in the midst of busy life. But any teacher and any student who's done intensive practice knows, and hopefully will say, that the path is the very opposite of blissful ignorance. We all have muck collecting at the bottom of our mental fishbowls, and when we shake things up, the muck gets stirred up as well.

Second, I want to give some place to the "story" in the unfolding of practice, even though doing so may contradict some of what I've said in Chapter Five about the nature of the developmental path. Clearly, Western Buddhism—particularly in the Theravadan traditions—has become overly confused with psychotherapy and personal growth. The Buddha did not, so far as I'm aware, instruct his students to sit and mull over their childhood trauma. On the other hand, when the Buddha was visited by Mara during his own "dark night," Mara said some very specific things about the Buddha's specific "stuff." People don't become liberated in general; we become liberated in our specificity, in our times and places and names. The only way out is through.

But I also want to question and perhaps undermine everything I've said so far. I want to entertain seriously the possibility that all the details of this story were just decoration on top of a predictable mental development. It might just be this: I passed through the A&P, and afterward came the dark night. All the rest, perhaps, is commentary; all the content was just a distraction. I am open to that possibility, and truthfully, on subsequent retreats, I've gotten less and less interested in this kind of content. This, too, has evolved. As time has passed, I find what works for me is practicing enough to upgrade the mind and build its emotional resilience, its ability to slide in and out of difficult (and pleasant) mind-states with less and less friction along the way. What doesn't work is indulging in story and thinking that I can solve whatever problem has arisen. To solve these problems doesn't take more tinkering—it takes a better set of tools—and acquiring those tools, not psychoanalysis, is what meditation does best. As much as I've gone into the story here, and as powerful as the experiences were for me—on a content as well as insight level—some teachers would say that all of this verbiage is just layers of rationalization atop a basically mechanistic process. In fact, some might even say that relating it is unskillful, as it might give the impression that a meditation retreat is just another psychotherapeutic modality, when in fact it's meant to do something completely different. On a personal level, I know I can get very attached to my own story of marginalization and victimization, even if it ends with me triumphing over those forces—my queer identity can become yet another form of identification, and a kind of political spiritual materialism. Whereas from some dharma perspectives, all of this story is just . . . story.

For me, the impersonality of the progress of the dharma has converged with the personal details I've shared in this chapter. The truth is, I don't feel today the way I felt nine years ago. I'm not wracked with guilt about my sexuality, I'm happily partnered, and while there are always new shadows that come up in practice, these particular ones really don't. I've seen them so many times, on and off retreat, that I recognize them for what they are: leftover memes from an earlier time in my life, and the traces of a homophobic society. Once in a while, I'll still have some sex-negative thought, or still experience a twinge of internalized homophobia. That doesn't mean it's true, or I am back to square one; to suppose these wrong views will simply disappear makes light of the depth of homophobia and homophobic acculturation. Being gay, when I was growing up, wasn't just an unfortunate characteristic, or a disfavored choice—I believed it was a curse. So, as I realized on that retreat years ago, it's unrealistic to suppose that all traces of the belief will simply vanish. But it has, over time, greatly diminished.

This process has unfolded precisely because I've been able to see it as *anatta,* as non-self, rather than in self-oriented psychological terms. For example, the facile belief that "your conscience should be your guide" is simply untrue. Your "conscience" isn't real; it's a series of responses that are conditioned by all sorts of social and other phenomena. The conscience of someone raised vegetarian recoils at the thought of eating meat; a carnivore's doesn't. My conscience recoils at eating shrimp, but yours probably doesn't. The conscience of someone from an older culture might be quite at peace with war and killing in the name of honor, or tribe; yours might not. There is no rhyme or reason to the operation of conscience; guilt adheres to sublime and ridiculous all the same. Often, there's a sense of attachment to some of these views: I am defined as someone who does this but not that, who acts this way but not that way. There's a weightiness there, a groundedness; this is who I am.

But all of that is illusion. Weightiness is a feeling-tone, groundedness is a sensation; they arise and pass due to conditions; they aren't "me"; and they don't even bring the lasting happiness that they promise. They are conditioned phenomena like everything else, and are almost mechanistic in nature. Play with a dog, and he'll want to play more. Give a man enough drinks, and he'll get drunk. Transgress old boundaries, and there will be guilt. Sometimes guilt obstructs love, and sometimes, let's be honest, it helps love grow by constraining our behavior, either with respect to other people or to life itself. But there's no there, there.

And yet, they are very powerful illusions. In my work with traditional religious communities, I've seen—no, I think I've felt—the power of this belonging, this connection. Traditional religious people (I've worked mostly with Christians and Jews) often have their entire sense of self bound up with a particular view of how the world is: that God created it, that the Bible is true. Take that groundedness away, and there's a terror there, a chaos that only the ordered norms of religion keep at bay. So too with many social conservatives, who fret, or maybe experience, that when traditional values are questioned, a kind of moral anarchy takes hold of them. Being in conversation with people who have these views—in my case, usually in the context of LGBT issues—has really been a revelation. I don't usually share my personal dharma journey with them, but I do see resonances of it: the unconscious holding-on, the identification with these views, and the enormously high stakes. What causes someone to believe that an omniscient deity would torture most of His creations for all eternity in hell? Can we untangle the knots of religious faith, not in a patronizing or reductive way (as nearly all the so-called neo-atheists have done), but by recognizing and empathizing with the operations of guilt and groundedness that so powerfully bind us to our views?

My work as a professional LGBT activist and my vocation as a dharma practitioner may sometimes seem quite distant from one another. But I could not do the latter without the former. Through the development of my own contemplative practice, I've seen and come to know the internal demons I share with others. I have tasted a form of groundedness that does not depend on causes and conditions, on behaviors done and not done. And from that place of internal stability, I am more able to do the work of reducing suffering where I find it.

This, then, is one example of how the dharma evolves *internally* —in one's own practice, according to the circumstances of one's own life. As we've seen in this second part of the book, the dharma's external evolutions reflect the developmental nature of the contemplative path itself. Sometimes this development can be charted in maps and models, but it can only be known directly, in one's own experience, according to the very specific terms and conditions of one's own humanity. This, I think, is true whether one is a beginning practitioner using meditation to ease the pain of disease, a maverick brainhacker exploring the potential of the human mind, or a dedicated practitioner following the traditional teachings of the Buddha. We are in the midst of a twenty-first-century experiment, in which technologies of mental fitness are being adapted and transmitted at a rate never seen before. No matter how many maps we carry, we don't really know where it will lead. But if my story and those of thousands of people like me are relatable, if it is true that the mind can be "upgraded" to enable more resilience, more compassion, and more happiness, then these external and internal evolutions indeed have the capacity for redemption.

part three

Fruition

CHAPTER 7

AFTER INTEGRATION

The Imperfect Is Our Paradise

"The point is to see the light in everyone and everything," Lama Surya Das once told me when, in an interview, I asked him about the meaning of life. In the years since he said it, I've returned to this simple formulation again and again, and it has held up well. At the early stages of the path, even to know that there is "light" is a revelation. This is what we've learned from practitioners of the kinds of applied mindfulness discussed in Part One: that the basic practices of the dharma give access to a way of being that is liberating. Eventually, some percentage of practitioners take further steps on their path, and the "light" evolves into all sorts of special experiences, mental developments, and dark places—this is what we've learned from the practitioners we met in Part Two. But for everyone, integration eventually becomes essential. Anyone can "see the light" under special circumstances, but what about in the midst of daily life, with its joys and sorrows and annoyances and stuff—

with what Jon Kabat-Zinn, quoting Zorba the Greek, called "the full catastrophe"?

This is the subject of the third part: how contemplative wisdom is integrated into daily life, either for those "returning" to it from extraordinary circumstances, or those who never left it in the first place. In this chapter, we'll explore what awakening in the midst of the world might actually look like, and delve into some of the controversies around whether the dharma has integrated *too* much into lives it really ought to transform. Next, we'll look at how one aspect of the dharma, the insight into non-self, intersects with spirituality, identity, and gender. And finally, we'll see how the evolving dharma is adapting itself to new modes of political activism, and (hopefully) learning from its own struggles with power and authority.

The evolving dharma has had to address these questions in entirely new ways. Never before has a formerly monastic contemplative practice been implemented in the offices of Google. And the jury is still out on its ultimate efficacy: to really hack the brain and optimize the mind may take a lot of commitment. This is why monks are monks and not householders. But news flash: most Western dharma practitioners are not going to spend the rest of their lives in monastic seclusion, and the expected fruition of the path must shift as a result. This is the karma of the West: we are humanists, often materialists, often deeply connected to values of family, home, and hearth. This is who we are.

You Must Change Your Life

I'm sitting at the Wisdom 2.0 conference in San Francisco, being serenaded by an über-California "social artist" telling us to open our hearts, while awaiting a program of millionaires and celebrities, half-envying and half-loathing the fact that many of the people here are filthy rich. Over the next three days, there are presentations on corporate efficiency with A-list tech names, product rollouts that range from the sublime to the ridiculous, and lots and lots of networking.

And as a blogger on the conference for *Tricycle* magazine, I'm reminded that a lot of this stuff pisses Buddhists off. We're clearly at an inflection point in the Western dharma right now: the last twenty years of secular, mainstreamed mindfulness will likely be nothing compared to the next twenty—not with healthcare, technology, and even the military coming around to the hard data on mindfulness's effectiveness. And that phenomenon, which we explored mostly in Part One, gives pause to a lot of the more intense practitioners we explored in Part Two. On the one hand, meditation might just save the world, and mainstreaming it—vulgarizing it, even—is how that will happen. On the other hand, what will be the price of this wider embrace? Just how crass, cheesy, or watered-down will things have to get?

Several times, in panels and private discussions, variations on this same question kept coming up in conversation: What is the real goal here? Is the goal to make unhappy vulture capitalists into happy ones? Or, if mindfulness works, will it cause them to, well, reconsider being vulture capitalists in the first place?

I asked this of Jon Kabat-Zinn on the last night, after his talk at the conference. I mentioned David Loy's open letter to William George, a longtime meditator also on the board of Goldman Sachs and Exxon Mobil.[1] The letter, entitled "Can Mindfulness Change a Corporation?" argued that if Mr. George were really seeing clearly in his practice, he couldn't serve in good conscience on the boards of corporations that have been involved in unethical business practices. It was a pointed and well-stated challenge.

So I was curious what Kabat-Zinn, who has consulted with numerous corporations and had just given a talk about mindfulness in business, had to say. Although he hadn't read the letter, his answer was surprisingly similar to Loy's. "This whole issue of ethics is really important," he said:

> It's not like Goldman Sachs can just do a little mindfulness
> and then be driven by greed, hatred, and delusion all the

more. That's not mindfulness. This is about restructuring things so that your business is aligned with the deepest domains of integrity and morality. You can make money in the service of creation of wealth, but not lying, cheating, and stealing, or cutting every corner.

Honestly, I was surprised by his answer. Sure, it's what one might expect from a longtime practitioner, son-in-law to Howard Zinn, and, not least, careful interview subject who knew he was talking to a *Tricycle* blogger. But if Kabat-Zinn is right, if serious mindfulness practice eventually erodes the foundations of certain businesses, aren't the critics right to criticize?

The issue arose again the next morning, in the panel with Evan Williams, the founder of Twitter. A questioner pointed out that Williams is no longer a twenty-something entrepreneur, maniacally focused on building his company; how can the values of balance, wisdom, and meditation be communicated to those who still are? Williams basically punted. He agreed that he got interested in a more balanced approach to work when he got older, and that most meditators at his new company, Obvious, were older as well. Indeed, it might be true that if you meditate and introspect, you'd get some perspective on your life—and thus forfeit your value as an out-of-balance, insanely driven worker bee at a tech company.

Kabat-Zinn, in our conversation, had made a similar point. "I did some mindfulness work with a major Boston law firm back in the day, and people ate it up—and then a whole bunch of them left. We have to be prepared for that. . . . These people were being given annual bonuses called 'no-life bonuses' because you had to work so many hours that you never saw your family."

Now, it may be that such a world is ultimately bad for business, but that's not my experience: when I was younger and working at a dot-com I co-founded, I put in sixty-, eighty-hour work weeks, and so did everyone else. The system is designed to make use of, leverage, or exploit the energy of young workers, who are usually quite willing to put in the time, if there's a chance of a Twitter-like payoff at the end. Eventually, yes, most of us get tired of the rat race, and either move up the ladder or, like Bartleby and Billy Joel, move out.

So won't a serious mindfulness disrupt this *ferkokte* system, which depends on lives out of balance? After all, as Krishnamurti said, "It is no measure of health to be well-adjusted to a profoundly sick society." Sometimes the unavoidable fact may be that our lives need to be adjusted to the dharma—if what we're after is deep change. And often, seekers (including this one) actually integrate too fast, moving too quickly from low-level spiritual states back into the conventional world, without adequately deepening the stages and insights they bring about. Sometimes, we use the rhetoric of "integration" to have our spiritual cake and eat it, too.

This is true even in Vajrayana Buddhism, which, unlike Theravadan practices, is designed to pursue enlightenment in daily life—especially in the Shambhala tradition created by Trungpa Rinpoche. And it is true at places like Naropa University, founded by Shambhala, which seek to bring Western and Eastern modes of personal flourishing together. After all, not all daily lives are created equal. Many of us want both the capitalist householder life with children and the rest, and, you know, peace and enlightenment. But what if such an "evolved" dharma is really a devolved one?

Even the core innovation of Western dharma, the marriage of monastic practice and lay life, may be part of the problem. Zen master John Daido Loori once complained that "most of the lay practice that goes on among new converts in America is a slightly watered-down version of monastic practice, and most of the monastic practice is a slightly glorified version of lay practice. . . . To me, this hybrid path—halfway between monasticism and lay practice—reflects our cultural spirit of greediness and consumerism. With all the possibilities, why give up anything? We want it all. Why not do it all?"[2]

Integrated dharma may also be cut off from the possibility of deeper transformation. Joseph Goldstein, in an interview quoted in Richard Seager's *Buddhism in America,* wondered openly "whether we, as a generation of practitioners, are practicing in a way that will produce the kind of real masters that have been produced in Asia. I don't quite see that happening."[3] Indeed, as we saw earlier, if we approach dharma practice with the intention of becoming more relaxed, we may be disturbed to learn that its Buddhist sources have the opposite intention.

Finally, just as premature integration can reinforce preconceptions about our lives and what matters within them, it can stand in the way of the changes we might need to make to those lives. Rilke's encounter with the numinous in his poem "Archaic Torso of Apollo" concludes with "You must change your life." Not "You must make small changes around the edges" or "You must find twenty minutes a day to meditate." Likewise with spiritual practice. I am often asked, at the end of a meditation retreat or other spiritual program, how the practice can be brought home, integrated into regular life. It's a natural question, and a good one, and I do my best to answer. But the real answer may be "You can't integrate it into regular life; you must change your life."

Some people don't want to hear that, of course. It feels much better to be told "Yes, just do this practice half an hour each day, watch what you eat, and you'll obtain all the benefits." But what if a deep process of introspection and contemplation is incompatible with working sixty hours a week, raising a family, and being surrounded by American media? What then? Letting go is great, but letting go into what? My life is often so cluttered with demands, to-do lists, and appointments that if I "let go" into that, I become a crazed and nervous wreck. The Hindu sage Ramakrishna once said that the mind is like fabric; it takes the color of the dye it's soaked in. Soak the mind in a quiet, relaxing environment and it will become quiet and relaxed. Soak it in floods of Facebook and, well. . . .

Now, let me pause this torrent of pessimism for a moment. Surely, in the tradition of the "Middle Way" there are productive methods of managing the complex dance of integration and commitment— to create what Jack Kornfield has called "the mandala of the whole."[4] I want to talk about three of them.

First, of course contemplative practice is not all-or-nothing; it's possible to make incremental progress, and we don't all have to be saints. There are numerous contemplative practices that may not accomplish the Great Goal but that can, incrementally, cultivate a little more peace, quiet, wisdom, and compassion; think of Western adaptations of Zen *oryoki* (eating meditation), Theravadan walking meditation, and the Tibetan encouragement to experience "small moments, many times." And I have seen, firsthand, that these practices work.

Now, does that mean they lead to full enlightenment, and the final extinction of sorrow, lamentation, and despair? No. But do they have no value as a result? Also no. Consider these two statements from Lama Surya Das. On the one hand, he said,

> Enlightenment has never been a small and easy matter. It's the great matter, the matter of life and death. If we would talk in English about becoming a saint or becoming one with God, we'd know that it's not something you get in a weekend. You don't become a wise philosopher by going to a weekend with a wise philosopher; it's not that simple.

And yet, on the other hand:

> Integration is the name of the game, not seclusion. We have to do it where we are, in our lives, except for those few who can renounce the world and go off for a good period of time and really devote themselves to it. . . . It would be heretical if any of us believed that people couldn't get enlightened today. The Buddha's message is that anyone can become enlightened and awakened. . . . We just may not get enlightened as soon as we want to.

This seems like a healthy balance. Practice may look different in different contexts. On retreat, one might get deeply concentrated and very quiet, and have one set of goals. But the goal of daily practice isn't the same as the goal of intensive practice. You're not trying to have the most exotic *samadhi* or mystical experience each day;

you're trying to develop a kind of spiritual resilience, a looseness and fluidity that enables you to move quickly and smoothly from mortgage payments to spiritual truths, from linear achievement to present-moment love. You don't need to discover new territory—only to return with ever-decreasing friction to what you know is truest, most authentic, most real.

Second, "integration" goes two ways. Vince Horn from Buddhist Geeks pointed out that "the normal idea is bringing your practice into your life, about taking what we learned in practice and applying it to life. But what about bringing your life into your practice? How many more hours do we spend living than practicing? Life changes our understanding about what practice is." There is, in other words, a two-way oscillation. On the one hand, one goes into intensive environments to train the mind to do certain things, to go certain places, to rest in certain ways. Then, in the rest of one's life, the mind practices doing that—alighting in a place of calm, amidst the rush-hour traffic. Finding an inner capacity of love, amidst cacophony and discord. And yet, the complementary motion is also essential: bringing the wisdom of the world, of our karma, into practice as well. When I sit—and I'll develop this more in the next chapter—I bring all of my sound and fury, my time and place, to the cushion.

I truly honor my monastic friends who have devoted themselves to a single goal. But, in Isaiah Berlin's terms, I am a fox, not a hedgehog; my humanist, post-whatever consciousness wants to sample some of everything—most of all the many delights of the world. As Lou Reed sang, "Some kinds of love, the possibilities are endless—and for me to miss one, would seem to be groundless." And then there's the highly un-quiet world of political engagement and activism. So, yes, I get highly involved in things that often lead to the traditional Buddhist "defilements" of greed, hatred, and delusion. This karma—by which I mean the social constructions of my particular Western subculture, which seem as much a part of "me" as anything—may well be holding me back from further advancement. Then again, this is also the "Tantric turn," the turn from enlightenment outside the world to enlightenment within it. It is what I called in an earlier book the "resanctification of the world," in which holiness is seen—as in Allen Ginsberg's "Footnote to Howl"—everywhere and in everything. And each time I re-ask whether it wouldn't be better to give up the fleshpots for the cloister, I hear a clear, humanistic "No" in response. What was it that Nisargadatta, the Vedanta sage, said? "Wisdom tells me I'm nothing. Love tells me I'm everything. In between, my life flows."

Third, let me return for a moment to the Wisdom 2.0 conference, home of the meditators from Mashable and yogis from Yahoo. On the last day of the event, we heard from Meg Pilasco, a former Marine. Pilasco, "born in the middle of nowhere, Oklahoma," served for several years in the unit guarding President George W. Bush. Tragically, she was sexually assaulted while serving, and subsequently suffered from PTSD as well as other trauma-related conditions. Making matters worse, her superiors chose not to pursue her case, and, like other veterans, Pilasco was afraid to go to the VA for fear of being labeled as damaged goods. She was eventually put on cocktails of meds, which she says didn't work, and she eventually hit bottom, ultimately attempting suicide and landing in the hospital.

Following her release from the hospital, Pilasco found her way into a program called "Honoring the Path of the Warrior," which included mindfulness and meditation, as well as a five-day retreat at the Tassajara Zen Center. "I thought meditation was for crazy hippies—no offense," she said to the laughs of the crowd. "But this program saved my life." Her depression lifted, her twice-nightly nightmares decreased in frequency and intensity, and by the time the program was over, she said, "I was ready to live my life again."

Coming on the heels of two days' worth of tech millionaires, celebrity idolatry, and high-powered networking, Pilasco's story reminded me of why we bother with this meditation thing in the first place. *Dukkha* is not the self-inflicted stress of a technology executive; it's the real stuff, the kind of suffering that merits the Pali word's original meaning: brokenness, stuckness. I'm delighted, really, that mindfulness can also relieve the stresses of privileged, fortunate people. But Pilasco's story, simple as it was—indeed, it is entirely un-unique—moved me to tears.

Real suffering, the kind Pilasco experienced—that's what animates those of us who not only meditate but teach, or write, or evangelize on the dharma's behalf. And "even" applied mindfulness can have a powerful impact. On the first page of the first chapter of Jon Kabat-Zinn's first book, he writes about teaching mindfulness to AIDS patients in the 1980s, to people recovering from crippling injuries, and ordinary people suffering from debilitating migraines.[5] For some people, sure, mindfulness simply greases the wheels, and makes an already fortunate life that much more pleasant. But I don't think that is true of most of the folks at Wisdom 2.0, or its organizers either. At worst, corporate mindfulness is a gateway drug that will bring some minority of practitioners into a more meaningful engagement with the reality of life. But I think it's better than that. I think that for a significant percentage—maybe significant enough to make a real difference—it will lead to the conclusion that, indeed, you must change your life.

Emotional Resilience

So, what's it like being enlightened in the so-called "real" world?

Perhaps the most important thing is what it is not. In both my (limited) personal experience, and the (less-limited) experience of many people I know, practice of the dharma does lead to more happiness, but only if happiness is defined in a particular way. It won't necessarily affect the balance of one's neurochemistry; if you tend toward depression, that may or may not shift. It won't fill your life with joyful occasions and remove sorrows; that would be magic, not meditation. It won't even necessarily add more moments of happiness, depending on what your life looks like. I think anyone who promises you these things is telling you a story.

Nor does enlightenment turn you into a sweet, beneficent Yoda figure. In fact, as Jack Kornfield has related at length, one can be an awakened, enlightened human being and still be a total schmuck, still be sad at times, still face doubt and insecurity.[6] Enlightenment does not have to do with being a nice person; it's about intuitively knowing all things to be totally conditioned and transitory and thus unclingable. Being a nice guy is something different, and enlightenment doesn't really help with it. Indeed, as I'll describe in a minute, it can often make things worse.

What practice does tend to do, and has done in my experience, is increase emotional resilience—a mental slipperiness, or looseness, which enables one to move from one mind-state to another. Ten years ago, moods lasted longer; I'd stay in a funk for a longer period of time, unable or unwilling to pull myself out of it. Now, the same melancholy that might have lasted two days lasts perhaps two minutes, if I'm attentive to it. Notice, the melancholy still arises—but it passes more quickly. Sometimes this is simply due to mindful attention: I am more attuned to my own emotional mind-state than I used to be, and in the moment when the mind recognizes "I am angry," in that moment, I am not angry—I am noticing, witnessing, becoming aware. Even if I revert immediately into anger, just the momentary interlude helps lessen the momentum. The mind "settles back," in the language several contemporary teachers use, instead of lurching forward into whatever difficult emotional state it had been in. The intuitive aspect is crucial, which is why the metaphor of upgrading the mind resonates with my experience. It's not about reading these words in a book, but actually retraining the mind. With enough practice, you react in a different way; you *think* in a different way. In my experience, the result is less about joy or freedom or enlightenment in any mystical sense, and more about a knowing of the deep, radiant restfulness of the mind, together with the resilience to slip back into it, easily, from whatever distracting or unpleasant mind-state happens to be arising.

Other times, there does seem to be a greater ease in letting go.

The mind-state arises—envy, anger, an unhelpful lust, whatever—and it becomes more and more possible to diagnose it, be aware of it . . . and let it go. For me, this is still a work in progress, but there has been progress. Sometimes, I'm able to even let go right in the middle of a difficult exchange with someone; instead of escalating a conflict, I've been able to notice the heat and disengage. This has been enormously helpful in my political activism, for example, as I've had conservative interlocutors hurl enormously offensive accusations at me: that my relationship with my husband is no different from bestiality, for example, or that I'm betraying the Jewish people by criticizing the actions of a right-wing Israeli government. I don't always succeed at this—and it's clearly the case that others do it better. But sometimes, if I'm lucky, even in the midst of one of those exchanges, I can let go of the emotion, or decline even to take the emotional bait in the first place, and respond in a skillful, tactical way. Letting go leads to a lot of personal peace, and it's also really useful at work.

But letting go is not the same as not having in the first place. If you choose to pursue a career that involves arguing with people about politics, conflict is going to arise, and the mind is going to react. That is just inevitable. But what is not inevitable is how those reactions affect you: how coolly or heatedly you reply. (Sometimes, of course, a little heat is useful; remember when President Obama occasionally needed to be reminded to get *more* upset, or at least seem that way to voters?) Similarly, if you have a family, particularly one with children, you are going to go on an emotional roller-coaster ride; that is the nature of raising a family. But what is up to you is how the roller-coaster feels: the ratio of anxiety to glee, fear to release.

Now, some might ask, is this how an "evolved" person is supposed to act—arguing about politics and still getting upset about stuff? Shouldn't s/he always be more gentle? Speak in a soft voice? Work as a holistic healer? Have only "mindful" sex, not drink, not get angry? Maybe give lots of money to charity?

I think these misconceptions confuse what the contemplative

path is and isn't, are exceedingly class- and culturally dependent, and get in the way of making progress on the spiritual path. They're also pretty annoying. Some forms of contemplative fitness absolutely lead to more sweetness and love. Some will curb your drinking and your sex life, or at least demand that you do so. Others, though, don't. In the case of the Buddhist path, there may well be a loosening of identification with the ego, and an intuitive understanding of the impermanence, ultimate unsatisfactoriness, and emptiness of all things. But it doesn't lead to the knowledge of how to change the oil in my car, and it doesn't lead to sympathy with crystal healing, patchouli, or hempseed vests.

It hasn't even led me to be more socially skillful. I remain somewhere on the autism scale when it comes to predicting how other people perceive me. I'm an introvert, and I neither understand nor particularly like complicated interpersonal interactions. My various dharma accomplishments have not changed this. On the contrary— sometimes they've made the behaviors worse. Because I don't get as bothered by a bit of negative energy here or there, I have grown even more oblivious to how deeply others are upset by it. Okay, somebody's having a meltdown. It'll be okay eventually; why does someone else now want to process it with me? In other words, in many ways I'm an even bigger jerk now than I was before I did my long meditation retreats.

Ethical lines of development are distinct from spiritual/transpersonal ones. They may be related, and we may point to ethical failings as evidence of spiritual flaws, but they are not identical. Contemplative practice doesn't do that work. For that, you need a therapist, or hard lessons, or drugs. Nor does meditation necessarily lead to a less sexual, less active, mundane life. It may, for some people, if only because mindfulness tends to point out how many of our most familiar habits are actually unpleasant or unhelpful. Particularly in a Western context, however, contemplative practice can sit right alongside active professional, political, sexual, personal, even hedonistic endeavors.

Doubtless, these misconceptions about what a spiritual life should look like alienate many cynics, skeptics, and, well, educated people from taking contemplative practice seriously. The last thing a hard-edged New Yorker wants to do is lose her edge, right? Moreover, this kind of spiritual confusion—mistaking a state for a stage, confusing a pleasant feeling with the happiness that does not depend on conditions—is particularly prevalent in places where the dharma has (d)evolved into self-help. The Buddha's dharma didn't teach peace and relaxation; it taught awakening—often rude awakening. But when it's translated into pop psychology, the potential for confusion only increases.

In fact, it's possible to be doing a lot of good work without even noticing it. Because contemplative fitness works on the brain like weight training works on the biceps; you may be doing just fine, even if you don't (yet) feel different, and even if you haven't bought any Yanni CDs. "What's wrong?" you might ask, "I'm doing all this work, but I still get pissed off at my mom!" Well, sure, welcome to being human. Maybe, over time, you'll notice that your anger lasts for less time, that you're less immediately reactive, that you pick fewer fights (or take the bait less often). But that may be all you can hope for. Meanwhile, the practice is doing its work.

Personally, I find all this to be liberating. One of my own greatest misconceptions was the view that enlightenment was about some big occult secret. In fact, the reality is that my most powerful insights have been shockingly banal. Indeed, despite having spent two decades studying the baroque mysteries of the Kabbalah, the intricacies of postmodern philosophy, and the endless inversions of gender and queer theory, and despite four (count 'em) graduate degrees, I find that the insights that affect me the most, and last the longest, are maxims you might find on any hybrid-SUV's bumper stickers. Love and Let Go. You are Okay. Trust the Part that Loves. It's ridiculous, really; having written more than two hundred essays and articles on the spiritual path, I'm at a loss to say anything original about what really matters to me. It all comes out sounding trite.

What has stuck are the fundamentals, which I tried to express at the beginning of the first chapter: We are animals descended from five billion years of wanting, striving, and seeking. And life just doesn't cooperate. So we suffer. And so the solution to that problem is to upgrade our minds, in a distinctly "unnatural" way, so that the mind clings less and lets go more.

This, you'll observe, has very little to do with esotericism, Kabbalistic coincidences, Atlanteans, Lumerians, entheogenic visions, theorizing, cognizing, faiths, anti-faiths, Bible Codes, Mayan calendar, or energy vortices. The fruits of the dharma are exceedingly simple: just a letting go, a disentanglement, and the discovery that there is a radiant peace, always accessible in the mind. This is the happiness that does not depend upon conditions. That's *it*? I guess it is.

Everything passes, everything changes. And when it doesn't change quickly enough, you do—your mind shifts, attention jumps, even the most solid-seeming of experiences actually strobes in and out of consciousness. And so the fundamental axis of the teaching is very, very simple: to understand, intuitively and deeply, that what Buddhists call "conditioned formations"—i.e., stuff, ideas, people, emotions, and everything else—are incapable of providing lasting, deep happiness. Formations change all the time. The joys they bring—though often wonderful, profound, and amazing—are short-lived. Even when we get exactly what we want, it gets old after a while, and we want something else.

And, most subtly but also most importantly, physical and mental formations just happen. They don't happen to you or to me. There's no one really minding your mental store—it's running on autopilot. Stimulus, response; cause, effect. We say "I am angry" but really all that's happening is "anger has arisen." More on this in the next chapter.

And while at the further stages of the spiritual path "letting go" becomes quite profound indeed, as it comes to include letting go of *everything*, even thought and consciousness and self, most of the time, it's just plain, ordinary letting go. Those things that have to get done—don't really have to get done. The dream that you have, which your life will be meaningless if you don't achieve—let it go, too.

Boring, right? No angels, demons, neo-Platonic spheres, noetic experiences of the union of all life. But it is "profound" in a different sense of the word, as in "profoundly difficult" or "profound change." It is a fundamental reordering of our most basic sense of the world. And so it does take a long time to really sink in. Can I really be equanimous as to pain and pleasure, love and its lack? Can I really remember, over and over again, that, contrary to all indications, fulfilling my desires will not be as satisfying as lessening them? Simple, but not easy.

The reason all this is liberating is that it's accessible. It's not even dependent on sitting for an hour a day, which, let's face it, is beyond the reach of most people who take up meditation.[7] Much of it is attitudinal: Jon Kabat-Zinn's attitudes of mindfulness, for example—non-judging, patience, beginner's mind, trust, non-striving, acceptance, letting go—may be practiced on the cushion but they are put *into* practice in the rest of life.[8] You build the mental muscles to do this in intensive practice, but ultimately life is your real practice. This, incidentally, is why Ñaniko, the monastic we met in Chapter Three, chose the monastic path. "Retreats," he said, "are so focused on formal meditation, they don't give as much emphasis to the rest of the Eightfold Path." Ironically, it is precisely those other aspects of the path—right conduct, right speech, and so on—that are most accessible to householders living in the Western world. You don't need extended concentration states to practice speaking more kindly. As Sylvia Boorstein put it to me, "This is a way of life, not apart from everyday life."

In Defense of Square One

Recently, I was having lunch with a yoga-teacher friend of mine who, after years of teaching, was beginning to get burned out. He still enjoyed the daily routine of teaching, and he was continuing to grow in how and what he taught. But over the years his own practice had evolved to the point where he had come to see his basic teaching work as, well, somewhat vulgar: cheap yoga thrills, low-level relaxation states, not really doing the deep work. Just rearranging the deck chairs on the *Titanic* of his students' lives. Sound familiar?

And yet, having critiqued special states in the previous chapter, and having questioned integration in this one, I now want to defend spiritual vulgarity, on several grounds.

First, let's remember that most people have still not had a taste, and my friend—who is quite good at what he does—has the job of providing it. It's a challenge, since his own practice is moving forward while his teaching stays at square one, to help the people who are still stuck there. But this is how it must be: to be authentic, we each need to move forward and be learning ourselves, growing, changing, evolving. Yet to be skillful, we need to come back to the beginning, every day.

Second, square one is a powerful place to be. "I felt connected to something bigger than myself." "It was as if time stopped, and the only thing in the universe was my baby daughter's face." "I have no words to describe it." Aren't these important moments? They show us that it's possible to get beyond the egoic self, that there is another way of being human. They give a taste of the light that is so delicious that we are impelled to practice more. And they can, in themselves, awaken love, wisdom, and compassion in the individual. If you've never had these experiences, please *go have them*. Maybe one day you'll tire of them, but in the meantime you'll be transformed.

And third, let's not forget that wherever one is on the contemplative path, reminders are always important. If it's true that awakening is not a permanent transformation into a beatific laughing Buddha, then life at any stage of the path will necessitate some remembering and forgetting, tightening and letting go. Square one, square ten, it doesn't really matter—and if someone else's ego-shattering peak experience is, for you, just a pleasant reminder of the truth of non-self or impermanence, well, that's alright. The dharma evolves in one's own practice, but the human mind still forgets.

Finally, if contemplative wisdom is going to change the world, vulgarity will have to lead. Yes, catalogs festooned with pictures of sunsets, advertising svelte yoga teachers and fancy dharma gear are cheesy. But I'm perfectly content for vulgarity to be the gateway drug for transformation. I've seen firsthand that the real work of social and environmental justice is going to happen within the human mind. And if that's true, the work of spiritual teaching and the work of social justice intersect not in the more esoteric or refined realms, but in what you could call the "retail business" of spirituality: bringing change to more and more people, usually in somewhat gross ways.

Eckhart Tolle, after the huge success of *The Power of Now,* took a year of silent retreat to discern what his next step should be—not as a matter of career, but as one of mission. What he did next was not unveil the next stage of the path, what lies beyond "now," but rather adjust the way he was teaching, simplify it, and, in a way, translate it into more coarse terms. The result was *A New Earth,* which was a worldwide success and gained him, through Oprah, the largest audience a spiritual teacher has received in recent years. Now, *A New Earth* is far less profound than Tolle's earlier work. Yet I stand in awe of Tolle's success at reaching a mass audience. He is giving over very powerful teaching, and he has figured out a container that makes it available to millions of people. Good for him—and for the rest of the world.

Dharma teachers still need to promise that you'll feel good, and deliver the goods. That's the only way to translate the truth into the lies of the ego. Wei Wu Wei, the British nondual teacher whose books from the middle of the last century are now gaining a wide audience, said that "in early stages, teaching can only be given via a series of untruths diminishing in inveracity in ratio to the pupil's apprehension of the falsity of what he is being taught."[9] That takes a little untangling, but it is the essence of the Buddhist doctrine of *upaya,* skillful means, which we've referred to several times already. What other way is there to somehow convince the human ego to sample a bit of the light beyond itself? You have to use the tricks of the prison to free the prisoner from it. Especially if the prisoner is you.

The fruition of the path may be occasioned by remarkable shifts and exciting mind-states. Then, as Jack Kornfield wrote, after the ecstasy, the laundry. We reintegrate into our lives, or maybe we change them. The developmental path develops, and yet we're still back with the furniture and the weather and the bills and the cat. Have we failed somewhere? Or is the deepest tantric truth, that emptiness and manifestation are one, that enlightenment happens in the world—actually true? To repeat: if it wasn't always there, it isn't "it." The timeless goal is, by definition, present right now. The dharma evolves, but if the ultimate *bodhicitta,* the awakened heart-mind, is not something that comes and goes, that means it hasn't gone anywhere at all. And that is true whether you're in an MBSR session at the medical clinic or sitting long hours in the zendo. All we're doing in intensive practice is getting a closer look at the obvious, so that we don't miss it for its ordinariness. Hacking the brain sounds like changing something, and in a sense it is, but what's really changing is only a way of seeing—not the what, but the how. Maybe let's put it this way: what would it take for you to know, to really know in your *kishkes,* that this—this moment, this mind, this place—was really *it*?

CHAPTER 8

AFTER THE SELF

Postmodernity, Spirituality, and Identity

As the dharma has taken hold in the West, it has entered cultural contexts with very different notions of individuality, group identity, and subjectivity than those of the cultures where Buddhism came into being. Western, and particularly American, society has tended to value the individual above the collective: conservatives recoil against socialism and collectivism, liberals against authoritarianism and fascism. The founding documents of the United States imbue individuals (some of them, anyway) with "natural" rights. And in a nation of immigrants, communal ties are often in tension with individualistic American dreams of prosperity. How then does a philosophical system with an emphasis on the illusory nature of the self translate into a society seemingly obsessed with it?

Of course, sometimes the translation is a bit rough. When Chogyam Trungpa Rinpoche coined the term "spiritual materialism," he was referring to the tendency to claim spiritual attainments or identities as badges of specialness—exactly the opposite of how they are meant to be. Little did he know how spiritual materialism would be reified into spiritual stuff: my favorite cushion, or "Zen" accessories for every personal aggrandizement.

Often, though, the translations are more interesting than that. For example, the Buddhist doctrine of non-self intersects in startling and provocative ways with contemporary notions of spirituality and identity. Ours is a postmodern moment in which the modern self is being seriously critiqued by philosophers, modern notions of identities are being questioned and "queered" by academics and activists, and modern conceptions of religious/ethnic identity are being mixed and matched by a new generation of spiritual DJs. Thus, whereas many of the evolutions we have explored so far consist of adaptations and mutations, this one is more of a convergence. Of course, Buddhist Abhidharma is quite different from post-structuralist philosophy; this is not an exercise in syncretism. But the convergences of postmodern and Buddhist (non-)identity are, as with other evolutions we have traced, pregnant with possibilities for the dharma's integration into the West.

BuJus in the Age of iSpirituality

I admit, I am a BuJu.

In this book, in contrast to my previous ones, I have chosen to focus on the Buddhist side of my contemplative path. Yet as readers of those earlier books know, I also have studied and taught Kabbalah for fifteen years, managed to get a PhD in Jewish Thought at Hebrew University, and have written two books and about a hundred articles on Jewish theology, culture, and spirituality. My personal practice includes keeping Shabbat in a fairly traditional way, and, more generally, a fairly serious engagement with the learning, practice, and teaching of Jewish spirituality. I speak Hebrew fluently (having lived in Israel for three years), I have sampled Jewish meditation traditions as well as Buddhist ones, and I am deeply invested in Jewish cultural and religious life as a committed, nondenominational American Jew.

So how does this all fit together? First I want to explore the cultural-sociological aspects, then the philosophical ones.

On a sociological level, I am far from the only one to practice this particular type of "double belonging."[1] Not only are a disproportionate number of American Buddhist teachers of Jewish backgrounds, but many Jews practice both Judaism and Buddhism—some of the better-known names include Sylvia Boorstein, Norman Fischer, Rodger Kamenetz, David Cooper, Brenda Shoshanna, Jeff Roth, Jonathan Slater, Judith Linzer, Rachel Cowan, and many others. Likewise Christians such as Professor Paul Knitter, author of *Without Buddha I Could Not Be a Christian*; Stuart Lord, recently president of Naropa University; blogger Bishop Craig Bergland; the many contributors to the wonderful anthology *Beside Still Waters: Jews, Christians, and the Way of the Buddha*; and many, many more.[2] (Interestingly, Thich Nhat Hanh's *Living Buddha, Living Christ* remains one of the best-selling Buddhist books of all time.) Although in an earlier period, the standard form of Jewish-Buddhist encounter was a secularized American or European Jew relinquishing one identity for another one,[3] today multiple, overlapping identities are widespread. It's now commonplace, in fact, to find meditation groups in any number of Jewish and Christian communities. I myself have taught insight meditation in synagogues, churches, and community centers of several denominations. The integration of Buddhist technologies of contemplative practice within Western spiritual paths is a widespread trend.

More broadly, such experimentation and hybridization is a common feature in what I have elsewhere called "iSpirituality."[4] By way of analogy, perhaps you remember, in the old days, how you used to buy music? Maybe you would go to a store and purchase a large plastic disk (later, a smaller plastic disc) that an expert had recorded, sequenced, and curated for you. Its style, and thus, secondarily, yours, was carefully thought out by an array of musicians, producers, art directors, and marketing men (generally, men). Not only that, but you probably had heard about it from another bevy of experts: radio programmers, promoters, and DJs. The style of the plastic music disc was generally uniform: if not created by a single artist, it at least hewed to a specific style, or theme, or genre. This is what it was to buy music, as recently as twenty years ago: a purchase of a single, coherent style organized by experts, arranged for your consumption.

If you're under thirty, this narrative isn't even nostalgic; it's Jurassic. Today, it's understood that participants (not consumers) buy, stream, download, or trade bits of music; that they (not experts) arrange them how they like; and that what makes a good playlist on Spotify or iTunes is not uniformity of style, but diversity. The expectation of younger people today is that they will cocreate their experience, whether it's a Tumblr, a playlist . . . or a religion.

All identity, but in particular "spiritual" or "religious" identity, is similar. The dharma is evolving in a multi-identity world—we live in the age of iSpirituality, no less than the age of the iPod. As with music, everything is now available all the time. Participants (formerly parishioners, consumers, or target markets) expect, not as a matter of *au courant* hipdom but simply as a matter of course, that they will have a role in constructing their identities and experiences—and that they will do so from a variety of different sources, in their own distinctive ways. Top-down curation, uniformity of program offerings, and mono-identity are as outdated as those old 33s. Whether that's a good thing or not remains to be seen. But even if it's not desirable, it is inevitable.

Really, this is more evolution than revolution. Modernity itself radically shook the existing foundations of identity, religion, and eternal values. Late modernity and industrialization radically destabilized class, and the twentieth century challenged racial and gender stratification. Yet postmodernity, enabled by information technology and the shattering of conventional identity markers, is of a different order of magnitude. Traditional definitions of "Buddhist" (to the extent they were even that traditional) are unlikely to appeal or apply to many, if not most, Westerners interested in Buddhist meditation, mindfulness, or other contemplative technologies. Purists can complain about hybridizers destroying the dharma,[5] but it's not just the dharma that's being hybridized but all forms of contemplative, religious, or personal-growth practices. Conversely, it should also be clear that such innovations will not replace traditional forms; as we saw in Chapter Three, many practitioners seem attracted precisely to a stable notion of Buddhist identity or tradition, perhaps for practical reasons, perhaps as a replacement for the religious community they've left behind, or perhaps as a link to a more secure-seeming past. Western dharma practitioners, whether they identify as Buddhist or not, should "let a thousand flowers bloom" in what is rapidly becoming an ecosystem marked by diversity, not monoculture.

These postmodern sociological and cultural conventions are half of the story. The philosophical zones of juncture and disjuncture are the other half. In my BuJu practice, there have been two major intersection points between my Judaism and my Buddhism: non-self (the subject of this chapter), and the way in which meditation and mindfulness complement and enhance the devotional elements of the Jewish path. I will briefly elaborate on the latter, before focusing on the former.

The Judaism I choose to practice is a way of being in relationship with that which is beyond my personal concerns and my human, self-centered nature. Judaism gives form to my life and a shared community of meaning with which to shape the sacred moments of life. It's also my cultural birthright, and the community in which I often feel the closest familial ties. In terms of spirituality specifically, Jewish practice has also given me ways to encounter what some call the sacred or holy aspect of human experience. This way of being in the world is accessible all the time, but for basically dharma-related reasons, it's difficult to access, because at almost all waking moments, the mind is busy going somewhere else. The

Hasidic master Rabbi Nachman of Bratzlav said: "The world is full of light and mysteries both wonderful and awesome, but our tiny little hand shades our eyes and prevents them from seeing."

In this context, meditation is one way to cultivate wonder at and gratitude for being alive; religious reminders, signs, and communities are another. The two practices can reinforce one another. First, as Kenneth Folk said to me, religious practice can be a form of contemplative fitness: "Even if you say 'Accept Jesus Christ!' that's fine if it gets you to stop getting lost in content of thoughts, which is the prerequisite to everything that I think of as contemplative fitness. Since this is really all about brainhacking, all about brain development, you can use whatever conceptual framework you want, as long as you do the work." And second, meditation can enhance religious practice. In Jewish and Kabbalistic traditions, meditation was often used as a preparation for other practices—prayer and Torah study, for example. The quiet mind absorbs sacred text much more readily than the busy mind does, and the presence of mind that comes from mindfulness (not a traditional Jewish form, though certainly a contemporary one) also enables a richer, juicier gratitude for life's many blessings. Indeed, for several years this was my main intention for mindfulness practice. (My book *God in Your Body: Kabbalah, Mindfulness, and Embodied Spiritual Practice* is, in large part, devoted to it.) Sylvia Boorstein, probably the world's most beloved BuJu, put it this way:

> These days it's normal for me not only to go to a synagogue and have people say "let's sit quietly for a few moments" but to really talk about what we're doing there in terms of the transformation of consciousness, of developing kindness and compassion. The message of dharma is more than just the practice of sitting—you can sit quietly and nothing can happen. It's about sitting quietly with the intention to notice those characteristics of heart and mind that lead to unhappiness, and those that lead to happiness, and therefore

"choose life." This is not just a groovy way to alter your consciousness, or feel a little bit high or a little bit relaxed, but really to see deeply into the nature of your own character and—whatever language you want to use—the glory of God, or the wonder of creation, or the awesomeness of being alive, and to have that vision transform you into the kindest and most courageous person that you can be for the duration of your lifetime.

As my Jewish and Buddhist practices evolved, though, a further resonance began to arise—with non-self as the essential point. This, in fact, was the focus of another of my books, *Everything Is God: The Radical Path of Nondual Judaism*—that the God understood by (parts of) the Jewish mystical tradition is not some deity that does or does not exist, but *Ein Sof,* the Endless, everything and nothing. For example, Moses asks how he's supposed to describe God, and gets the reply "I Am That I Am," *Ehyeh Asher Ehyeh,* variously rendered as "I Will Be What I Will Be," "I Am What I Am," or, without the pronoun, "It Is What It Is." Of course, many Jews have much more anthropomorphic notions, of a creator god, a judging god, a god who prefers Jews to everyone else, and so on. But this more mystical conception is as traditional a Jewish notion as theirs, and I have little need to justify it.

As heterodox as it may sound, I see very little difference between the nondual God YHVH ("It Is What It Is") and the Buddhist Dharma with a capital "D." As Ajahn Sumedho once wrote, one goal of meditation is to see all arising phenomena as dharma, and not self. Replace "dharma" with "God" and the theistic and nontheistic paths converge. It is what it is—that's all there is to it. This is how God is always present, even with prophets in jail and saints in death camps, because the present is always present. Can I repeat the Ramana Maharshi quotation from the end of Chapter Five? "Let come what comes, let go what goes. See what remains."

In the dharma, what remains is dharma; empty phenomena,

rolling on; the way things are. In nondual traditions, including Jewish ones, what remains is the All, the One, That Which Is, the Atman, the I-I. Of course there are differences among the different nondual paths, and even larger differences between them and Buddhist ones. But the destination, I have found, is more alike than different. Whether everything is nothing or Nothing does matter to theologians, perhaps, but only a little to contemplatives. Obviously, even if the destinations are similar, the paths diverge. Meditation begins from observable experience, from the epistemological bottom upward; religion often begins from a religious/ontological assertion, and proceeds from the top downward. For example, the great Kabbalist Rabbi Moshe Cordovero wrote: "Realize that the Infinite exists in each thing. Do not say 'This is a stone and not God.' Rather, all existence is God, and the stone is a thing pervaded by divinity." God first, then down to us.

Yet in both cases—and also as between Theravada and Mahayana Buddhism, which differ on how "emptiness" is to be understood—contemplative practice has roughly the same task: to see clearly, and thus see through, the conventional self, to get beyond its illusions of solidity, to either work with what is there (what Theravadans call purification of mind, Jews call *Kapparah,* as in Yom Kippur) or rest beyond it (what Dzogchen practitioners call *rigpa,* Jews call God's point of view).

In general, I find the bottom-up, Buddhist path to this realization to be easier to communicate than the Jewish one, because it takes nothing for granted and proceeds from no premises other than what can be observed and experienced. Yet on an emotional level, I sometimes find the top-down "God" more available and more helpful. In this way, the Buddhist and the Jewish map onto the contemplative and the devotional aspects of religious life. The brain is Buddhist, the heart is Jewish. Western religious devotional language addresses all that is not only as a net of causes and conditions, but as You. Dharma practice, and Western skeptical doubt, cause me to question whether this You is merely a projection of the mind—and generally answer in the affirmative. But the mind is not the only locus of meaning, and within the heart I often find myself turning to the very You I can't explain.

I've never been one to cover over the differences between these paths, however. I'm not interested in saying that Jewish practice is actually a mindfulness practice, for example. It isn't, though it can certainly be adapted for that purpose if you like. Nor do I want to iron out any troubling creases in Jewish theology to make them Buddhist-kosher. I'd rather see these paths as equally human, equally partial perspectives, and appreciate the varying consciousnesses that brought them about. For example, among the sharpest differences between the dharma and Western religious paths are not matters of theology or ontology, but the purpose of practice itself. Different practices lead to different goals. For example, I've met Sufis who are really, really loving, but who are also pretty "attached" in a dharma sense. So they "fail" a Buddhist test, but they pass a Sufi test with flying colors. This makes sense: they've focused on working out the love muscles and they're really juicy, and it's beautiful. Here's Kenneth Folk again, when I shared that example with him:

> Yes—that's based on their values. . . . We have finite capacities, both physical and mental. So if I want to optimize my own potential for long-distance running, I'm going to train for that, but I'm going to have to give up something because I can't simultaneously be a marathoner and a power-lifter. . . . This happens with the brain as well. We can't do everything. If I want to do Sufi practice, I can get as good as I can get being a Sufi, but I'm not going to be a very good Buddhist. This has to do with different goals and different practices that lead to those goals.

And yet, while one cannot become a marathoner and a power-lifter at the same time, from an integrated fitness perspective these differences among contemplative modalities are strengths. There are reasons, for example, why even monastic Buddhists take refuge in the Buddha, dharma, and sangha; why they bow to Buddha statues and chant twice a day. Human beings are embodied and emotional creatures, not merely intellectual ones. We are comforted by ritual, connected by bonds of community and teaching, and we often yearn for "refuge," for the sense that there are larger forces holding us even when we cannot hold ourselves. Obviously, I appreciate the extrapolation of mindfulness from religion into science, and the secularization of Buddhism in America. But I also appreciate the richness of ritual and myth, and the power of religious community. Certainly, there is little place in my worldview for primitive notions of reward and punishment, outdated myths about cosmology, or religious ethnocentrism. I also do not see either my Jewish or dharma practices as pointing to some fixed "identity." Yet I think precisely because my dharma practice tends to de-emphasize the devotional and the ritual, there remains a space in my life for religious practice that includes them—not as a matter of fact, but as one of the heart.

This, of course, is but one idiosyncratic way in which these traditions can reinforce one another, among many that have been explored by others. For me, the Buddhist teachings on non-self, emptiness, and dependent origination (all of which I see as pointing to the same non-thing) are among the deepest liberation teachings of the dharma, precisely because they point to what is leftover after the self is taken away. Over the years, whether I capitalize the word "What" or not, that question has remained a koan of infinite depth.

The Selfless Meme

The radical questioning of the self is not confined to various forms of contemplative practice, (i-)spirituality, or mysticism. For the last fifty or so years, postmodern philosophers of mind have critiqued the modern view of the subject, that basically rational, coherent self who, according to about three hundred years of Western philosophy, makes decisions, has various rights, and is the modern citizen of the modern state. This subject, an array of postmodernists have observed, is a social construction—not necessarily a bad construction, but a construct nonetheless. Human beings are not essentially rational, or essentially selfish, or essentially anything; we all have various attributes, some of which are deemed by some people to be essential. Moreover, these attributes are conditioned by the cultures in which all of us grew up. In some places, dogs are pets; in others, dogs are food. A Canadian who eats dogs might be seen as aberrant, but a Chinese person who eats dogs is perfectly normal. The modern subject, far from being a stable "self," is actually a social construction, an assemblage of memes, narratives, and values entirely made up of historically conditioned factors.[6] My supposed need for security, home, and hearth is a late-capitalist, bourgeois affectation conditioned by nineteenth- and twentieth-century advertising and cultural production. My tastes, preferences, styles, and self-identifications all are cultural constructions. So, too, every notion that you have, about politics, justice, identity, music, love, whatever, is a meme, constituted outside of "you" and replicated in sophisticated ways. To think that they are "you" is what epistemologist Wilfrid Sellars called "the myth of the given." It's what happened when Descartes moved from the arising of thought (*cogito*) to the existence of the full-on modern subject (*sum*). A postmodernist would reply: Yes, the thought arose—but that doesn't mean there was a "you" thinking it. There was just a set of memes thinking the thought, interpreting it, and constructing a self on the basis of it.

Philosopher Susan Blackmore,[7] drawing on the now-ubiquitous terminology of Richard Dawkins, calls human minds "meme machines."[8] Memes are bits of information that drift about, and replicate themselves with varying degrees of success. Most memes fail: New Coke, Google Wave. But some succeed, and a few succeed astonishingly well: regular Coke, or regular Google, or that old standby that our God is better than your God. (Memes succeed or fail not based on how morally or aesthetically good they are, but on how effectively they replicate. Some can be outright disastrous.[9]) Look at how you're dressed right now. Chances are, even if you're a non-conformist like Susan Blackmore (whose hair is often pink and sometimes purple), your look is entirely a collection of various memes that have drifted through culture and into your brain. Pants and shirts, for a start. Patterns that have come to be associated with this or that social role. Colors—remember that scene in *The Devil Wears Prada,* where a few fashion elites decide on the colors that millions of people eventually wear? Not to mention signifiers that you may have adopted: wedding rings, nose rings, earrings.

In fact, there's nothing in your mind *but* memes. Writes Daniel Dennett, "The human mind is itself an artifact created when memes restructure a human brain in order to make it a better habitat for memes . . . human consciousness is itself a huge complex of memes."[10] We imagine that in our brains is what Dennett calls a "Cartesian theater," where all the various sense data comes together and "we" watch the result.[11] But this is just not how the brain works. Actually, the Buddhist notion that when there is a sound, "sound-consciousness" arises is a better representation of what actually takes place; there is no place in the brain where all these sense impressions are assembled. Things happen, and our brains make coherence out of them. There is no homunculus outside the neurobiological system.[12] The "self" is born in the blur.

As we've suggested, this empirically and analytically derived view of the (non-)self is remarkably and usefully similar to the Buddhist experiential one.[13] This is not a simple comparative game; Stephen Batchelor, whom we encountered earlier, suggests that these parallels are "not purely academic at all. There needs to be an encounter between Buddhism and Western philosophical traditions to get over this kind of Western chauvinism." Like postmodern philosophers from Derrida to Rorty, the Buddha, too, was teaching in a context in which the self *(atman)* was seen as fundamental—even the only true reality. He asked his followers to inquire into where this self actually existed, and when it actually did anything. What he found, and what you can find if you look closely, is that every action you take is caused by various conditions which are not the "self":

your upbringing, your genetic constitution, your gender, your sex, your values (which, of course, you learned from somewhere), your intellectual capacities. Each of these individually may be *yours*, but none of them individually is *you*. "You" are a collection of these qualities, tendencies, views, and opinions. Beautiful, unique, interesting—but not one iota more than all of these non-you aspects bundled together with string.

One of the Buddha's ways to explain the non-self-ness of objects was to have his monks mentally take apart a chariot and ask where "chariot" comes into being, what "chariot" does as opposed to constituent parts like wheels, carriage, etc. Ultimately, even those parts are reduced to the four elements (in traditional science) or, in our science, to the properties of their molecules, atoms, and subatomic particles. If you don't have a chariot handy, consider a chair. Is the "chair" holding you up right now? Or is it really the various molecular bonds in the wood, metal, or plastic? Is the "chair" white, or black, or another color, or is it the molecular properties of the pigmentation? And do you perceive the "chair," or rather, different elements of it, like its size, color, and texture? And so on.

In some forms of meditation practice, it's possible to observe the process of "selfing" directly. One can note, with a high degree of attention, the arising of all kinds of impulses, ideas, and notions, including notions of the self—and yet none of those actually is "you." Consciousness arises if the conditions are present; and that's it.[14] Moreover, just like Susan Blackmore and Meryl Streep told us, each of these comes from somewhere else. In Blackmore's words, "In a very real sense they are not 'our' thoughts at all. They are simply the memes that happen to be successfully exploiting our brain-ware at the moment."[15] More specifically, in the words of writer Fred Pfeil, "Is it not possible, at least at some moments within one's meditation practice, to know by taste and sense and feeling, not analytically but experientially, the culturally and historically specific contingency of each and all our senses of things, including and especially of those things we each and all call our separate selves?"[16]

It is. If you're in the mood for a simple experiment, raise your right hand right now. Go ahead, just pause for a moment, raise your right hand, and then put it down. Now, whether you did or didn't raise your hand, reflect on what actually happened. Did the thing you call "you" really raise your right hand? In fact, what likely happened were a series of mental processes, all of which were conditioned from outside of "you." Maybe a sense of curiosity, or playfulness, or even obedience, arose, which was probably learned when you were a small child, or which maybe has something to do with your genetic predispositions. Or maybe some feeling of laziness, obstinacy, or contrariness arose—just as much learned from experience, from other people, from a thousand outside sources. Sure, the collection of all of those feelings, plus myriad more, is conventionally referred to as "you." But the collection, as such, never actually does anything—it's a label, nothing more. What actually acts, thinks, feels, dreams are one or more of those pieces, usually in combination, all of which come from outside "you" and none of which is actually "you." They are the conditions that are necessary for the action to take place—not "you." Who moved? The conditions moved.

In fact, all of your hopes, fears, dreams, loves, hates, tastes, predilections; each instance of who you are is wholly caused and constituted by non-you elements. Now, we may get very used to these movements of the mind and come to understand them as ourselves. But while that's a very useful and conventional way of seeing, it is a way of seeing, not a reality. As Joseph Goldstein put it, the self is like the Big Dipper; it's a pattern that emerges when you look from one perspective, but of course, it's not really there.[17] Labels of identity, gender, group belonging—are any of these *you*? Take a look for a few minutes (or hours, or weeks). As a reaction, idea, or emotion arises in the mind, try to notice it (obviously, a concentrated mind makes this easier) and query whether it's "you" or something that is "not-you." What I think you'll find is what Blackmore has said: "We, our precious, mythical 'selves,' are just groups of selfish memes that have come together by and for themselves."[18] Or as David Hume wrote, prefiguring Postmodernity by several hundred years:

I may venture to affirm to the rest of mankind that they are nothing but a bundle or collection of different perceptions, which succeed each other with an inconceivable rapidity, and are in a perpetual flux and movement . . . nor is there any single power of the soul, which remains unalterably the same, perhaps for one moment. The mind is a kind of theatre, where several perceptions successively make their appearance; pass, repass, glide away and mingle in an infinite variety of postures and situations."[19]

A Queer Example

Now, postmodernity and its various philosophical agendas may seem rather remote from the ways in which most of us live our lives day-to-day. Actually, though, we are enmeshed in the postmodern condition: how we conceive identity, how our culture is suffused by hyper-capitalism and the increasingly fragmented ways in which "mass" production is "personalized," and, not least, how the dominant culture and various subcultures conceive gender, race, sexuality, class, nationality, and the intersections between them. One of the most profound areas in which postmodern deconstructions of the self have been applied is in the area of sexuality and gender. Queer theory, the academic discipline that grew out of gay and lesbian studies in the 1970s and 1980s, has long held among its central tenets the notion that gender is socially constructed. One's biological sex is essentially (though not entirely) anatomical, but gender—as the saying goes, it has more to do with what's between your ears than what's between your legs. Confounding assumptions and conventions about gender animates drag performance, camp, rejections of gender binarism (no, Virginia, the world is not divided into masculine and feminine), articulations of queer sexuality (no, neither one of us is the "man" or the "woman"), and countless other aspects of LGBTQ existence. In terms of gender, I am neither man nor woman, except insofar as I participate in cultural discourses of masculinity or femininity—and neither is anyone else. And like other cultural discourses, what is "manly" shifts over time and place: there are cultures, today, in which holding hands with other men, wearing skirts, wrestling naked, and even engaging in forms of same-sex activity are all seen as entirely "manly."

To be sure, in the dharma world, there have been many LGBTQ voices that have made themselves heard within Buddhist communities—but they have been focused on healing, not on the intricacies of postmodern queer theory. In an earlier time, much of the work was focused on the ravages of the AIDS plague; Issan Dorsey, a gay Zen roshi, was one of the first religious leaders to reach out to San Francisco's gay community during those horrible years.[20] Today, in my experience, most LGBTQ teachers are focused on healing the particular forms of *dukkha* experienced by the gay community; for example, Larry Yang, who had led numerous retreats for LGBTQ people, told me that much of his work is "shepherding ourselves through the collective traumatization that we have as LGBT folks . . . the level of traumatic response is much greater than the mainstream population that doesn't necessarily experience these things of oppression or exclusion or overt discrimination." There are several LGBTQ sitting groups across the country, such as Queer Dharma and Queer Sangha, as well as two *Queer Dharma* anthologies,[21] and other essays and books.[22]

There have also been attempts to find ourselves, or legitimate ourselves, in Buddhist communities and traditions. The Dalai Lama has been asked for his opinions about homosexuality, and reproved for not offering progressive enough ones.[23] Buddhist scriptures have been scoured for references to homosexuality (for monks, it is a form of improper sexuality roughly equivalent to other violations of celibacy; for others, the texts vary),[24] while the Japanese tradition of same-sex love among monks and samurais has received some scholarly attention,[25] though like most such traditions, it is scarcely known among laypeople.

While this is all noble and important work, the more interesting questions, I think, are just beginning to be asked. I'm interested not just in building inclusive communities and finding ourselves in history, though both are obviously very important, but also in how queer theory and LGBTQ experience enrich all of our conceptions of gender and destabilize all of our notions of the self. I'm interested in how queering the sangha problematizes the ways in which patriarchy is perpetuated (more on that in the next chapter), and how Buddhist notions of non-self call all of us who work in "identity politics" to question how we may be reinscribing oppression by defining our identities in response to it. As Rita Gross has pointed out, gender constructs and gender identity are aspects of the ego.[26] Queer theory, like feminism, by pointing out the non-essentialistic nature of these egoic conditions, can thus be "useful to Buddhists," regardless of their sexual or gender identity.[27] Questioning our supposedly innate characteristics—that women are supposedly one way and men another; that women and men are a stable, binary map of all gender identity; that to be a "man" involves certain essential traits—is a gesture toward a more robust self-understanding and a more enlightened one. It's all drag, really: the identities, genders, gender roles, gender expressions. Queer theory and evolving dharma meet at the juncture of non-self.

Sometimes, even queer identity (which is practically an oxymoron) can sometimes reinscribe a kind of self-definition, and thus a certitude where perhaps there should be aporia. Of course I support queer people having positive experiences in Buddhist communities, and Larry has been quite careful to frame LGBT-specific retreats not as cul-de-sacs of identity politics but as "doors into our spiritual life . . . Wherever you are in your particular life, that's a door into these teachings, *and* there's so much more beyond the door." That is a crucial corrective, to which I would add that there are also many doors beyond inclusion, healing, and safe spaces; the more challenging intersections of non-self and contemporary identity promise much more than that.

Queer theory can seem rather abstract, and many of its academic proponents prefer it to remain that way. Yet it also captures much about how I experience my gender identity: as not fitting into boxes (including "gay"), as being defined according to a variety of contingent cultural conditions, and as intersecting with other vectors of oppression far more interesting than the gender of my emotional and physical life-partner. But let me try to bring it down to earth even more, and say something about gender theory, postmodernity, memes, the illusion of free will, and the liberation of non-self—with a quaint dharma story about a dog.

Once, on a meditation retreat a few years ago, I had been struggling with one of the petty irritations that meditators work with all the time: restless yogis making noise. This one shifted on her cushion, that one adjusted his blankets—it was like Grand Central Station in there. I know, we're all meant to be learning to accept what is, be in the moment, and so on. But who can work under such conditions?

This particular retreat was in the summertime, so after "noticing" my annoyance and irritation for a while, I decided to give myself a break and spend one session sitting outside. I sat far away from the main buildings, on a bench overlooking a beautiful valley. Inspired by the wind and the quiet, and relieved to be away from people shifting on their cushions, I quickly fell into a groove of watching my breath, and noting sensations, just as instructed. Now that's more like it!

Not ten minutes after I sat down, however, a dog appeared. Panting heavily in the heat, she invited me to play with her by dropping a stick in my lap. I tried to ignore her, but she was persistent. Okay, I thought: this is what is happening . . . I surrender. So I threw the stick, and the dog retrieved it. I threw it again, and she brought it back again. After a few minutes, the game had worn thin (for me) and I decided to return to my meditation practice. I decided to sit still, no matter what.

The dog was having none of it. She wanted to keep playing, and was not interested in my being a good meditator. She picked the stick up with her mouth and dropped it on my lap—over and over again. Maybe I didn't understand how to play; maybe I needed a hint.

In an instant, the frustration I had been experiencing earlier came into new perspective. Of course I wasn't angry at the dog—she was doing what her conditioning (genetic, environmental, training, whatever) caused her to do. So why was I angry at my fellow yogis for what their conditioning caused them to do? And perhaps even more important, why be angry at myself for being frustrated? My conditioning, the world in which I had been living—all these causes and conditions were giving rise to their inevitable result, just like the dog and the yogis.

Sure, the dog had a personality—but "personality" is just a label atop an amalgamation of behaviors and preferences, each of which is wholly caused by other things. The learned behavior of playing, the desire for companionship, the physical act of chasing the stick—the dog was doing just what it had to do. There was really no dog there—just all those conditions.

And me, too, and the other yogis, and the teachers, and everyone else I knew. The conditions caused the dog to play, other conditions caused me to be variously charmed, impatient, insistent, and indulgent. We were all just acting out our infinitude of conditions. For humans, there are more conditions, and far more complicated motives and factors at play—but the principle is the same. There is simply, as Sartre said, a great emptiness where we expect to find agency. Conditions are present, things move, anger arises, breezes blow—and there's no one minding the store.

Some time later, I remember sitting at Penn Station in New York one morning while around me thousands of people were replicating memes installed by culture, religion, education, and family. Habits learned, dispositions, instincts, and quite natural, evolutionarily beneficial desires to make more, do more, be more. Cause and effect, non-self—this, as I have experienced it, is the liberation of the machine, found precisely where some grieve the self's absence. I don't mean to dehumanize us with these metaphors and analogies;

on the contrary, I mean to draw us into the same vast matrix of causes and conditions, and in some small way, forgive. That morning in Penn Station, tired and awaiting the train platform to be called, there was little present save an impulse toward compassion and joy.

CHAPTER 9

AFTER THE FALL

Occupy Buddhism

Since the nineteenth century, Westerners have complained that Buddhism is pessimistic, passive, and world-renouncing. In the Victorian period, Buddhism was seen as nihilistic, offering no vision of hope, in contrast to Christianity. More recently, it has been seen as part of Sixties/Boomer spirituality, narcissistic and soothing. If only we were more angry, this particular theory goes, we would be more motivated to change the world. Dropping out, calming the mind—this only mutes our righteous political indignation.

This view is offensive and incorrect in just about every way. It generalizes from a perception of a handful of dabblers to condemn millions of Asian and Western practitioners of the dharma. It ignores the contemporary roles of monks in Burma, Thailand, and other societies in pushing for democracy and reform, or the peacemaking work of Thich Nhat Hanh and the Dalai Lama. And it is simply not the case even among the Western practitioners the contemporary stereotype seeks to critique. In fact, there are numerous examples of Western dharma practitioners motivated by their Buddhist practice to get more involved in social justice, environmental issues, peace activism, direct service, you name it, part of the movement known as Engaged Buddhism.[1] Moreover, with only a few exceptions (Zen in imperial Japan, for example, and some libertarian neo-Buddhists today) dharma practice tends to inspire a certain style of political commitment: one oriented toward more compassion. As I will suggest in this chapter, this fundamental orientation is the essence of a progressive political worldview, much more so than any slogans or platforms.

To be fair, there are challenges in pursuing an Engaged Buddhism, i.e., a dharma practice concerned and engaged with problems of justice. There is a tendency in any contemplative practice to focus on one's own "stuff," because that's what contemplatives do: we turn inward. And within Buddhism in particular, one can find world-renouncing and quietistic teachings, especially within the Theravadan tradition; those allegations of pessimism are not entirely without merit. Indeed, the very notion of a monastic community implies some degree of retreat from the problems of the world into a cloistered existence focused on other things. These tensions are present in all of us who take seriously the mandates to cultivate both wisdom and compassion. I've seen it myself in my own activist work, and many of my dharma friends have as well.

And then there's the tendency to overlook one's own shortcomings while preaching against the sins of others. Alas, this is not only the purview of closeted evangelicals inveighing against gay people; it is true in the Buddhist community as well, where power, as it always is, has been abused. If we're interested in justice, there is work we have to do at home, in the sangha. Thus, we will spend some of this last chapter exploring these particular shadows as well.

I think, though, that we have reason to be optimistic. The increases in non-hierarchical, participant-driven dharma communities—and the successes that traditional ones have had in becoming that way—have the capacity both for more effective political engagement and more effective internal reform. It is possible to "Occupy Buddhism"—possible, and powerful.

Why Meditation Really Will Save the World

For twenty years, I've been engaged—maybe obsessed—with the question of why some people turn out conservative, and others liberal. Each time I focus on political activism, whether environmental activism in the 1990s, local political activism in my hometown, or LGBT activism over the last ten years, I'm struck by how the parameters of the possible sometimes seem predefined at the outset. There are only this many swing voters, that many undecideds; public opinion will support this change, but not that one. In electoral politics, the numerical calculus of change is perhaps most obvious, but it's true more broadly as well. How can we change those parameters, those of us interested in promoting justice and equality? How are minds made up?

We've learned some of the answers, over the years. In the marriage equality battles of 2012, for example, I was a small part of a large movement to engage seriously with the "movable middle," those people whose minds were not made up one way or the other. Contrary to the shouting one often hears at the extremes, there were (and are) millions of folks in the middle who are not bigoted, not homophobic, but sincerely concerned and confused about perceived changes to our society's moral values. They were not receptive to sloganeering about equal rights, but they were open to hearing people's stories, to finding common ground, and to revising their opinions in the face of this new information. The progress we made in 2012 was incremental and incomplete, but I found it inspiring. Having those one-on-one conversations really gave me a sense of hope—that it's possible for minds to be open.

This, to me, is why contemplative practice is so essential to a political movement focused on caring more for those who are suffering the most. Political decisions often come down to some basic principles. Are we helping one another too much, or too little? Should government basically leave us alone, or do each of us owe the weaker among us a duty, with government being the all-too-imperfect means of fulfilling it? The answers to these political questions are not political at all—but ethical, and, for want of a better word, spiritual. At the end of the day, when moderates pull the lever one way or the other, they are swayed by competing impulses that are not reducible to political commitments, but, rather, precede them. How much do I care? How much do I give?

In Western religious traditions, it is understood that human beings may be selfish by nature, but also that it is possible to cultivate empathy that counteracts it. "You shall not mistreat a stranger, nor oppress him, for you were strangers in the land of Egypt," says Exodus 22:21. The baseline here is the acknowledgment of human nature. Left to our own devices, we would indeed mistreat and oppress the stranger, precisely because he is a stranger. All of us feel love for those close to us, like us, in our family or tribe. But morality (of an individual, a nation, or a country) is not measured based upon how we treat those close to us; it is tested on how we treat those unlike us—especially those who are weaker or poorer or "other." Exodus 22:21, then, is a spiritual exercise. It demands that each of us, regardless of our individual circumstances, remember or imaginatively remember our shared experience of being a stranger. We are somebody else's They. From that remembrance—which in the Jewish tradition is meant to occur every time the liturgy reminds us of how 'we' were once slaves in Egypt; i.e., several times a day, and several more on most of our holidays—springs compassion. And from compassion springs answers to the political questions asked above.

What Western traditions often lack, however, are technologies to actually do that work. Of course, I've met Christians, Jews, and Muslims who are genuinely motivated by their faith traditions to be kinder, gentler, and more just in their private and public lives. But obviously there are others who simply chant the words of justice, and traditions that merely dangle preposterous claims of a cosmic Santa Claus who knows who's been naughty and nice. Contemplative practice has a different message: that goodness evolves. Not on its own; it takes reflection and observation, as well as inclining the mind toward basic values of lovingkindness and compassion. But the same growth in the prefrontal cortex that enables me to be a little less reactive also enables me to be more empathetic toward others, and less likely to rely on those tendencies of mind that tell me to toughen up, blow them off, not care, leave them to their own devices, and let the chips fall where they may. These are all natural tendencies of mind. It's only human to want to be big cavepeople with huge houses and huge SUVs, and climate change be damned. But it's not compassionate to pursue these things.[2]

The contemplative practice of seeing clearly—not superimposing moral thinking atop a rotten foundation, but just seeing what is—leads to more justice and more peace. You can't see clearly, cause suffering, and be okay about it. And indeed, as we saw in Chapter Two, there is data showing that meditation improves the capacity for compassion, and that practicing lovingkindness meditation for just a few weeks lessens the activity of the amygdala when it is shown provoking images.[3] That reflexive anger we all feel when we see images of violence, that instinctual response to lash out—is actually lessened with just a bit of meditation practice.[4]

Now, I know that there are some conservatives who really believe that they are helping the poor by reducing government benefits; that if we just tax the ultra-rich even less, the benefits will trickle down to everyone; and that if we pursue a tough, militaristic foreign policy the world will be safer as a result. And there are some who have proposed that we understand conservative values as reflecting different iterations of the moral conscience.[5] Yet even apart from the issues of fact (Has trickle-down economics really helped the least fortunate? Has war made the world safer? Is climate change science really uncertain?) are the questions of values. Look inside. When you think of someone powerless, impoverished, unfortunate, what do you feel? Do you feel they must deserve it somehow? Are they "the stranger" to you? Have you, like most of us, had to wall yourself off from feeling too much about such people? Have you ever felt, toward an enemy or outside group, that you wish they could just disappear from the face of the earth? If we're truthful with ourselves, most of us have to admit that we sometimes answer affirmatively to one of more of these questions; this is part of being human. But if we answer yes to any of them, we must second guess ourselves, do the work, and strive to cultivate stronger capacities of empathy and compassion.

The peril of comfortable Westerners (e.g., most presumptive readers of this book) is not falling into abjection but slipping into apathy. We don't see the stranger often, and when we do, we don't talk to him or her. We're not evil; we're human. We can do better.

Let me share a very trivial example from my own practice, and then less trivial ones from my activist work. I remember one time when I was leading a meditation "sit" at a retreat. My eyes were open at the time—a combination of practicing Dzogchen and wanting to stay awake—and I saw someone readjust her posture. As meditators know, this can be very annoying, and I admit that most of the time when someone moves I get annoyed. This time, however, the genuine first thought that came into my mind was one of compassion: I hope she's okay, I hope she's not disturbed or feeling bad that she had to move, and so on. It wasn't "ought-to" compassion, which I usually find insufferable. It was that somewhere in there, marinating in my concentrated mind, was an impulse toward compassion rather than irritation, solidarity rather than blame. It was a small moment—but one that showed the possibility of a much larger transformation.

Such insights get put to the test every day in my work. I mentioned in Chapter Six that I routinely get attacked by folks who are anti-gay, or who disagree with this or that political view. Obviously, what's skillful in such contexts is to respond intelligently, bearing in mind that the goal is not to persuade the bigot but to address those who might be witnessing the interchange. On one far-right radio show, for example, the radio host told me that my marriage to my partner was no different from the sexual abuse of an animal. My meditation practice was the main reason I didn't curse him out on the air. What was really going on? Well, I thought to myself, this individual had this meme implanted in his brain, and it is lodged in there for all kinds of deep psychological reasons, and it is expressing itself in this odious way. Meanwhile, thousands of listeners—some of whom are probably struggling with sexuality themselves—are waiting to see whether I'll be reasonable or extreme, respectful or enraged. What can I say to them, to comfort the afflicted and afflict the comfortable? Can I detach enough from my personal responses to remember that there's something far more important here than how I feel? Of course, I wanted to register *some* emotion; that was called for by the moment. But mostly I wanted to think tactically, to respond effectively. And I think I did. But that was only because I was able to detach momentarily from my amygdala's fight-or-flight response, let the prefrontal cortex do its work, and create some mental spaciousness to think in terms of martial arts rather than blitzkrieg.

Likewise in other political debates, about Israel/Palestine, or the economy, or social justice, or climate change, or Tibet, or other issues in which I've become politically involved. There is, seemingly inherent in political life but amplified by our current social and technological structures, a tendency to praise anger, to defend "righteous indignation," and to reward brashness and zeal. On Fox News, the angriest commentator wins. In some radical-left environments, the most offended voice is the most rewarded. In my own work, I sometimes feel like a zealot for ambivalence, complexity, nuance, and uncertainty. It doesn't win me many allies. Yet I am convinced that if we're able to see the darker emotions—anger, fear—that often motivate political decisions, we'll be able to see other people's manipulation of them. We can be more in control of our political lives, and steer them toward generosity, precisely by seeing how politics tugs on our most primitive instincts.

These small movements of the mind, to me, are the reasons contemplative practice really might save the world. I've seen them work on political battlefields, and in quiet meditation halls. And they give me hope that, as contemplative fitness and optimizing the mind become values even in corporate boardrooms, there might be a welcome unintended consequence of more generosity and gentleness in our public life. So, too, in the very antithesis of corporate boardrooms, the Occupy movement. Adam Bucko, founder of the Reciprocity Foundation, which provides disadvantaged young adults with "programs that combine contemplative, therapeutic, and creative tools for personal transformation with business skills," found that the circular, consent-based, and process-oriented nature of the Occupy movement transformed some of its participants, particularly those who had come from underprivileged groups. The processes of Occupy "give them permission to express a part of themselves that they didn't know they had," Adam told me. Listening nonjudgmentally, noticing reactions, slowly moving to consensus—it's not just that Occupy fits neatly with contemplative practice. Occupy *is* the practice.

More specifically, within Western Buddhist communities there have been numerous initiatives that have defied the simple equating of spirituality with narcissism, of contemplation with quietism.[6] Despite a complicated set of traditions—the Buddha warned monks to stay out of politics, for example[7]—the movement known as "Engaged Buddhism," now forty years old and counting, draws on Buddhist emphases on compassion and lovingkindness, Buddhist political movements in Asia, the idealism of the Sixties/Boomer generation, and on interpretations of Mahayana nondualism that hold all things to be connected.[8] James Coleman has helpfully defined the movement as "a broad range of approaches, unified by the notion that Buddhist teachings and practices can be directly applied to participation in the social, political, economic, and ecological affairs of the non-monastic world."[9] Lawrence Sutin has proposed that Engaged Buddhism be seen as the fourth *yana*, or vehicle, of the dharma itself.[10]

Engaged Buddhism has many faces. Thich Nhat Hanh, one of the pioneers of Engaged Buddhism and perhaps the second most famous Buddhist teacher in the world after the Dalai Lama, coined the term "interbeing" from the Vietnamese words *tiep* (to be in touch) and *hien* (to manifest), and possibly coined the term "Engaged Buddhism" itself based on an existing Vietnamese tradition of Buddhist social justice activism, particularly in the years of the Vietnam War.[11] The Buddhist Peace Fellowship, probably the best known Engaged Buddhist organization, was founded in 1978 and has led numerous campaigns related to human rights, relief work, and peace activism.[12] Zen roshi Bernie Glassman has been doing peacemaking and social justice work for over thirty years: founding the Zen Peacemakers organization, courageously reaching out to AIDS patients when clergy of other religions shunned them and said they were being punished by God, creating the Greyston Bakery to invest in his own local community in Yonkers (and now many others), and leading "street sits" on the streets of New York.[13] In an interview, Glassman said that his work has two parts: "The social engagement part would be working with aspects of oneself and society that are underserved (that's my definition for social engagement). The Buddhist part (for me) means doing that work coming from the standpoint of nonduality and, in doing that work, trying to help people realize the interconnectedness and oneness of life. So that's the basis, the foundation from which I do the work."[14] Many other organizations, such as The Zen Peacemaking Order, The Buddhist Alliance for Social Engagement (BASE), and others, have brought together contemplative practice and social justice or social action work. And, yes, there were dharma practitioners in Zuccotti Park and elsewhere around the country during the Occupy movement;[15] in such contexts, as we've already noted, Engaged Buddhism doesn't just flow from dharma practice—it is the practice itself.

Women, in particular, have taken leadership of dozens of social justice projects and movements around the country.[16] For example, Joanna Macy has fused contemplative wisdom with ecological consciousness to find new ways for activists to appreciate the enormity of the ecological crisis without falling into despair.[17] Rita Gross has written persuasively about how feminism and the dharma reinforce each other, as both are concerned with the value of one's own experience, courageously fighting against the grain, mental constructs that block liberation, the ethic of non-harming, and liberation as a goal.[18] This despite the frequent blindness on the part of Western Buddhists toward androcentrism and patriarchy within Buddhism itself.[19]

All of this is profoundly good stuff. Yet I maintain the perhaps idealistic view that the dharma's most significant contribution to political life will come not from liberal organizations or Buddhist-specific organizations—not to demean any of that work—but from installing better cognitive software in people of all political persuasions. My friend Ñaniko, the monastic we met in Chapter Three, has struggled with the choice between working in Engaged Buddhist settings and teaching meditation. For now, he says, "as much as I believe in and support other forms of social engagement and healing, I also recognize that we need people to teach meditation . . . and maybe that's my bit, you know. And could I be content with that." I'd like to question the entire dichotomy. Rather than this or that specific political question, to me the fundamental factors that will determine our political futures are whether we can open our eyes (and heart) to suffering, whether we can see when we are being controlled by anger or fear, whether it's possible to speak and act more skillfully. I think we can.

Learning about Power the Hard Way

One risk in writing a book like this is sounding like a cheerleader. Because the dharma—meditation, mindfulness, and a life lived in the light of the teachings of the Buddha—has been so good to me, because it's changed my life, naturally I have some of the zeal of the converted. At the same time, I'm also aware of how annoying that is. No one wants to be told how to make their lives better and more exciting by doing what someone else suggests. At least I don't. So I've tried to temper my presentation of the dharma not just with a little irony, but with a sense of the imperfections, the places where the great translation of ancient Buddhist wisdom into Western postmodern life . . . gets lost.

Nowhere is this more apparent than in the dark shadow side of the Western dharma world, which is—not to put too fine a point on it—the seemingly inexhaustible desire of straight male Buddhist teachers to have sex with their female students. Sorry, did I say that out loud? If I did, it's because I'm tired of the niceties, the cover-ups, and the excuses. These serve no one other than the sexual predators—almost always heterosexual males in positions of power. Many of these men are still teaching, independently or in dharma centers, and I'm sure there are many more who have yet to be exposed.

The sordid history is by now well-known and well-documented.[20] Sandy Boucher, in her landmark volume *Turning the Wheel: Women Creating the New Buddhism,* devotes fifty pages to discussing it in detail (while at the same time maintaining a high degree of nuance and rigor),[21] and Jan Chozen Bays has done some outstanding reflection and reformation of her own community, as someone on the student side of (but she declines to say victimized by) a teacher-student sexual relationship.[22] To be sure, this phenomenon is not everywhere, and not involving anywhere near a majority of dharma teachers,[23] but it goes right to the top of some of the most important Buddhist lineages. Osel Tendzin, the successor to Chogyam Trungpa Rinpoche, believing himself to be magically protected from transmitting STDs, knowingly infected sex partners with HIV—and this in the 1980s, when doing so was tantamount to murder.[24] The brilliant Zen teacher Genpo Roshi/Dennis Merzel, whose retreats I've attended, has been dogged by repeated scandals involving extramarital affairs with students. Los Angeles Zen Center abbot Maezumi Roshi struggled with sex and alcohol throughout much of his teaching career[25]—as did Trungpa Rinpoche himself, though unlike other teachers he did not hide his sexual or alcoholic behaviors, and to this day his students are divided as to whether they represent failures, lifestyle choices, or even advanced teachings.[26] Even Sogyal Rinpoche, one of the most respected Tibetan lamas, has been the subject of not only rumors of sexual impropriety, but lawsuits, quietly settled out of court under the veil of nondisclosure agreements. Oh, and this is just the beginning. Leading Zen teachers like Richard Baker Roshi (San Francisco Zen Center),[27] Eido Shimano Roshi (New York Zen Center), Joshu Sasaki Roshi[28]—the list goes on.

I want to make three points about this phenomenon, hopefully in the service of the dharma. First, I want to affirm cultural difference and sex-positivity, and yet still condemn these teachers' abuse of power. Second, I want to observe that this really is all about power, not sex. And finally, I want to say that, believe it or not, the scandals are but one aspect of power relationships that have a long, long lineage—but that, I think, are being fast eroded by the new generation of dharma practitioners.

First, what one sometimes hears from these teachers and their defenders is that we Westerners just don't understand exotic Oriental culture. These teachers are *Asians,* you see; they have a different set of values from you and me. Indeed, it would be *Eurocentric* to imagine that Asian teachers are capable of understanding that abusing power relationships is inappropriate no matter the context. This, to me, is racism masquerading as anti-racism. Of course, Tibetan and Japanese teachers come from different cultures, and the sociological model is ill-suited to contemporary Western society. But cultural difference is not the same as moral relativism. These teachers are not infants; they are grown men with a deep understanding of the teacher-student relationship. And of course, this claim also

ignores the many Western teachers implicated in such scandals—
unless, perhaps, predatory sexual mores are passed on with *inka*.

Now, while I do want to condemn sexual abuse and exploitation
in all its forms, I'm also unwilling to jump on the sex-negative bandwagon and insist that everyone's sexual values be exactly the same—
or, worse, that they equal the most prudish common denominator.
First, sex-negativity is, itself, an oppressive value, and one that per-
petuates the problem of sexual abuse by repressing, stigmatizing,
and closeting sexual desire.[29] Second, many women who have had
sexual relationships with their teachers have said that they did not
find the relationships abusive. This is most famously the case with
Trungpa Rinpoche, whose students (male and female, but predomi-
nantly female) would actually vie for his attention, and who was
quite open about his sexual liaisons, his drinking, and his taste for
expensive material possessions.[30] And while I still have my qualms,
I want to respect these women, too, as responsible agents, in control
of their own bodies and their own decisions—although I think we
also need to hear the voices of the philandering teachers' spouses,
which may not be as supportive, as well as those who did not experience such liaisons as consensual. So while I am not here to judge
others' sexual behavior—quite the contrary; as a queer person who
spent years condemning my own, I'm loathe to pass judgment—
sex-positivity should not be a cover for abuse.

Really, though, there is one thing all these scandals have in common: power. These abuses take place in contexts where a power relationship exists between teacher and student. Indeed, that's what
makes them abuses. Take out the power relationship, and what's left
is an affair, rather than abuse. This, I think, is why the scandals are
more prevalent in Tibetan guru traditions and authority-centered
Zen ones than in other forms of Buddhism where the teacher's authority is less central.[31] As Zen teacher Norman Fischer put it, "The
Roshi comes out of the Sino-Japanese-Confucian worship-your-
ancestors tradition. Put that beautiful Roshi in the middle of our
Freudian Oedipal will-to-power tradition and it is little wonder that

people are going to be confused for a hundred years or so."[32] And as Buddhist feminist Rita Gross points out, focusing only on episodes of misconduct misses the more basic issues of authority, patriarchy, and secrecy.[33]

In other words, the power is the problem. And with this, we return to themes we explored in the beginning of this book. It's time to Occupy Buddhism—by which I mean not just bring the dharma to the Occupy movement as Adam Bucko described, but also to bring the ethos of Occupy, anti-globalization movements, Burning Man, and other participant-created communities to the dharma. Of course, teachers are still important; these are the people who have traveled where you want to go. They have acquired useful skills. But as Gross also points out, being wise, experienced, and good at meditation does not mean one is all-wise or all-perfect; gurus are not Mommy or Daddy, however much a student may wish them to be.[34] For Gross, the source of this healthy skepticism is feminism: "Being a feminist before I became a Buddhist has perhaps stood me in good stead in not expecting too much from a guru, in not expecting someone I can completely model myself after, someone who will never disappoint me, or someone who is always all wise."[35] Likewise with other liberation movements such as queer politics, Occupy, anti-racism movements, all of which share this mistrust of power; though I was formed in their crucibles rather than those of feminism, I couldn't agree more with Gross's assessment.

This, I think, is one of the ways in which the encounter with the West will improve the dharma. Respect our teachers, yes; grant them control and power over institutions and over the lives of adherents, no. Learn from teachers, yes; create small fiefdoms where they operate without oversight and transparency, no.

I'll go so far as to make a prediction here, which is that the guru-centered model is going to implode on its own accord. First, power corrupts, and religious power corrupts religiously. Those centers that minimize the concentration of power will have fewer disruptive scandals than those that do not. Second, as the dharma evolves beyond the needs of spiritual seekers, who may very well be look-ing to teachers precisely for parent-like authority, it will move into contexts where the same power games that might be appealing to would-be cult followers are an immediate turnoff. Not to get too buzzwordy here, but people under thirty have grown up on Web 2.0, with its user-generated content and socially generated market-ing, not to mention Pinterest and Tumblr. To return to the meta-phor from Chapter Eight, a previous generation may be used to DJs curating their musical taste, and buying LPs of music by a single artist—but this one is used to iTunes, playlists, and making a vir-tue of individual tastes rather than label-dictated listening formats. This ethos will impact (productively, I think) iSpirituality as much as iTunes. For example, I asked Lama Surya Das (who once warned his students, "Don't give away your authority to a teacher"[36]) how he deals with the guru phenomenon, particularly as an American teaching in a guru-centric Tibetan lineage. His response?

> It's never been a secret. I try to demystify it. I act normal. I don't go around in expensive brocade robes setting myself apart from everybody else and trying to collect money to support that lifestyle. I don't think that's where it's at today.

Personally, I gave up looking for a guru ten years ago—which not coincidentally is when my spiritual practice began in earnest. I realized that there was not going to be anyone who would "get" all of me: the Jewish, the Buddhist, the queer, the earth-based, the plugged-in, the geeky, the freaky, the square, and the shy. And there was no one who was going to be all of those shifting, constructed identities in the mirror—not least because they were always works in progress for me as well. I feel blessed to have learned from so many different kinds of teachers, and I don't envy those who have found The Guru whom they trust above all. On the contrary—that kind of trust makes me uncomfortable. Not only because of the poten-tial for abuse, but because that's just not how I want to live. I'm not interested in molding myself in someone else's image, or assuming that all of who I aspire to be can or should be reduced to a single iteration of a single tradition. And I don't think I'm alone in feeling that way.

Now, that may just be one taste among many. I know people who benefited from their guru relationships, and some people just go in for that sort of thing. For those who do, though, it is worth learning from communities that work with power and submission all the time—specifically, BDSM sexual communities, which guru/disciple settings often resemble. If people want to negotiate a guru/disciple relationship, they should recognize it as a dom/sub relationship: a role play in which one party is allowing the other to dominate them. By all means, they should go ahead and set that relationship up—but with clear boundaries, safe words, and agreements, as the kink community does. Otherwise, such a relationship is unsafe. To dangle promises of enlightenment in front of vulnerable people and then have them unwittingly surrender their bodily integrity as part of a blank check—to me that's blackmail, not consent. No S/M relationship would ever be forged on such a dubious basis, and no teacher/student one should be either.

As Foucault tried to tell us, any dissemination of information—which the dharma is—is inherently an exercise of power. As such, any claim that "I've got the answer" is also a claim of authority, of "listen to me." Yet for all the venerable guru traditions in Buddhism, I am struck by how different the Buddha himself was when it came to questions of authority, asking monks to inquire into their own experience, using the Socratic method rather than a dictatorial one, and offering an almost empiricist form of contemplative practice. So whatever precedent there is for those who say that surrender to the guru is an essential part of the spiritual path, there is also ample precedent on the other side.

This shadow side of Western dharma can also teach us about the limitations of liberation. Depending on one's model of liberated consciousness, "enlightenment" may bring about a total perfect saintlihood, or just a release from the usual patterns of craving and suffering. Even if it's the former, saints who live in the material world have to deal with material challenges, and unless your model of enlightenment is that it comes with total omniscience and omnipotence—in which case, judging from human experience, it seems rather difficult to attain—life in this world will continue to occasion pain, disease, and, at the very least, inconvenience.

In fact, the model that I've sketched out here, which (in this form or another one) animates most of the dharma practitioners I know, promises far less. Not only will liberated beings continue to have to deal with the same external stuff as the rest of us—they'll have much of the same internal stuff as well: uncertainty, sadness, desires of various kinds. And that's only the fully liberated ones; the rest of us partially liberated people still have most of the neuroses and melancholies we've had all our lives. In my own experience, dharma practice has lessened these only a bit; as I wrote about earlier, what it's done is increase the looseness, the slipperiness, of these mind-states such that they catch me less, and hold on less. But they still arise.

Rather than find this a cause for despair, I think the limitations of liberation are encouraging.[37] These various ethical failings might serve as a useful reminder that you might not be as far off as you think you are; if a Zen master still gets angry when she's stuck in a traffic jam, maybe you're not doing so bad yourself. They also counter the fear that many of us have had, that to become liberated is to become a lifeless zombie, apathetic and detached. I've met some pretty awakened people over the years, and none of them fits that description. If nothing else, these libidinal failings of enlightened Buddhist masters is a useful reminder that zombiehood is not the goal.

Occupying Buddhism means many things: political engagement, a questioning of authority, a social realism, and also a sense that yes, you are entitled to occupy this space on the Earth and to pursue contemplative practice and its goal of liberation from suffering. As Lama Surya Das told me, "We have to occupy the dharma, occupy the spirit, not just leave it for the one percent, the Dalai Lamas and Thich Nhat Hanhs. Occupy the dharma—that's the Buddha's intention." The dharma is not unattainable, not just for saints and mystics—you can do it. In this way, the ethical concerns of this chapter bring us back to the methodological and pedagogical innovations of the first part of this book. Occupying the dharma means ending authoritarian structures within it, healing the Buddhist community's own wounds while enabling a new generation to take hold of it. It means accommodating the teaching to new contexts and new forms, extending *upaya,* skillful means, into some highly unlikely locations.

Finally, the limitations of liberation should be a reminder of why basic ethical behavior remains important, even amidst all the bells and whistles of contemplative practice. As we discussed in Chapter Seven, we all evolve along different lines of development. Getting a PhD doesn't improve your physical health (quite the contrary), and getting stream entry doesn't necessarily improve your ethical health. You can be an *arahant* and still be an asshole. Indeed, you might even act worse, since you worry less about what people think about you. These are all different lines of development, and advanced status in one by no means assures advancement in another.

This is why, whether it's in the context of Buddhist sex scandals or everyday personal interaction, I often come back to the five basic precepts: not harming, not stealing, not committing sexual misconduct, not lying, and not being too intoxicated to care.[38] This is not a book on the precepts, and others have written far more eloquently about them than I can, but they are an apt place to conclude, precisely because they are where most practitioners are taught to begin. It's only in the last century that folks have been told that meditation alone will make them kinder and more generous. (On the contrary, meditation has been taught in Japan to help warriors and businessmen be more ruthless.) In Buddhist tradition, more is needed, and virtue *(sila)* is a prerequisite to gaining wisdom and building concentration. If your life is filled with unethical choices and relationships, you're not going to be able to concentrate or turn the mind to dharma—you'll be too busy dealing with the nasty stuff that comes up when you meditate. Meditation is not a practice of self-deception; contrary to popular presentation, it is often about searing honesty, and facing precisely that which we might prefer to ignore. For this reason, ethical action is not some moralizing side note; without it, your meditation will not progress. All those realizations into non-self, that everything is one and that your own life is a ripple on a very large cosmic ocean—all of that nice stuff can lead to some very not-nice behavior, because the ripples in your particular consciousness are still conditioned by the five billion years of dissatisfaction with which we began this book. You don't escape from being human, even if you do get enlightened. You may think you do—you may enter into some exalted states, gain psychic powers, and attract followers who think you're an avatar of the Divine. But that is just delusion.

The precepts don't have any foundation. There's no Zarathustra moment, no thunder and lightning at Sinai. They're described in the Pali Canon as "gifts." Not requirements, or revelations—just, here, here are the gifts. No one is going to punish you for not obeying them, though it's possible that you'll punish yourself if you ever lift the veil of ignorance to examine your actions. There may be karma—cause and effect—but there's no way of predicting how that will come around in your life, or even in your future lives, if you believe in that. Really, there's no basis for these precepts at all, save that they seem to work as general guidelines and help us keep our all-too-human desires in check, so that we can coexist with other people.

In the famous Zen ox-herding sequence, the process of gaining enlightenment is analogized to finding and taming a wild ox. As is well known, the final stage of that process is not nothingness, not pure transcendence, but returning to the marketplace with the ox. The ultimate stages of the contemplative path are, finally, a return to where it began. Everything is the same, and yet much has evolved.

AFTERWORD

The Future

What's next for the evolving dharma?

I hate making predictions. There are always so many factors to consider, and the most important ones tend to be unforeseen. Hardly any futurists predicted the rise and importance of the Internet, for example: they thought the future would be about flying cars and robots, not cloud storage and streaming-everywhere multimedia. Statistical studies have shown that pundits are generally right about 50 percent of the time—as long as there are only two choices. The wisest course seems to be that of Stephen Batchelor, who told me:

> Forty years ago, when I was a Tibetan monk in the Himalayas, if someone would have told me that mindfulness would be taught at the National Health Service and debated in the houses of Parliament, I'd have dismissed them as a fantasist.

So I can put my hand on my heart and say I do not know what the next forty years will bring.

That said, we are clearly at a turning point in the American dharma. Applied, secular mindfulness is about to break wide open—bigger than the yoga craze, for sure, and possibly bigger than the physical fitness craze that began in the 1980s and is still going strong at a Pilates studio near you. Once the scientific data becomes better known, and the packaging of mindfulness and meditation better meets the needs of contemporary people, the mainstreaming of secular mindfulness seems almost inevitable, purely as a matter of economics. In fact, fifteen years into the contemplative neuroscience field, maybe what's needed most is not scientific data but economic data. This, surprisingly, was Richard Davidson's view. "From a pragmatic perspective," he told me:

> I think the most important work that has to be done has nothing to do with the kind of research that I do, but is research that examines the economic impact of meditation practice, particularly on healthcare utilization. . . . If it is found that the regular practice of these methods leads to a decrease in healthcare utilization, every corporation and every health insurance company in the country is going to want to be on this bandwagon. I think that's when you'll see this work crossing the tipping point.

This seems right to me. Just consider the numbers. If MBSR can reduce the length and duration of hospital visits at low cost; if Search Inside Yourself–style corporate mindfulness can improve productivity, again at a relatively low cost; if even the short-term effects of mindfulness practice become as readily apparent as the benefits of exercise, then market forces alone seem likely to encourage the (secular) dharma not just to grow—but to explode.

What we've seen so far is only the prelude. Sure, we've seen meditation mainstreamed, and covered by major media outlets, but it still carries the whiff of exoticism and bourgeois indulgence, like yoga or sushi once did. Imagine what will happen once the benefits of applied secular mindfulness become more widespread. Those associations will lessen—as, indeed, they have for yoga and sushi, both of which were weird thirty years ago and are quite ordinary today. Congressman Tim Ryan is one of those who have pressed for serious investment in mindfulness-based interventions. He told me, with a sense of urgency, that:

> I hope that the people who have the means recognize that mindfulness and some of these other alternative therapies are having a significant impact in transforming schools, prisons, the healthcare system, veterans who need our help, a military that needs this, and so on. What we need to do is ramp it up through foundations, and corporations who can push it out into the world. And to have that being expressed in a room where you have some of the highest concentration of wealth in our country is a heck of an opportunity.

Of course, notwithstanding all the evidence that Congressman Ryan refers to, the data may yet come out the other way. In our conversation, Davidson returned multiple times to the issue of how little we actually know—about consciousness, about neuroplasticity, and emerging frontiers in epigenetics and the modulation of genomic processes. Or, who knows, the studies Willoughby Britton and her team are doing may show that meditation works *too* well—that it enlightens those who weren't even trying to get enlightened, but just wanted to relax a bit at work.

But I don't think so. If the past thirty years are any indication, the next thirty should see the scientific and clinical data growing even more solid and even more quantifiable. Like Davidson, I think applied mindfulness will soon be everywhere. It's simple economics.

I wonder, though, if these kinds of applied meditation are only an intermediate stage. Some have already begun to wonder what

will happen if our neuroscientific understanding of meditation becomes more refined. Will we be able to increase cortical thickness
with medication one day? Surgery? Maybe implanted computing
devices? "Brainhacking" today is meant to be a metaphor. But if improvements in nanotechnology and wearable devices continue, and
if the scientific understanding of mindfulness does as well, then it
stands to reason that we should be able to devise brain-machines or
brain-medications that stimulate the neural growth that right now
is done the old-fashioned way. If this seems fanciful, consider how
we understand melancholy today, as compared with thirty years
ago. Once, sadness was a font of poetry and music. Now it's something to be medicated. Are we that far off from the *moksha* medicine
of Aldous Huxley's *Island,* a psychedelic-like substance without the
side effects of current chemical compounds, but with the capacity to
enlarge wisdom and compassion? Or, more darkly, are we closer to
the *soma* of Huxley's *Brave New World,* which stupefies more than
it enlightens?

"We still have not even scratched the surface on the fundamental hard problem of consciousness," Davidson told me. "I think
that a serious reckoning of that problem will occur and may lead
to some really radical and fundamental reconceptualizations of our
understandings of mind and brain." His student Joe Wielgosz upped
the ante even further:

> Brain-machine interfaces and robotics and AI—these pose
> some serious problems for your average person's theory of
> mind and self. They don't fit into any religious tradition, in-
> cluding Buddhism. There's never been precedent for that.
> What if you can stimulate the temporal lobe accurately and
> give someone transformative experiences? What are the
> ethics of that? What are the implications for practice? This
> is real. It seems like science fiction, but it's already no big
> deal that you can write Tweets with your mind, or can con-
> trol prosthetic limbs with electrodes in the brain. Now flash

forward ten years—these things will not be just sideshows but major parts of our lives. . . . The line is blurring between machine technology and human minds. That is totally unexplored territory for anybody.[39]

It's interesting to speculate about a future, perhaps only a few decades from today, in which psychopharmacology includes not only the crude uppers and downers prescribed today, but insight-enhancers, compassion-inducers, and other wisdom pills. One wonders if there will really be a market for the best of these—after all, one side effect of Buddhist wisdom is you tend to chase after material goods a little less zealously. Not exactly the kind of behavior that maximizes profit for pharmaceutical companies. Maybe there'll be competition among different mystical-experience purveyors. Rumitocin provides a rush of universal love, but Sariputtax gets you into seventh *jhana.* Corporate suits like Samadhin, because it helps them focus. But beware of Maggaphalin—it'll mess with your motivation. All this, of course, is mere speculation. It could be that nanotechnology will render even pharmaceuticals hopelessly crude. If you want to grok impermanence, just select the right procedure and the nanites will boost up your Left PFC function, and you're set.

Obviously, there's a dystopian tone to such speculation; it's not too dissimilar to Ramez Naam's recent novel, *Nexus,* in which a similar biotechnology is used for pleasure, coercion, and mind control. But if you take seriously the proposition that brainhacking can upgrade the human brain hardware, and that doing so will, more or less, save the world, maybe the possibilities aren't so scary. After all, love is also a chemical phenomenon, but we still seem interested in it.[40] Here's Kenneth Folk one more time:

I think everything we're doing, whether we're taking medication, or are hanging out with our friends, or watching movies, or meditating, we're hacking the chemical soup in the brain. And if we can be really honest about that and say that, ultimately, all we're trying to do is have a good life, to feel good and to extend that to the community . . . so just this search for well-being is motivating everything. And our experience of that always comes down to the chemical soup in the brain. If you get really practical about it, what difference does it make how that gets hacked? I'm fine with any of it.

I tend to agree. If enlightenment comes in a pill, well, I hope people take it.

So much for mass-market, secular mindfulness. What about the hardcore—the spiritual adventurers, the ones mad to live and mad to meditate, aiming toward enlightenment (or at least stream entry) and exploding in mad fireworks of *jhana*?

It's harder to say. Certainly, there has been an interesting uptick in serious contemplative practice, not just among Buddhists but in the wider population as well. But as it has been throughout history, the contemplative life remains a boutique, rather than mass-market, phenomenon, and honestly I don't see that changing. Millions may meditate a little bit, if it really helps improve longevity and reduce stress, but only a few, I think, will meditate a lot. Perhaps this is just a matter of taste. People like different things—some sports, others spirituality; some body-building, others brain enhancement. I am not one of those contemplatives who claim that, conveniently, contemplative practice is the reason we're here on Earth. I do it because I like it and I appreciate its effects (to understate the matter somewhat). But not everyone does.

I do think that serious practitioners will find the path much changed, and much enriched, by new communities, new ways of teaching, and, hopefully, new questions asked of old authoritarian models. Clearly, there is a greater degree of interplay and intermixing between dharma communities and less attachment to sectarian orthodoxies,[41] and there is a greater appreciation of the multiple ways in which "contemplative fitness" might be developed. In Daniel Ingram's fast-paced words:

There are all these different skill sets you can develop, all these different attributes you can develop. . . . Does every-body do everything equally well? No, clearly not. And peo-ple, based on their own aesthetics, history, based on what they think available and on what they can do, definitely op-timize for different aspects of this thing. Now there are some aspects that I still consider more important than others: the dissolution of the sense of any of these phenomena being a separate, in-control entity is of tremendous value. The dis-solution of the sense of agency, the dissolution of the sense of separateness, I think those make tremendous differences.

There is also far more access to these teachings. Just forty years ago, your only way to meditate for an extended period was to learn from an Asian master, or fly off to Asia yourself. Just twenty years ago, you still had to go to a retreat center somewhere. Now, not only is the dharma online, but legions of Buddhist Yelpers are happy to offer you their opinions, experience, and critiques. Like the rest of social media, this situation is more confusing but vastly more informed as well. I hunted for *Practical Insight Meditation* in used bookstores—and even that was a huge leap forward. Now, not only is it on Ama-zon, but you can download a PDF for free, listen to podcasts about it, and join in a discussion about whether the "fear of dissolution" *nyana* made you dizzy.

This, too, may be only the beginning. When I asked Daniel about the future of the dharma, he got excited about the nexus be-tween neuroscience and the developmental path:

Obviously what people want to know is: How do you do emotional transformation? How do you change the way the system relates to the impulses, the chemical stimulus, to the adrenaline rushes, the neurapine and dopamine, and all the interesting things the brain does in response to exter-nal stimuli? I think that's where the most interesting work is coming. How does that fit into the contexts and the models, and what might actually be possible, and what might you gain and lose by doing that? Those are some of the most fascinating questions.

Lama Surya Das told me that "in 2013, the dharma is in its early teens. In the '90s and '80s, it was like an elementary school kid, and in the 1950s and 60s, infancy." With this coming of age, innocence has turned to experience. As a result, some of the Sixties idealism has faded—but in my opinion, just as the human conscience productively evolves as it matures from youth to age, so, too, has the collective understanding and application of the dharma evolved, grown, and ripened over time. It's a good thing that we're more sober, more cynical, more cautious—particularly because the signs point to this phenomenon exploding in the next few years. Indeed, what has happened communally reflects a personal evolution as well. All of us who have taken up meditation in a serious way have our fond memories of that first retreat or first peak experience, when all the joys were new and a whole new way of being human seemed possible. I treasure these memories. But they are memories only, and I would not choose to reinhabit them if it meant giving up the more profound, if more subtle, shifts I have experienced since.

Which brings me to my boldest, perhaps most foolhardy, prediction yet. There is no question that technologies of destruction have evolved in terrifying ways in the past several decades. Nuclear and chemical weapons were bad enough when they were in the hands of two superpowers, but now they seem likely to fall into the hands of madmen. And ecological collapse, biodiversity loss, habitat loss, climate change—all these are even more grave threats to our continued existence, not to mention fanaticism, economic instability, and the creeping oligarchy of the super-rich. So what can we do? It's no longer realistic to pursue a kind of global gun control, hoping that dangerous technologies can be restricted or eliminated. Nor is it realistic to pine for an archaic, edenic pre-capitalist time before all this mess came about—or yearn for the New Age to come when we will live like that again, homesteading and bartering for all our needs. You can't homestead a triple bypass.

What we've got to do, it seems to me, is get through this awkward in-between stage in our human evolution. Not only the dharma is in its teens right now—the human race is, too, in the middle of an adolescent growth spurt, charged up with hormones, and strong enough to do some real damage to itself and others. So we've got to stay in school. We've got to find a way to grow up as a species, to evolve our minds and brains enough to rise above our natural instincts, at least a little bit. As Larry Yang put it, quite simply, "as we pay attention, we actually learn to love ourselves and each other." And however corny it may sound, this is exactly what we need. So far, our age has been one of improved means for unimproved ends. Our amygdala's fight-or-flight instincts haven't been transcended— they've been indulged, by billion-dollar industries figuring out how best to maximize their effects. All this is only natural; it, too, is just the dharma unfolding.

But freedom evolves as well. At the same time as I can select food, entertainment, and pornography according to a choice engine's precise calibration of my not-yet-articulated desires, I also have access to the world's contemplative wisdom, in forms that might make it more appealing and more widespread than ever. As the great human problem has loomed more obvious, perhaps a solution has as well.

Who knows, maybe we really are in some kind of great cosmic race between wisdom and ignorance, our better natures and our craven ones, with the future of humanity at stake. Or maybe not. Either way, if the stakes are as high as they seem to be, these evolving technologies of mind are more than merely useful. To paraphrase the great dharma sage Obi Wan Kenobi, they might just be our only hope.

BIBLIOGRAPHY

Books and Articles

Aamodt, Sandra. Interview with Eric Nestler. "The Dark Side of Brain Plasticity: How Learning Contributes to Depression or Addiction." *Being Human,* November 6, 2012.

Analayo. *Satipatthana: The Direct Path to Realization.* Cambridge, UK: Windhorse, 2004.

Arden, John B. *Rewire Your Brain: Think Your Way to a Better Life.* Hoboken, NJ: Wiley, 2010.

Arrowsmith-Young, Barbara. *The Woman Who Changed Her Brain: And Other Inspiring Stories of Pioneering Brain Transformation.* New York: Free Press, 2012.

Axelrod, Jim. "Ohio Congressman's Meditation Crusade." *CBS News.* February 9, 2013. www.cbsnews.com/8301-18563_162-57568552/ohio-congressmans -meditation-crusade/.

Batchelor, Stephen. "The Agnostic Buddhist." In Watson, Batchelor, and Claxon, *The Psychology of Awakening,* 23–29.

Batchelor, Stephen. *The Awakening of the West: The Encounter of Buddhism and Western Culture.* Berkeley, CA: Parallax, 1994.

Batchelor, Stephen. *Buddhism Without Beliefs: A Contemporary Guide to Awakening.* New York: Riverhead Books, 1997.

Batchelor, Stephen and John Peacock. "Uncertain Minds: How the West Misunderstands Buddhism." Lecture presented at St. Paul's Cathedral, London, March 21. http://secularbuddhism.org/2011/11/14/uncertain -minds-how-the-west-misunderstands-buddhism/.

Baumann, Martin. "American Buddhism: A Bibliography on Buddhist Traditions and Schools in the U.S.A. and Canada." *Journal of Global Buddhism,* June 1999. www.globalbuddhism.org/bib-ambu.htm.

Baumann, Martin. "The Dharma Has Come West: A Survey of Recent Studies and Sources." *Journal of Buddhist Ethics* 4 (1997): 194–211.

Begley, Sharon. *Train Your Mind, Change Your Brain: How a New Science Reveals Our Extraordinary Potential to Transform Ourselves.* New York: Ballantine Books, 2007.

Berman, Morris. *The Reenchantment of the World.* Ithaca, NY: Cornell University Press, 1981.

Bhushan, Nalini, Jay L. Garfield, and Abraham Zablocki, eds. *TransBuddhism: Transmission, Translation, and Transformation.* Amherst: University of Massachusetts Press, 2009.

Blackmore, Susan. *The Meme Machine.* New York: Oxford University Press, 1999.

Blackmore, Susan. "Waking from the Meme Dream." In Watson, Batchelor and Claxon, *The Psychology of Awakening,* 112–22.

Boucher, Sandy. *Turning the Wheel: American Women Creating the New Buddhism.* Updated and expanded edition. Boston: Beacon, 1988.

Boorstein, Sylvia. *That's Funny, You Don't Look Buddhist: On Being a Faithful Jew and a Passionate Buddhist.* New York: HarperCollins, 1997.

Boyce, Barry, and Editors of the *Shambhala Sun,* ed., *The Mindfulness Revolution: Leading Psychologists Scientists, Artists, and Meditation Teachers on the Power of Mindfulness in Everyday Life.* Boston: Shambhala, 2011.

Brach, Tara. *Radical Acceptance: Embracing Your Life with the Heart of a Buddha.* New York: Bantam, 2004.

Brahm, Ajahn. *Mindfulness, Bliss, and Beyond: A Meditator's Handbook.* Somerville, MA: Wisdom, 2006.

Brasington, Leigh. "Sharpening Manjushri's Sword: The Jhanas in Theravadan Buddhist Meditation." December 4, 2005. www.leighb.com/jhana2a.htm

Britton, Willoughby B. "The Dark Night Project." *Buddhist Geeks* audio podcast, 26:31. www.buddhistgeeks.com/2011/09/bg-232-the-dark-night-project/.

Britton, Willoughby B. "Mindful Binge Drinking and Blobology," *Buddhist Geeks* video, www.buddhistgeeks.com/2012/11/video-mindful-binge-drinking -and-blobology/.

Brodie, Richard. *Virus of the Mind: The New Science of the Meme.* New York: Hay House, 1996.

Bush, Mirabai. "Knowing Every Breath You Take." *New York Times.* January 5, 2013.

Butler, Judith. *The Psychic Life of Power: Theories in Subjection.* Stanford, CA: Stanford University Press, 1997.

Cabezon, Jose Ignacio, ed. *Buddhism, Sexuality and Gender.* Albany: State University of New York Press, 1992.

Carroll, Michael. *Awake at Work: 35 Practical Buddhist Principles for Discovering Clarity and Balance in the Midst of Work's Chaos.* Boston: Shambhala, 2004.

Carroll, Michael. *Fearless at Work: Timeless Teachings for Awakening Confidence, Resilience, and Creativity in the Face of Life's Demands.* Boston: Shambhala, 2012.

Catherine, Shaila. *Focused and Fearless: A Meditator's Guide to States of Deep Joy, Calm, and Clarity.* Somerville, MA: Wisdom, 2008.

Chapman, David. "'Nice' Buddhism." *Meaningness* (blog). http://meaningness .wordpress.com/2011/06/10/nice-buddhism/

Claxton, Guy. "Neurotheology: Buddhism, Cognitive Science, and Mystical Experience." In Watson, Batchelor, and Claxon, *The Psychology of Awakening,* 90–111.

Claxton, Guy. *Noises from the Darkroom: The Science and Mystery of the Mind.* Detroit: Aquarian, 1994.

Coleman, James W., *The New Buddhism: The Western Transformation of an Ancient Tradition.* New York: Oxford Univeristy Press, 2001.

Cook, Francis Dojun. *How to Raise an Ox: Zen Practice as Taught in Zen Master Dogen's Shobogenzo.* Somerville, MA: Wisdom, 2001.

Dalai Lama. *Stages of Meditation.* Translated by Geshe Lobsang Jordhen, Losang Choephel Ganchenpa, and Jeremy Russell. Ithaca, NY: Snow Lion, 2001.

Davidson, Richard J., and Sharon Begley. *The Emotional Life of Your Brain: How Its Unique Patterns Affect the Way You Think, Feel, and Live—and How You Can Change Them.* New York: Hudson Street Press, 2012.

Davis, Jake H. and Evan Thompson. "From the Five Aggregates to Phenomenal Consciousness: Toward a Cross-Cultural Cognitive Science," in *A Companion to Buddhist Philosophy,* ed. Steven Emmanuel. Hoboken, NJ: Wiley-Blackwell, 2012.

Dennett, Daniel. *Consciousness Explained.* Boston: Little, Brown and Co., 1991.

d'Estries, Michael. "Bill Clinton Embraces Buddhist Meditation." *Mother Nature Network.* August 21, 2012. www.mnn.com/health/fitness-well-being/blogs /bill-clinton-embraces-buddhist-meditation.

Dispenza, Joe. *Evolve Your Brain: The Science of Changing Your Mind.* Deerfield Beach, FL: Health Communications, 2007.

Doidge, Norman. *The Brain That Changes Itself: Stories of Personal Triumph from the Frontiers of Brain Science.* New York: Penguin, 2007.

Dowman, Keith, ed. *Flight of the Garuda: The Dzogchen Tradition of Tibetan Buddhism.* Somerville, MA: Wisdom, 1994.

Droit, Roger-Pol. *Cult of Nothingness: The Philosophers and the Buddha.* Translated by David Streight and Pamela Vohnson. Chapel Hill: University of North Carolina Press, 2003.

Ellison, Katherine. "Mastering Your Own Mind." *Psychology Today,* September 1, 2006.

Faure, Bernard. "A Gray Matter: Another Look at Buddhism and Neuroscience." In *Tricycle,* Winter 2012.

Faure, Bernard. *Double Exposure: Cutting Across Buddhist and Western Discourses.* Stanford, CA: Stanford University Press, 2004.

Fields, Rick. *How the Swans Came to the Lake: A Narrative History of Buddhism in America.* Boston: Shambhala Publications, 1992.

Folk, Kenneth. "Developmental Window for Contemplative Fitness." *Kenneth Folk Dharma* (blog), http://kennethfolkdharma.com/2013/01 /developmental-window-for-contemplative-fitness-brainstorm/.

Fronsdal, Gil. "Insight Meditation in the United States." In Prebish and Tanaka, *The Faces of Buddhism in America,* 164–180.

Gaussen, Terence. "The Development of Personhood and the Brain." In Watson, Batchelor, and Claxton, *The Psychology of Awakening,* 123–34.

Goldstein, Joseph. *The Experience of Insight: A Simple and Direct Guide to Buddhist Meditation.* Boston: Shambhala, 1976.

Goldstein, Joseph. *Insight Meditation: The Practice of Freedom.* Boston: Shambhala, 2003.

Goldstein, Joseph. *One Dharma: The Emerging Western Buddhism.* New York: HarperCollins, 2002.

Goleman, Daniel. *Emotional Intelligence: Why It Can Matter More Than IQ.* New York: Bantam Books, 1995.

Goleman, Daniel. *The Meditative Mind: The Varieties of Meditative Experience.* New York: Putnam, 1988.

Glassman, Bernie. Interview by *Sweeping Zen.* Transcribed by Jason Nottestad. April 24, 2012. http://sweepingzen.com/bernie-glassman-interview/.

Greenland, Susan K. *The Mindful Child: How to Help Your Kid Manage Stress and Become Happier, Kinder, and More Compassionate.* New York: Free Press, 2010.

Gross, Rita M. *Buddhism After Patriarchy: A Feminist History, Analysis, and Reconstruction of Buddhism.* Albany: State University of New York Press, 1993.

Gross, Rita M. "Helping the Iron Bird Fly: Western Buddhist Women and Issues of Authority in the Late 1990s." In Prebish and Tanaka, *The Faces of Buddhism in America,* 238–52.

Haidt, Jonathan. "The Moral Roots of Liberals and Conservatives." *TED Talks* video. September 2008. www.ted.com/talks/jonathan_haidt_on_the _moral_mind.html.

Hanson, Rick. *Buddha's Brain: The Practical Neuroscience of Happiness, Love, and Wisdom.* With Richard Mendius. Oakland, CA: New Harbinger, 2009.

Hanson, Rick. *Just One Thing: Developing a Buddha Brain One Simple Practice at a Time.* Oakland, CA: New Harbinger, 2011.

Hanson, Rick and Richard Mendius. *Meditations to Change Your Brain: Rewire Your Neural Pathways to Change Your Life.* Louisville, CO: Sounds True, 2009. Audiobook.

Harris, Sam. "Killing the Buddha." *Shambhala Sun.* March 2006.

Harvey, David. *The Condition of Postmodernity: An Enquiry into the Origins of Cultural Change.* Malden, MA: Blackwell, 1990.

Heaversedge, Jonty, and Halliwell, Ed. *The Mindful Manifesto: How Doing Less and Noticing More Can Help Us Thrive in a Stressed-Out World.* Carlsbad, CA: Hay House, 2012.

Hoffman, Claire. "David Lynch Is Back . . . as a Guru of Transcendental Meditation." *New York Times,* Feb. 22, 2013.

Hsieh, Tony. *Delivering Happiness: A Path to Profits, Passion, and Purpose; A Round Table Comic.* Mundelein, IL: Round Table Comics, 2012.

Imamura, Ryo. "Buddhist and Western Psychotherapies: An Asian American Perspective." In Prebish and Tanaka, eds., *Faces,* 228–37.

Ingram, Daniel. *Mastering the Core Teachings of the Buddha: An Unusually Hardcore Dharma Book.* London: Aeon Books, 2008.

Jackson, Phil, and Hugh Delehanty. *Sacred Hoops: Spiritual Lessons of a Hardwood Warrior.* New York: Hyperion, 1995.

Kabat-Zinn, Jon. *Full Catastrophe Living: Using the Wisdom of Your Body and Mind to Face Stress, Pain, and Illness.* New York: Bantam Dell, 1990 edition.

Kabat-Zinn, Jon. *Wherever You Go, There You Are: Mindfulness Meditation in Everyday Life.* New York: Hyperion, 1994.

Kabat-Zinn, Jon. "Indra's Net at Work: The Mainstreaming of Dharma Practice in Society" in Watson, Batchelor, and Claxton eds., *Psychology of Awakening,* 225–49.

Kabat-Zinn, Jon and Myla Kabat-Zinn. "Parenting with Mindful Awareness." In Boyce, *Mindfulness Revolution,* 227–35.

Kasimow, Harold, John P. Keenan, and Linda Klepinger Keenan. *Beside Still Waters: Jews, Christians, and the Way of the Buddha.* Somerville, MA: Wisdom, 2003.

Khema, Ayya. *Being Nobody, Going Nowhere: Meditations on the Buddhist Path.* Somerville, MA: Wisdom, 1987.

Khema, Ayya. *When the Iron Eagle Flies: Buddhism for the West.* Somerville, MA: Wisdom, 2000.

Khyentse, Dzongsar Jamyang. *What Makes You Not a Buddhist.* Boston: Shambhala, 2007.

Knitter, Paul F. *Without Buddha I Could Not Be a Christian.* Croydon, UK:
    Oneworld, 2009.
Konnikova, Maria. *Mastermind: How to Think Like Sherlock Holmes.* New York:
    Penguin, 2013.
Kornfield, Jack. *Meditation for Beginners.* Louisville, CO: Sounds True, 2008.
Kornfield, Jack. *After the Ecstasy, the Laundry: How the Heart Grows Wise on the
    Spiritual Path.* New York: Bantam Books, 2000.
Kornfield, Jack. *A Path with Heart: A Guide Through the Perils and Promises of
    Spiritual Life.* New York: Bantam Books, 1993.
Kornfield, Jack. "Is Buddhism Changing in North America?" In Don Morreale,
    ed., *Buddhist America,* xi–xxiii. Santa Fe: John Muir Publications, 1988.
Lazenby, Roland. *Mindgames: Phil Jackson's Long Strange Journey.* New York:
    McGraw-Hill, 2001.
Levine, Noah. *Dharma Punx: A Memoir.* New York: Harper Collins, 2003.
Levine, Noah. *The Heart of the Revolution: The Buddha's Radical Teachings on
    Forgiveness, Compassion, and Kindness.* New York: HarperCollins, 2011.
Leyland, Winston, ed. *Queer Dharma: Voices of Gay Buddhists.* Volume 1. San
    Francisco: Gay Sunshine Press, 1997.
Leyland, Winston, ed. *Queer Dharma: Voices of Gay Buddhists.* Volume 2. San
    Francisco: Gay Sunshine Press, 1999.
Linzer, Judith. *Torah and Dharma: Jewish Seekers in Eastern Religions.*
    Northvale, NJ: J. Aronson, 1996.
Lopez, Donald S. *The Scientific Buddha: His Short and Happy Life.* New Haven,
    CT: Yale University Press, 2012.
Lopez, Donald S. "The Scientific Buddha." *Tricycle,* Winter 2012. www.tricycle
    .com/feature/scientific-buddha.
Lowe, Donald M. *History of Bourgeois Perception.* Chicago: University of
    Chicago Press, 1982.
Loy, David. "Can Mindfulness Change a Corporation?" Turning Wheel Media,
    Feb. 19, 2013. www.buddhistpeacefellowship.org/can-mindfulness-change
    -a-corporation/.
Lutz, Antoine, John D. Dunne, and Richard J. Davidson. "Meditation and
    the Neuroscience of Consciousness." In *The Cambridge Handbook of
    Consciousness,* ed. Philip David Zalano, Morris Moscovich, and Evan
    Thompson. New York: Cambridge University Press, 2007.
Lynch, Aaron. *Thought Contagion: The New Science of Memes; How Beliefs
    Spread Through Society.* New York: Basic Books, 1996.
Mahasi Sayadaw, "The Progress of Insight (Visuddhiñana-katha)" translated
    from Pali Nyanaponika Thera (Kandy, Sri Lanka: Buddhist Publication
    Society, 1994). *Access to Insight.* www.accesstoinsight.org/lib
    /authors/mahasi/progress.html.
Mahasi Sayadaw, *Practical Insight Meditation: Basic and Progressive Stages.*

Translated by U Pe Thin and Myanaung U Tin. Kandy, Sri Lanka: Buddhist Publication Society, 1971.

Mann, Gurinder Singh, Paul David Numrich, and Raymond B. Williams. *Buddhists, Hindus, and Sikhs in America*. New York: Oxford University Press, 2001.

Maull, Fleet. *Dharma in Hell*. Kate Crisp, ed. Boulder, CO: Prison Dharma Network, 2005.

McCauley, Robert N. *Why Religion is Natural and Science is Not*. New York: Oxford Univ. Press, 2011.

McCown, Donald, Diane Reibel, and Marc S. Micozzi. *Teaching Mindfulness: A Practical Guide for Clinicians and Educators*. New York: Springer, 2010.

Metzinger, Thomas. *The Ego Tunnel: The Science of the Mind and the Myth of the Self*. New York: Basic Books, 2010.

Michaelson, Jay. *God vs. Gay? The Religious Case for Equality*. Boston: Beacon Press, 2011.

Michaelson, Jay. *Everything Is God: The Radical Path of Nondual Judaism*. Boston: Trumpeter Books, 2009.

Michaelson, Jay. *God in Your Body: Kabbalah, Mindfulness and Embodied Spiritual Practice*. Woodstock, VT: Jewish Lights, 2007.

Michaelson, Jay. "Get Ready for iSpirituality." *Forward*, February 6, 2013.

Michaelson, Jay. "Nonduality, Neuroscience, and Postmodernism: The Dream of the Self." *Reality Sandwich*, April 11, 2011. www.realitysandwich.com /dream_of_self.

Morreale, Don, ed. *The Complete Guide to Buddhist America*. Boston: Shambhala, 1998.

Naam, Ramez. *Nexus*. Nottingham, UK: Angry Robot, 2012.

Norberg-Hodge, Helena. "Compassion in the Age of the Global Economy." In Watson, Batchelor, and Claxon, *The Psychology of Awakening*, 55–67.

Numrich, Paul D. *Old Wisdom in the New World: Americanization in Two Immigrant Theravada Buddhist Temples*. Knoxville: University of Tennessee Press, 1999.

O'Connell, Matthew. "Post-Traditional Buddhism: The Quiet Revolution?" *Elephant Journal*, November 20, 2011. www.elephantjournal.com/2012/11/post -traditional-buddhism-the-quiet-revolution-part-one-matthew-oconnell/

Oppenheimer, Mark and Ian Lovett. "Zen Groups Distressed By Accusations Against Teacher." *New York Times*, February 11, 2003.

Peltz, Lawrence. "Mindfulness and Addiction Recovery." In Boyce, *Mindfulness Revolution*, 159–165.

Pfeil, Fred. "Subjects Without Selves: Contemporary Theory Accounts for the 'I.'" In Watson, Batchelor, and Claxon, *The Psychology of Awakening*, 40–54.

Prebish, Charles S. *Luminous Passage: The Practice and Study of Buddhism in America*. Berkeley: University of California Press, 1999.

Prebish, Charles S., and Kenneth K. Tanaka, eds. *The Faces of Buddhism in America.* Berkeley: The University of California Press, 1998.

Quart, Alissa. "Neuroscience Under Attack." *New York Times,* November 23, 2012.

Queen, Christopher S., ed. *Engaged Buddhism in the West.* Somerville, MA: Wisdom, 2000.

Queen, Christopher and Duncan Ryuken Williams, eds. *American Buddhism: Methods and Findings in Recent Scholarship.* New York: RoutledgeCurzon, 1999.

Ricard, Matthieu. "This Is Your Brain on Mindfulness." In Boyce, *Mindfulness Revolution,* 127–35.

Rothberg, Donald. "Responding to the Cries of the World: Socially Engaged Buddhism in North America." In Prebish and Tanaka, *The Faces of Buddhism in America,* 266–86.

Rutter, Peter. *Sex in the Forbidden Zone: When Men in Power—Therapists, Doctors, Clergy, Teachers and Others—Betray Women's Trust.* New York: Ballantine Books, 1997.

Ryan, Tim. *A Mindful Nation: How a Simple Practice Can Help Us Reduce Stress, Improve Performance, and Recapture the American Spirit.* Carlsbad, CA: Hay House, 2012.

Saikaku, Ihara. *The Great Mirror of Male Love.* Translated by Paul Gordon Schalow. Stanford: Stanford University Press, 1991.

Salzberg, Sharon. *Real Happiness: The Power of Meditation: A 28-Day Program.* New York: Workman, 2010.

Seager, Richard H. *Buddhism in America.* New York: Columbia University Press, 1999.

Schalow, Paul Gordon. "Kukai and the Tradition of Male Love in Japanese Buddhism." In Cabezon, *Buddhism, Sexuality and Gender,* 215–30.

Schmidt, Marcia Binder, ed. *Dzogchen Primer: An Anthology of Writings by Masters of Great Perfection.* Boston: Shambhala, 2002.

Schwartz, Jeffrey M., and Sharon Begley. *The Mind and the Brain: Neuroplasticity and the Power of Mental Force.* New York: Regan Books, 2002.

Shankman, Richard. *The Experience of Samadhi: An In-depth Exploration of Buddhist Meditation.* Boston: Shambhala, 2008.

Shoshanna, Brenda. *Jewish Dharma: A Guide to the Practice of Judaism and Zen.* Philadelphia: Da Capo, 2008.

Siegel, Daniel J., *The Mindful Brain: Reflection and Attunement in the Cultivation of Well-Being.* New York: W.W. Norton, 2007.

Siegel, Daniel J., *Mindsight: The New Science of Personal Transformation.* New York: Bantam Books, 2010.

Siderits, Mark, Evan Thompson, and Dan Zahavi, eds. *Self, No Self? Perspectives from Analytical, Phenomenological, and Indian Traditions.* New York: Oxford University Press, 2010.

Siff, Jason. *Unlearning Meditation: What to Do When the Instructions Get in the Way*. Boston: Shambhala, 2010.

Silberman, Steve. "Digital Mindfulness." In Boyce, *Mindfulness Revolution*, 84–90.

Silverman, Kaja. *The Subject of Semiotics*. New York: Oxford University Press, 1984.

Smalley, Susan L., and Diana Winston. *Fully Present: The Science, Art, and Practice of Mindfulness*. Philadelphia: Da Capo, 2010.

Smith, Huston. *Cleansing the Doors of Perception: The Religious Significance of Entheogenic Plants and Chemicals*. New York: Penguin, 2000.

Smithers, Stuart. "Occupy Buddhism, Or Why the Dalai Lama Is a Marxist." *Tricycle*, June 12, 2012.

Snyder, Stephen and Tina Rasmussen. *Practicing the Jhanas: Traditional Concentration Meditation as Presented by the Venerable Pa Auk Sayadaw*. Boston: Shambhala, 2009.

Sponberg, Alan. "Attitudes Toward Women and the Feminine in Early Buddhism." In Cabezon, *Buddhism, Sexuality and Gender*, 3–36.

Storhoff, Gary and John Whalen-Bridge, eds. *American Buddhism as a Way of Life*. Albany: State University of New York Press, 2010.

Surya Das. *Awakening the Buddha Within: Tibetan Wisdom for the Western World*. New York: Broadway Books, 1997.

Sutin, Lawrence. *All Is Change: The Two-Thousand-Year Journey of Buddhism to the West*. New York: Little, Brown, 2006.

Taylor, Charles. *Sources of the Self: The Making of the Modern Identity*. New York: Cambridge University Press, 1989.

Taylor, Steve. "Can Meditation Change the World?" *Out of the Darkness: The Science of Post-Traumatic Growth (blog)*. *Psychology Today*. www.psychology today.com/blog/out-the-darkness/201212/can-meditation-change-the-world.

Taylor, Steve. *Back to Sanity: Healing the Madness of Our Minds*. Carlsbad, CA: Hay House, 2012.

Tamney, Joseph B. *American Society in the Buddhist Mirror*. New York: Routledge, 1992.

Tan, Chade-Meng. *Search Inside Yourself: The Unexpected Path to Achieving Success, Happiness (And World Peace)*. New York: HarperOne, 2012.

Thich Nhat Hahn. *Being Peace*. Edited by Rachel Neumann. Berkeley: Parallax, 1987.

Thompson, Evan. *Waking, Dreaming, Being: New Light on the Self and Consciousness from Neuroscience, Meditation, and Philosophy*. New York: Columbia University Press, forthcoming 2013.

Thurman, Robert. *Inner Revolution: Life, Liberty and the Pursuit of Real Happiness*. New York: Riverhead Books, 1998.

Tolle, Eckhart. *A New Earth: Awakening to Your Life's Purpose*. New York: Penguin, 2008.

Tonkinson, Carole, ed. *Big Sky Mind: Buddhism and the Beat Generation.* New York: Riverhead Books, 1995.

Tweed, Thomas A. *The American Encounter with Buddhism, 1844–1912: Victorian Culture and the Limits of Dissent.* Chapel Hill: University of North Carolina Press, 2000.

Van Esterik, Penny. *Taking Refuge: Lao Buddhists in North America.* Tempe, AR: Arizona State University, Program for Southeast Asian Studies, 1992.

Wallace, Alan. *The Attention Revolution: Unlocking the Power of the Focused Mind.* Boston: Wisdom, 2006.

Wallis, Glenn. "Nascent Speculative Non-Buddhism." glennwallis.com.

Wallis, Glenn. "X-Buddhist Provocateurs?" http://speculativenonbuddhism .com/2012/12/09/x-buddhist-provocateurs/.

Warner, Brad. *Hardcore Zen: Punk Rock, Monster Movies, and the Truth About Reality.* Somerville, MA: Wisdom, 2003.

Warren, Jeff. *The Head Trip: Adventures on the Wheel of Consciousness.* New York: Random House, 2007.

Watson, Gay, Stephen Batchelor, and Guy Claxon, eds. *The Psychology of Awakening: Buddhism, Science and Our Day-to-Day Lives.* London: Rider, 2012.

Wei, Wu Wei. *Ask the Awakened: The Negative Way.* Boulder, CO: Sentient, 2002.

Woods, Judith. "Now's the Moment for Mindfulness." *The Telegraph,* December 31, 2012.

Zwilling, Leonard. "Homosexuality As Seen in Indian Buddhist Texts." In Cabezon, *Buddhism, Sexuality and Gender,* 203–14.

Abhisanda Sutta, Anguttara Nikaya 10.176

Cula Malunkya Sutta, Majjhima Nikaya 63

Cunda Kammaraputta Sutta, Anguttara Nikaya 8.39

Khuddaka Nikaya, Theragatha 1024

Satipatthana Sutta, Majjhima Nikaya 10

Scientific Studies and Presentations

Baer, R. A., Smith, G. T., Hopkins, J., Krietemeyer, J., and Toney, L. "Using Self-Report Assessment Methods to Explore Facets of Mindfulness." (2006) Assessment 13 (1), 27–45.

Black, David. "Hot Topics: A 40-Year Publishing History of Mindfulness," *Mindfulness Research Monthly* 1, no. 5 (June 2010): 1–2. www.mindfulexperience.org/resources/files/MRM_V1N5_june.pdf

Brewer, Judson, and Patrick D. Worhunsky, Jeremy R. Gray, Yi-Yuan Tang, Jochen Weber, and Hedy Kober. "Meditation Experience Is Associated with Differences in Default Mode Network Activity and Connectivity."

Proceedings of the National Academy of Arts and Sciences 108, no. 50 (December 2011): 1–6. doi:10.1073/pnas.1112029108.

Britton, Willoughby B., Patricia L Haynes,Keith W. Fridel, and Richard R Bootzin. "Mindfulness Training Improves Polysomnographic and Subjective Sleep Profiles in Antidepressant Medication Users with Sleep Complaints." *Psychotherapy and Psychosomatics 81* (2012): 296–304. doi: 10.1159/000332755.

Cahn, Rael. "Cultivation of Awareness: Neural Correlates to the Enhanced Clarity and Decreased Automated Reactivity During Vipassana Meditation." Lecture presented at Advances in Meditation Research Conference, New York, January 17, 2013.

Cahn, B. Rael and J. Polich. "Meditation States and Traits: EEG, ERP, and Neuroimaging Studies." Psychological Bulletin 132, no. 2 (March 2006): 180–211. doi: 10.1037/0033-2909.132.2.180.

Chiesa, A., A. Serretti, Jakobsen A. C., "Mindfulness: Top-down or Bottom-up Emotion Regulation Strategy?" *Clinical Psychology Review* 33, no. 1 (February 2013): 82–96. doi: 10.1016/j.cpr.2012.10.006.

Davidson, Richard J., Jon Kabat-Zinn, Jessica Schumacher, et al. "Alterations in Brain and Immune Function Produced by Mindfulness Meditation." *Psychosomatic Medicine* 65, no. 4 (July/August 2003): 564–570. doi: 10.1097/01.PSY.0000077505.67574.E3.

Fox, K. C. R., Zakarauskas, P., Dixon, M. L., Ellamil, M., Thompson, E., and Christoff, K. "Meditation Experience Predicts Introspective Accuracy." PLoS ONE, 7(9), e45370. (2012)

Gard, Tim. "Meditation Effects on Protecting Against Age-related Deficits in Cognition and Associated Neuroimaging Measures." Lecture presented at the Advances in Meditation Research Conference, New York, January 17, 2013.

Holzel, Britta K., Sara W. Lazar, Tim Gard, Zev Schuman-Olivier, David R. Vago, Ulirch Ott. "How Does Mindfulness Meditation Work? Proposing Mechanisms of Action from a Conceptual and Neural Perspective." *Perspectives on Psychological Science* 6, no. 6 (November 2011): 537–59. doi: 10.1177/1745691611419671.

Ioannidis, John P. A. "Why Most Published Research Findings Are False," *PLoS Medicine* 2 no. 8 (August 2005): e124. doi:10.1371/journal.pmed.0020124.

Josipovic, Zoran. "Duality and Nonduality in Meditation Research." *Consciousness and Cognition* 19, no. 4 (December 2010): 1119–1121. doi: 10.1016/j.concog.2010.03.016.

Josipovic, Zoran, Ilan Dinstein, Jochen Weber, and David J. Heeger. "Influence of Meditation on Anti-correlated Networks in the Brain." *Frontiers of Human Neuroscience* 5, no. 183 (January 2011): 1–11. doi: 10.3389/fnhum.2011.00183.

Kabat-Zinn, Jon. "Mindfulness-Based Interventions in Context: Past, Present, and Future." *Clinical Psychology: Science and Practice* 10, no. 2 (June 2003): 145–46. doi: 10.1093/clipsy.bpg016.

Kabat-Zinn, Jon, L. Lipworth, R. Burney, and W. Sellers. "Four-year Follow-up of a Meditation-based Program for the Self-regulation of Chronic Pain; Treatment, Outcomes, and Compliance." *The Clinical Journal of Pain* 2, no. 3 (1986): 159.

Kornfield, Jack. "Intensive Insight Meditation A Phenomenological Study." *The Journal of Transpersonal Psychology*, 1979, Vol. 11, No. 1.

Krusche, Adele, Eva Cyhlarova, Scott King, J. Mark Williams. "Mindfulness Online: a Preliminary Evaluation of the Feasibility of a Web-based Mindfulness Course and the Impact on Stress." *BMJ Open* 2, no. 3 (May 2012) doi: 10.1136/bmjopen-2011-000803.

Lazar, Kerr Sara Lazar, Rachel H. Wasserman, et al. "Meditation Experience Is Associated with Increased Cortical Thickness," *Neuroreport* 16, no. 17 (November 2005): 1893–1987. www.ncbi.nlm.nih.gov/pmc/articles /PMC1361002/.

Loizzo, Joseph, Janey C. Paterson, Mary E. Charlson, et al. "The Effect of a Contemplative Self-healing Program on Quality of Life in Women with Breast and Gynecological Cancers." *Alternative Therapies* 16, no. 3 (May 2010): 30–38. www.scribd.com/doc/31007722/The-Effect-of-a-Contemplative-Self-healing-Program-on-Quality-of-Life-in-Women-With -Breast-and-Gynecologic-Cancers.

Luders, Eileen, Kristi Clark, Katherine L. Narr, and Arthur W. Toga. "Enhanced Brain Connectivity in Long-term Practitioners." *NeuroImage* 57, no. 4 (August 2011): 1308–1316. doi: 10.1016/j.neuroimage.2011.05.075.

Lutz, Antoine, and Evan Thompson. "Neurophenomenology: Integrating Subjective Experience and Brain Dynamics in the Neuroscience of Consciousness." *Journal of Consciousness Studies*, 10, No. 9–10, 2003, pp. 31–52.

"Meditation: An Introduction." National Center for Complementary and Alternative Medicine. National Institutes of Health. February 2006. http://nccam.nih.gov/health/meditation/overview.htm

Moss, Aleeze Sattar, Nancy Wintering, Hannah Roggenkamp, et al. "Effects of an Eight-Week Meditation Program on Mood and Anxiety in Patients with Memory Loss." *Journal of Alternative and Complementary Medicine* 18, no. 1 (2012): 48–53. 10.1089/acm.2011.0051.

Newberg, Andrew. "Meditation and Neurodegenerative Disease." Lecture presented at the Advances in Meditation Research Conference, New York, January 17, 2013.

Newberg, Andrew B., N. Wintering, D. S. Khalsa, H. Roggenkamp, M. R. Waldman. "Meditation Effects on Cognitive Function and Cerebral Flow in Subjects with Memory Loss: A Preliminary Study." *Journal of Alzheimer's Disease* 20, no. 2 (2010): 517–526. doi: 10.3233/JAD-2010-1391.

Pagnoni, Giussepe and Milios Cekic. "Age Effects on Gray Matter Volume
     and Attentional Performance in Zen Meditation." *Neurobiology of Aging* 28,
     no. 10 (October 2007): 1623–1627. doi:10.1016/j.neurobiolaging.2007
     .06.008.

Plassman, Brenda L., John W. Williams Jr., James R. Burke, Tracey Holsinger,
     Sophiya Benjamin. "Systematic Review: Factors Associated With
     Risk for and Possible Prevention of Cognitive Decline in Later Life."
     Annals of Internal Medicine 153, no. 3 (August 2010): 182–197. doi:
     10.1059/0003-4819-153-3-201008030-00258.

Shapiro, Deane H. "Adverse effects of meditation: A preliminary investigation
     of long-term meditators." *International Journal of Psychosomatics*, Vol 39(1-
     4), 1992, 62-67.

Shapiro, Shauna L., Roger Walsh, and Willoughby B. Britton. "An Analysis of
     Recent Meditation Research and Suggestions for Future Directions." *Journal
     for Meditation and Meditation Research 3* (2003): 69–90. http://brittonlab
     .files.wordpress.com/2011/03/pdf4.pdf.

Tang, Yi-Yuan. "The Advances in Meditation Research: Achievement and
     Challenge." Lecture presented at the Advances in Meditation Research
     Conference, New York, January 17, 2013.

Tang, Yi-Yuan, Mary K. Rothbart, and Michael I. Posner, "Neural Correlates
     of Establishing, Maintaining, and Switching Brainstates," *Trends in
     Cognitive Sciences* 16, no. 6 (June 2012): 330–337. doi: 10.1016/j.tics
     .2012.05.001.

Tang, Yi-Yuan, Yinghua Ma, Yaxin Fan, et al. "Central and Autonomic Nervous
     System Interaction Is Altered by Short-Term Meditation." *Proceedings of the
     National Academy of Arts and Sciences* 106, no. 22 (June 2, 2009): 8865–
     8870. doi:10.1073/pnas.0904031106.

Taylor, Veronique, Veronique Deneault, Joshua Grant, et al. "Impact of
     Meditation Training on the Default Mode Network During a Restful State."
     Social Cognitive and Affective Neuroscience 8, no. 1 (January 2013): 4–14.
     doi: 10.1093/scan/nsr087.

Travis, Fred and Jonathan Shea. "Focused Attention, Open Monitoring and
     Automatic Self-transcending: Categories to Organize Meditations from
     Vedic, Buddhist and Chinese Traditions." *Consciousness and Cognition* 19,
     no. 4 (December 2010): 1110–1118. doi: 10.1016/j.concog.2010.01.007.

Vago, David R. and David Silversweig. "Self-awareness, Self-regulation,
     and Self-transcendence (S-ART): a Framework for Understanding the
     Neurobiological Mechanisms of Mindfulness," *Frontiers of Human
     Neuroscience* 6, no. 296 (October 2012): 1–30. doi:10.3389/fnhum
     .2012.00296.

Wheeler, Mark. "Meditation Reduces Loneliness." *UCLA Newsroom*, August 14,
     2012. http://newsroom.ucla.edu/portal/ucla/meditation-reduces
     -loneliness-237463.aspx.

Blogs and Websites

Applied Buddhism: Living Life Fully. appliedbuddhism.wordpress.com
Being Human. www.beinghuman.org
Brasington, Leigh. www.leighb.com
Buddhanet: Buddha Dharma Education Association Inc. buddhanet.net
The Buddhist Blog. thebuddhistblog.blogspot.com/ (contains updated blogroll)
Buddhist Geeks: Discover the Emerging Face(s) of Buddhism. www.buddhist
    geeks.com
Chapman, David. *Meaningness* (blog). meaningness.wordpress.com
Dharma Overground. www.dharmaoverground.org/web/guest/home
Dharma Seed. www.dharmaseed.org
Elephant Journal: Yoga, Sustainability, Politics, Spirituality. www.elephant
    journal.com
Kenneth Folk Dharma. kennethfolkdharma.com
The International Symposia for Contemplative Studies. contemplativeresearch.
    org
Prison Mindfulness. prisonmindfulness.org
Sangha of Thousands of Buddhas. Website of Spirit Rock Meditation Center.
    www.thousandsofbuddhas.org
Speculative Non-Buddhism. speculativenonbuddhism.com
Sweeping Zen: The Definitive Online Who's Who in Zen. sweepingzen.com
Tricycle: Buddhist Wisdom, Meditation, and Practices for Daily Life.
    www.tricycle.com
YourMorals.Org. yourmorals.org

Magazines

Buddhadharma
Dharma Today
Inquiring Mind
Mandala Magazine
Mindful
non + x
Shambhala Sun
Tricycle
Turning Wheel
Western Buddhist Review

Applied Mindfulness and Mindfulness Research Institutions

Association for Mindfulness in Education
Center for Compassion and Altruism Research and Education
Center for Contemplative Mind in Society
Center for Investigating Healthy Minds
Center for Mindfulness in Medicine, Health Care, and Society
Clinical and Affective Neuroscience Laboratory
Cognitive Neuroscience of Thought Laboratory
Contemplative Studies Initiative
Duke University Integrative Medicine
Garrison Institute
Greater Good Science Center
Institute for Mindful Leadership
Mind and Life Institute
Mind Body Awareness Project
Mind Fitness Training Institute
Mindful Awareness Research Center
Mindful Living Programs
Mindfulness Practice Center at University of Missouri
Mindfulness Research Monthly
Mindfulness-Based Childbirth and Parenting Program
Mindfulness-Based Relapse Prevention
Mindsight Institute
Penn Program for Mindfulness
Search Inside Yourself Leadership Institute
Stressed Teens
Wisdom 2.0

NOTES

Introduction

1. See Chade-Meng Tan, *Search Inside Yourself* (New York: HarperOne, 2012). Though I believe "upgrading the mind" to be my coinage, the language of optimization is taken from Chade-Meng Tan, the founder of Google's Search Inside Yourself program.

2. David Black, "Hot Topics: A 40-year Publishing History of Mindfulness," *Mindfulness Research Monthly* Vol. 1, No 5 (2010); Yi-Yuan Tang, "The Advances in Meditation Research: Achievement and Challenge" (lecture, Advances in Meditation Research Conference, New York, January 17, 2013).

3. See Daniel Siegel, "The Proven Benefits of Mindfulness," in *The Mindfulness Revolution,* ed. Barry Boyce (Boston: Shambhala, 2011), 136–39; Lawrence Peltz, in Boyce, "Mindfulness and Addiction Recovery" in *Mindfulness Revolution,* 159–165; and sources cited in Chapters One and Two.

4. Kenneth Folk, "Developmental Window for Contemplative Fitness," *Kenneth Folk Dharma* (blog), http://kennethfolkdharma.com/2013/01 /developmental-window-for-contemplative-fitness-brainstorm/. In a sense, "contemplative fitness" is a subset of "Brain Fitness," made famous in the 2008 PBS series. See "The Brain Fitness Program PBS 16x9 NEW Trailer,"

YouTube video (3:00). http://www.youtube.com/watch?v=4b3XcNENTLk.
Neuroplasticity and "brain fitness" are discussed in Chapter Two.

5. Katherine Ellison, "Mastering Your Own Mind," *Psychology Today*
    September 1, 2006. http://www.psychologytoday.com/articles/200608
    /mastering-your-own-mind.

6. "Meditation: An Introduction." National Center for Complementary and
    Alternative Medicine. National Institutes of Health February 2006.
    http://nccam.nih.gov/health/meditation/overview.htm.

7. In my own, Theravadan Buddhist tradition it's actually pronounced
    "dhamma," but I will use the conventional Western word here. The word
    "evolving," incidentally, has been used by all kinds of contemporary teachers
    to refer to various new iterations of spiritual practice. I am not referring to
    any of those particular teachers here.

8. See Marcia Binder Schmidt, ed., *Dzogchen Primer* (Boston: Shambhala,
    2002).

9. Jon Kabat-Zinn, *Wherever You Go There You Are* (New York: Hyperion,
    1994), 4.

10. Barry Boyce, "Introduction," *Mindfulness Revolution,* xi.

11. Jan Chozen Bays, "What Is Mindfulness?" In Boyce, *Mindfulness
    Revolution,* 3.

12. Jack Kornfield, "A Receptive, Respectful Awareness," in Boyce, *Mindfulness
    Revolution,* 8.

13. Joseph Goldstein, "Here, Now, Aware," in Boyce, *Mindfulness Revolution,* 21.

14. Daniel Siegel, *The Mindful Brain: Reflection and Attunement in the
    Cultivation of Well-Being* (New York: W.W. Norton, 2007), 91.

15. The Pali Canon is one of the three "baskets" of the tripitaka, the
    authoritative scriptures of Theravadan Buddhism. (The other two are the
    abhidharma, the psychological/philosophical literature, and the vinaya,
    the monastic code.) The term *tripitaka* eventually becomes synonymous
    with "Buddhist scripture" more generally, and is expanded in Mahayana
    traditions. The term "Pali Canon" helpfully distinguishes the older
    Theravadan/Hinayana texts from the subsequent Mahayana ones.

16. For example, www.jackkornfield.com/2011/02/sitting-meditation/; www
    .mindful.org/mindfulness-practice/mindfulness-the-basics; www.how-to
    -meditate.org; zenhabits.net/meditate/; Shambhala Sun, "How to Meditate,"
    http://www.shambhalasun.com/index.php?option=content&task=view&id
    =26&Itemid=161.

17. Some from my own tradition include Jon Kabat-Zinn, *Full Catastrophe
    Living* (New York: Bantam Dell, 1990); Ayya Khema, *Being Nobody, Going
    Nowhere: Meditations on the Buddhist Path* (Somerville, MA: Wisdom,
    1987); Joseph Goldstein, *Insight Meditation: The Practice of Freedom*
    (Boston: Shambhala, 2003); Jack Kornfield, *Meditation for Beginners*

(Louisville, CO: Sounds True, 2008); Sharon Salzberg, *Real Happiness: The Power of Meditation: A 28-Day Program* (New York: Workman, 2010).

Chapter 1

1. See Kabat-Zinn, *Full Catastrophe Living*, 248-53; Noah Levine, *The Heart of the Revolution* (New York: HarperCollins, 2011), 13.
2. See Cheng-Meng Tan, *Search Inside Yourself* (New York: HarperOne, 2012).
3. See Stephen Batchelor, *The Awakening of the West* (Berkeley, CA: Parallax, 1994), 206–15.
4. See Batchelor, *Awakening*, 235 (noting there is no term for Buddhism in Asia).
5. See Rick Fields, *How the Swans Came to the Lake* (Boston: Shambhala Publications, 1992), 141. It is also unfortunately common.
6. Richard Seager, *Buddhism in America* (New York: Columbia University Press, 1999), 9–10. See also Fields, *Swans*, 70–82, 339–58.
7. Other valuable studies include Lawrence Sutin, *All Is Change* (New York: Little, Brown, 2006); James W. Coleman, *The New Buddhism* (New York: Oxford, 2001); Joseph B. Tamney, *American Society in the Buddhist Mirror* (New York: Routledge, 1992); Seager, *Buddhism in America*; Penny Van Esterik, *Taking Refuge* (Tempe, AR: Arizona State University, 1992); Paul D. Numrich, *Old Wisdom in the New World* (Knoxville: University of Tennessee Press, 1999); Christopher Queen and Duncan Ryuken Williams, eds., *American Buddhism* (New York: Routledge, 1999). See generally Martin Baumann, "The Dharma Has Come West. A Survey of Recent Studies and Sources." *Journal of Buddhist Ethics*, 4, 1997, 194–211; Martin Baumann, "American Buddhism: A Bibliography on Buddhist Traditions and Schools in the U.S.A. and Canada." *Journal of Global Buddhism*, June 1999. http://www.globalbuddhism.org/bib-ambu.htm.
8. See Charles Prebish, *Luminous Passage* (Berkeley: University of California Press, 1999), 58–63. The distinction between the "two Buddhisms" was coined by Charles Prebish in 1979. The current population estimates are 3–4 million total Buddhists in the U.S., of whom 2.2 million are Asian and 800,000 are non-Asian. Excellent studies of Asian American Buddhist communities include the essays in Charles Prebish and Kenneth Tanaka, ed., *The Faces of Buddhism in America* (Berkeley: The University of California Press, 1998), 13–161; and Prebish, *Luminous Passage*, 7–147. Seager differentiates between recent Asian immigrants (who arrived subsequent to the immigration reforms of the 1960s) and long-term Asian-Americans, noting several differences in community and practice. See Seager, *Buddhism in America*, 9–10; 235–248. For our purposes, however, "two Buddhisms" is sufficiently distinctive.

9. See Prebish, *Luminous Passage*, 23–26l; Seager, *Buddhism in America*, 70–89. Today, there are many Western Soko Gakkai practitioners, distinguished by the focus on the mantra *nam myoho renge kyo* and distinctive rituals and beliefs.

10. See Prebish, *Luminous Passage*, 20–23; Seager, *Buddhism in America*, 51–69.

11. See Rick Fields, "Divided Dharma: White Buddhists, Ethnic Buddhists, and Racism," in Prebish and Tanaka, *Faces of Buddhism*, 196–207.

12. On the BCA, see Seager, *Buddhism in America*, 51–69.

13. See Fields, *Swans*, 9–10 (discussing transformation of Buddhism into a religion with the Buddha living in heavenly realms surrounded by supernatural retinues).

14. See Batchelor, *Awakening*, 161–83.

15. Fields, *Swans*, 20.

16. See Fields, *Swans*, 34–53.

17. See Fields, *Swans*, 55–69.

18. See Batchelor, *Awakening*, 239–42.

19. Fields, *Swans,* 105–15.

20. Thomas A. Tweed, *The American Encounter with Buddhism, 1844–1912*, 2–68 (Chapel Hill: University of North Carolina Press, 2000). Tweed notes that Buddhism was interpreted and appreciated differently by those he calls intellectuals, esoterics, rationalists, and romantics. See also Prebish, *Luminous Passage*, 3–7.

21. See Tweed, *American Encounter*, 31–33; Fields, *Swans*, 119–45.

22. Fields, *Swans*, 129.

23. Fields, *Swans*, 69; Tweed, *American Encounter*, 29.

24. Fields, *Swans*, 101–106; Batchelor, *Awakening*, 267–71.

25. Tweed, *American Encounter*, 133–53; Prebish, *Luminous Passage*, 7; Sutin, *All Is Change*, 107–43.

26. See Fields, *Swans*, 196–97, 204–07; Seager, *Buddhism in America*, 40.

27. Fields, *Swans*, 190–95; Prebish, *Luminous Passage*, 8–20.

28. Seager, *Buddhism in America*, 90–91. Seager points out that the Zen of the early Western transmitters was largely the result of nineteenth-century reform and modernization movements.

29. See Fields, *Swans*, 187–91; Sutin, *All Is Change*, 292–97; Seager, *Buddhism in America*, 40–41.

30. See Fields, *Swans*, 210-14; Seager, *Buddhism in America*, 41–42; Carole Tonkinson, ed. *Big Sky Mind: Buddhism and the Beat Generation* (New York: Riverhead Books, 1995), 1–20.

31. Fields, *Swans*, 248–49. On the early years of the SFZC and Tassajara, see Fields, *Swans*, 25–265. Interestingly, during the spread of Zen, traditional distinctions remained in place. Shunryu Suzuki taught in the Soto Zen school, emphasizing gradual enlightenment and "just sitting." D. T.

Suzuki studied in the Rinzai school, emphasizing *kensho* enlightenment experiences.

32. See Fields, *Swans*, 249–51. Transcendental Meditation, or TM, has been both popular and controversial, not least owing to the way the Maharishi is regarded as almost godlike, and the somewhat cult-like features of the TM community. It appears that since the Maharishi's death, these trends have decreased. Interestingly, filmmaker David Lynch has played a significant role in TM's upsurge and rehabilitation. See Claire Hoffman, "David Lynch Is Back . . . As a Guru of Transcendental Meditation," *New York Times*, Feb. 22, 2013, www.nytimes.com/2013/02/24/magazine/david-lynch -transcendental-meditation.html.

33. See Fields, *Swans*, 273–303, 308–18; Prebish, *Luminous Passage*, 40–46.

34. Seager, *Buddhism in America*, 147; Prebish, *Luminous Passage*, 148–58. On Denison, see Sandy Boucher, *Turning the Wheel: Women Creating the New Buddhism* (Boston: Beacon, 1988), 177–84.

35. Fields, *Swans*, 374–78.

36. Seager, *Buddhism in America*, 133–34.

37. Lama Surya Das, *Awakening the Buddha Within* (New York: Broadway Books, 1997), 382–95. See also Prebish, *Luminous Passage*, 264–65; Fields, *Swans*, 371 (calling lay practice "the real heart and koan of American Buddhism").

38. Jack Kornfield, "Is Buddhism Changing in North America?" in Don Morreale, ed., *Buddhist America* (Santa Fe: John Muir Publications, 1988), xi-xxiii.

39. Fields, "Divided Dharma," pp. 196–98.

40. Quoted in Gil Fronsdal, "Insight Meditation in the United States," in Prebish and Tanaka, *Faces*, pp. 164–180, 167.

41. Sutin, *All Is Change*, 162.

42. Quoted in Maria Konnikova, *Mastermind: How to Think Like Sherlock Holmes* (New York: Penguin, 2013), 3.

43. See Goldstein, *Insight Meditation*, 93–105. See also Ryo Imamura, "Buddhist and Western Psychotherapies: An Asian American Perspective," in Prebish and Tanaka, eds., *Faces*, 228–37.

44. Quoted in Jon Kabat-Zinn, "Indra's Net at Work: The Mainstreaming of Dharma Practice in Society," in Watson, Batchelor, and Claxon, eds., *Psychology of Awakening* (London: Rider, 2012), 225–49, 227.

45. Fields, *Swans*, 8.

46. See Seager, *Buddhism in America*, 148–49.

47. See Batchelor, *Awakening*, 344–48.

48. Satipatthana Sutta, Majjhima Nikaya, 10. See Batchelor, *Awakening*, 341–44; Analayo, *Satipatthana: The Direct Path to Realization* (Cambridge, UK: Windhorse, 2004).

49. Fronsdal, "Insight Meditation," 167–68.
50. Batchelor, *Awakening*, 346-48; Goldstein, *One Dharma*, 20.
51. Seager, *Buddhism in America*, 138–43.
52. See Seager, *Buddhism in America*, 137.
53. Don Morreale, *The Complete Guide to Buddhism in America* (Boston: Shambhala, 1998), xvii.
54. Khuddaka Nikaya, Theragatha, 1024.
55. For a concise summary of the distinctions between the three vehicles, see Seager, *Buddhism in America*, 21–32.
56. Joseph Goldstein, *One Dharma* (New York: HarperCollins, 2002), 26.
57. Quoted in Prebish, *Luminous Passage*, 262.
58. See Kabat-Zinn, *Full Catastrophe Living*.
59. See Susan L. Smalley and Diana Winston, *Fully Present* (Philadelphia: Da Capo, 2010), 218–20; Susan K. Greenland, *The Mindful Child* (New York: Free Press, 2010).
60. See, e.g., Michael Carroll, *Awake at Work* (Boston: Shambhala, 2004); Michael Carroll, *Fearless at Work* (Boston: Shambhala, 2012); Chade-Meng Tan, *Search Inside Yourself*. There has recently been increased data supporting workplace happiness more generally as a contributor to productivity and sustainability. See, e.g., Tony Hsieh, *Delivering Happiness*.
61. Matthieu Ricard, "This Is Your Brain on Mindfulness," in Boyce, *Mindfulness Revolution*, 134. On the study itself, see Ricard, 129–33.
62. See Seager, *Buddhism in America*, 213–14.
63. Boyce, *Mindfulness Revolution*, xiii.
64. See Siegel, *Mindful Brain*, 18.
65. Jon Kabat-Zinn, quoted in Seager, *Buddhism in America*, 214.
66. See Tan, *Search Inside Yourself*.
67. See Phil Jackson and Hugh Delehanty, *Sacred Hoops* (New York: Hyperion, 1995).
68. Tim Ryan, *A Mindful Nation: How a Simple Practice Can Help Us Reduce Stress, Improve Performance, and Recapture the American Spirit* (Carlsbad, CA: Hay House, 2012). See Jim Axelrod, "Ohio Congressman's Meditation Crusade," *CBS News*, February 9, 2013. www.cbsnews.com/8301 -18563_162-57568552/ohio-congressmans-meditation-crusade/.
69. Ryan, *Mindful Nation*, 116–24; Judith Woods, "Now's the Moment for Mindfulness," *Telegraph*, December 31, 2012. www.telegraph.co.uk/health/wellbeing/9772911/Nows-the-moment-for -mindfulness.html.
70. Fleet Maul, *Dharma in Hell* (CO: Prison Dharma Network, 2005); http://prisonmindfulness.org/. See also Kabat-Zinn, "Indra's Net" in Watson, Batchelor and Claxton, eds., *Psychology of Awakening*, 225–49, 245–46.
71. Smalley and Winston, *Fully Present*, 112–18.

72. Siegel, *Mindful Brain,* 15.
73. Hoffman, "David Lynch."
74. See Barry Boyce, "Creating a Mindful Society," in Boyce, *Mindfulness Revolution,* 256–57; See also *Against the Stream: Buddhist Meditation Society* (blog), www.againstthestream.org.
75. Ryan, *Mindful Nation,* 164.
76. Ryan, *Mindful Nation,* 80–82.
77. Carroll, *Awake at Work;* Carroll, *Fearless at Work;* "Awake at Work with Michael Carrol." www.awakeatwork.net/.
78. Boyce, "Creating a Mindful Society," in Boyce, *Mindfulness Revolution,* 259–61. Examples of mindfulness in law projects include Berkeley's Initiative for Mindfulness in Law (www.law.berkeley.edu/mindfulness.htm) and Pepperdine's "Tools of Mindful Awareness" classes (http://law.pepperdine.edu/straus/training-and-conferences/professional-skills-program-summer/mindfulness-conflict.htm).
79. Michael d'Estries, "Bill Clinton Embraces Buddhist Meditation," *Mother Nature Network,* August 21, 2012. www.mnn.com/health/fitness-well-being/blogs/bill-clinton-embraces-buddhist-meditation.
80. Mirabai Bush, "Knowing Every Breath You Take," *New York Times,* January 5, 2013.
81. See Prebish, *Luminous Passage,* 69–81, and discussion in Chapter Three.

Chapter 2

1. See Richard Davidson, *The Emotional Life of Your Brain* (New York: Hudson Street Press, 2012), 183–97, describing the (very) rough early days of the field.
2. Black, "Hot Topics," 1–2; Tang, "Advances in Meditation Research."
3. Some of the recent studies include Judson Brewer et al., "Meditation Experience Is Associated with Differences in Default Mode Network Activity and Connectivity," *Proceedings of the National Academy of Arts and Sciences* 108, no. 50 (2011); Willoughby Britton et al., "Mindfulness Training Improves Polysomnographic and Subjective Sleep Profiles in Antidepressant Medication Users with Sleep Complaints," *Psychotherapy and Psychosomatics* 81, no 5. (2012); B. Rael Cahn and John Polich, "Meditation States and Traits: EEG, ERP, and Neuroimaging Studies," *Psychological Bulletin* 132, no. 2, (2006); A. Chiesa, A. Serretti, Jakobsen A.C., "Mindfulness: Top-down or Bottom-up Emotion Regulation Strategy?" *Clinical Psychology Review* 33, no. 1 (2013); Veronique Taylor, et al. "Impact of Meditation Training on the Default Mode Network During a Restful State," *Social Cognitive and Affective Neuroscience* 8, no. 1 (2013); Britta K. Holzel, et al., "How Does Mindfulness Meditation

Work? Proposing Mechanisms of Action from a Conceptual and Neural Perspective," *Perspectives on Psychological Science* 6, no. 6 (2011); Zoran Josipovic et al., "Influence of Meditation on Anti-correlated Networks in the Brain," *Frontiers of Human Neuroscience* 5, no. 183 (2011); Joseph Loizzo et al., "The Effect of a Contemplative Self-healing Program on Quality of Life in Women with Breast and Gynecological Cancers," *Alternative Therapies 16, no. 3* (2010); Eileen Luders, "Enhanced Brain Connectivity in Long-term Practitioners," *NeuroImage* 57, Issue 4 (2011); Andrew B. Newberg et al., "Meditation Effects on Cognitive Function and Cerebral Flow in Subjects with Memory Loss: A Preliminary Study," *Journal of Alzheimer's Disease* 20, no. 2 (2010); Aleeze Sattar Moss et al., "Effects of an Eight-Week Meditation Program on Mood and Anxiety in Patients with Memory Loss," *Journal of Alternative and Complementary Medicine* 18, no. 1 (2012); Fox, K.C.R., Zakarauskas, P., Dixon, M. L., Ellamil, M., Thompson, E., and Christoff, K. (2012), "Meditation Experience Predicts Introspective Accuracy," PLoS ONE, 7(9), e45370.

4.   See Boyce, *Mindfulness Revolution,* xiv.

5.   Jon Kabat-Zinn, L. Lipworth, R. Burney, and W. Sellers, "Four-year Follow-up of a Meditation-based Program for the Self-regulation of Chronic Pain; Treatment, Outcomes, and Compliance," *The Clinical Journal of Pain,* 3 no. 1 (1987).

6.   See Susan L. Smalley and Diana Winston, *Fully Present,* 105; Siegel, "Proven Benefits," in Boyce, *Mindfulness Revolution,* 138; Richard J. Davidson, *The Emotional Life of Your Brain* (New York: Hudson Street Press, 2012), 204.

7.   Smalley and Winston, *Fully Present,* 108; Jeffrey M. Schwartz and Sharon Begley, *The Mind and The Brain* (New York: Regan Books, 2002), 249–50.

8.   See Mark Wheeler, "Meditation Reduces Loneliness," *UCLA Newsroom* (website), August 14, 2012, http://newsroom.ucla.edu/portal/ucla /meditation-reduces-loneliness-237463.aspx.

9.   Siegel, "Proven Benefits," 138; Jon Kabat-Zinn, "Indra's Net at Work: The Mainstreaming of Dharma Practice in Society," in Watson, Batchelor, and Claxton eds., *Psychology of Awakening,* 225–49, 241–44.

10. Richard J. Davidson "Alterations in Brain and Immune Function Produced by Mindfulness Meditation," *Psychosomatic Medicine,* Vol. 65 No. 4 (2003).

11. Lawrence Peltz, "Mindfulness and Addiction Recovery," in Boyce, *Mindfulness Revolution,* 159–165.

12. Smalley and Winston, *Fully Present,* 219.

13. Davidson, *Emotional Life,* 201.

14. Ibid.

15. Smaley and Winston, *Fully Present,* 155.

16. Ibid.

17. Ibid.

18. Andrew Newberg, "Meditation and Neurodegenerative Disease" (lecture, Advances in Meditation Research Conference, New York, January 17, 2013). Remarkably, Newberg's study showed changes in brain function after only eight weeks of practice.

19. Tim Gard, "Meditation Effects on Protecting against Age-related Deficits in Cognition and Associated Neuroimaging Measures" (lecture, Advances in Meditation Research Conference, New York, January 17, 2013). Lifestyle factors such as cognitive training, exercise, social engagement, and diet can also modify the rate of decline. Brenda L. Plassman et al., "Systematic Review: Factors Associated With Risk for and Possible Prevention of Cognitive Decline in Later Life," *Annals of Internal Medicine* 153, no. 3 (2010).

20. Yi-Yuan Tang, et al. "Central and Autonomic Nervous System Interaction Is Altered by Short-Term Meditation," *PNAS*, Vol. 106 No. 22 (2009).

21. R. A. Baer, et al, "Using Self-Report Assessment Methods to Explore Facets of Mindfulness." (2006) Assessment 13 (1), 27–45. See Siegel, *Mindful Brain*, 91–95.

22. See Jeff Warren, *The Head Trip* (New York: Random House, 2007), 300.

23. Norman Doidge, *The Brain That Changes Itself* (New York: Penguin, 2007).

24. Doidge, *Brain That Changes*, 109–12. Plasticity also accounts for how brains can become addicted. See www.beinghuman.org/article/interview-eric -nestler-dark-side-brain-plasticity.

25. Doidge, *Brain That Changes*, 114.

26. See Doidge, *Brain That Changes*, 113–14.

27. Rael Cahn, "Cultivation of Awareness: Neural Correlates to the Enhanced Clarity and Decreased Automated Reactivity During Vipassana Meditation" (lecture, Advances in Meditation Research Conference, New York, January 17, 2013).

28. Davidson, *Emotional Life*, 213–14.

29. Davidson, *Emotional Life*.

30. Davidson, *Emotional Life*, 208–09.

31. Smalley and Winston, *Fully Present*, 157.

32. Siegel, *Mindful Brain*, 111–114, citing Cahn and Polich, "Meditation States and Traits."

33. Davidson, *Emotional Life*, 216, citing Davidson (2007). Interestingly, the most experienced meditators showed less activity, suggesting the concentration practice was easier for them.

34. Eileen Luders, "Exploring Age-related Brain Degeneration in Long-Term Meditation Practitioners" (lecture, Advances in Meditation Research Conference, New York, January 17, 2013).

35. Eileen Luders et al., "Enhanced Brain Connectivity in Long-term Practitioners," *NeuroImage* Vol. 57, Issue 4 (2011). The subjects of Luders's

study used a variety of different practices, primarily Samatha, vipassana, and Zen, and had an average of twenty-three years of meditation experience.

36. Sara Lazar, et al, "Meditation Experience Is Associated with Increased Cortical Thickness," *Neuroreport* Vol. 16, No. 17 (2005).

37. Giussepe Pagnoni and Milios Cekic, "Age Effects on Gray Matter Volume and Attentional Performance in Zen Meditation," *Neurobiology of Aging* Vol. 28, Issue 10 (2007).

38. Davidson, *Emotional Life*, 184.

39. Ryan, *Mindful Nation*, 75–77.

40. Davidson, *Emotional Life*, at 222, citing Davidson 2007.

41. See Siegel, *Mindful Brain*, 337–362.

42. Davidson, *Emotional Life*, 204.

43. Quoted in Terence Gaussen, "The Development of Personhood and the Brain" in Watson, Batchelor, and Claxton, eds., *Psychology of Awakening*, 123–34.

44. On the methodological challenges, see Yi-Yuan Tang, Mary K. Rothbart, and Michael I. Posner, "Neural Correlates of Establishing, Maintaining, and Switching Brainstates," *Trends in Cognitive Sciences* 16, no. 6 (2012). On the limitations of small-scale research studies in general, see John P.A. Ioannidis, "Why Most Published Research Findings are False," *PLoS Med* 2 no. 8 (August 2005): e124. On the limitations of self-reporting, Baer, et al, "Using Self-Report Assessment Methods;" Willoughby Britton, "Mindful Binge Drinking and Blobology," Buddhist Geeks, www.buddhistgeeks .com/2012/11/video-mindful-binge-drinking-and-blobology/.

45. See Britton, "Mindful Binge Drinking and Blobology."

46. See David R. Vago and David Silversweig, "Self-awareness, Self-regulation, and Self-transcendence (S-ART): A Framework for Understanding the Neurobiological Mechanisms of Mindfulness." *Frontiers of Human Neuroscience*, Vol. 6 No. 296 (2012).

47. Alissa Quart, "Neuroscience Under Attack," *New York Times,* November 23, 2012. www.nytimes.com/2012/11/25/opinion/sunday/neuroscience -under-attack.html. But see Gaussen, "Development," in Watson, Batchelor and Claxton, *Psychology of Awakening,* 124–25, noting that material-neurological and psychological accounts describe different levels of phenomena, and one need not reduce to the other.

48. Bernard Faure, "A Gray Matter: Another Look at Buddhism and Neuroscience," *Tricycle,* Winter 2012, 73. Unfortunately, Faure himself overgeneralizes as well, describing mindfulness as "usually regarded as a rudimentary practice," for example. This may be true of Vajrayana practitioners, but the Buddha described it as "the direct path to realization"—hardly rudimentary. Faure also alleges that the neuroscientific

studies are in the service of a dark, pharmaceutical conspiracy. Since I am sure Faure knows as many of the researchers personally as I do, I am not sure how he can possibly make that charge. The ones I have met are sincerely motivated by curiosity and an optimism that the dharma can reduce suffering. If they wanted to make money from drug companies, they could have sold out long ago. Unfortunately, much of Faure's article is a rant by an Orthodox Buddhist and Buddhist scholar who is unhappy that the dharma has evolved beyond its traditional containers and contexts.

49. Donald S. Lopez, *The Scientific Buddha* (New Haven, CT: Yale University Press, 2012), Chapter Four.

50. Donald S. Lopez, "The Scientific Buddha." *Tricycle*, Winter 2012. www.tricycle.com/feature/scientific-buddha.

51. Lama Surya Das, *Awakening the Buddha Within*, xiii.

52. Batchelor, *Buddhism Without Beliefs* (New York: Riverhead Books, 1997), 10.

53. See Smalley and Winston, *Fully Present*, 108.

Chapter 3

1. Jack Kornfield, "American Buddhism," in Don Morreale, ed., *The Complete Guide to Buddhist America*, xxi–xxx.

2. See Boucher, *Turning the Wheel*; Rita M. Gross, *Buddhism After Patriarchy: A Feminist History, Analysis, and Reconstruction of Buddhism* (Albany: State University of New York Press, 1993); Rita M. Gross, "Helping the Iron Bird Fly: Western Buddhist Women and Issues of Authority in the Late 1990s," in Prebish and Tanaka, *Faces of Buddhism*, 238–52; Seager, *Buddhism in America*, 188–94.

3. See, e.g., Boucher, *Turning the Wheel*, 326–335; Coleman, *The New Buddhism*, 83–85. Of course, there have also been controversies and disputes. See also Boucher, 154–61.

4. Boucher, *Turning the Wheel*, 117. Sandy Boucher has suggested that, in fact, early Buddhist communities invested monks with a high degree of autonomy, and it was only later that the more authoritarian models arose.

5. See Prebish, *Luminous Passage*, 250.

6. Kornfield, "American Buddhism," xxix.

7. For some of the early history of the "cybersangha," see Prebish, *Luminous Passage*, 203–32; Steve Silberman, "Digital Mindfulness," in *Mindfulness Revolution*, 84–90.

8. David Chapman, *Meaningness* (blog), http://meaningness.wordpress.com/

9. See Batchelor, *Awakening*, 212; Prebish, *Luminous Passage*, 8–20.

10. Chapman, "'Nice' Buddhism," *Meaningness* (blog), http://meaningness .wordpress.com/2011/06/10/nice-buddhism/. "The subliminal message of

much of its marketing is 'if you belong to our religion, then you are allowed to feel you are ethical enough.'"

11. Cula Malunkya Sutta, Majjhima Nikaya, 63.

12. See Batchelor, *Buddhism without Beliefs*, 14.

13. See Stephen Batchelor and John Peacock, "Uncertain Minds: How the West Misunderstands Buddhism" (lecture presented at St. Paul's Cathedral, London, March 21, 2001).

14. See Sam Harris, "Killing the Buddha," *Shambhala Sun,* March 2006. For example, "neo-atheist" Sam Harris, never one to spare reductionism when it comes to a religion, claims that "In many respects, Buddhism is very much like science." This, of course, is as absurd as it is offensive. Clearly, Buddhism generally and Buddhist meditation may be scientific, or they may not be. Harris makes a strong case for extracting Buddhist meditation from Buddhism, with which this book is centrally concerned, but these ahistorical and incorrect claims about what Buddhism "is" are inaccurate, Eurocentric, and arrogant.

15. Matthew O'Connell, "Post-Traditional Buddhism: The Quiet Revolution?" *Elephant,* www.elephantjournal.com/2012/11/post-traditional-buddhism -the-quiet-revolution-part-one-matthew-oconnell/.

16. O'Connell, "Post-Traditional Buddhism?"

17. O'Connell, "Post-Traditional Buddhism?"

18. Glenn Wallis, "X-buddhist Provocateurs?" http://speculativenonbuddhism .com/2012/12/09/x-buddhist-provocateurs/.

19. Wallis, "X-buddhist Provocateurs?"; Glenn Wallis, "Nascent Speculative Non-Buddhism," glennwallis.com.

20. Lopez, *Scientific Buddha,* 67.

21. Imamura, "Buddhist and Western Psychotherapies," 235.

Chapter 4

1. See Huston Smith, *Cleansing the Doors of Perception* (New York: Penguin, 2000); Jack Kornfield, *After the Ecstasy, The Laundry* (New York: Bantam Books, 2000), 16–20. Kenneth Folk compared psychedelics and meditation this way: "LSD, although it does hack the brain in really useful ways, has got its downsides: you come down after you get high; you can have a bad trip; you can't control the dosage; and you haven't gained the facility to reproduce these experiences on demand. So for me it's a profoundly unsatisfactory way to hack the brain. And so one reason I have so enthusiastically embraced meditation as a way to hack the brain over the years is these states and insights that we get from meditation are reproducible."

2. Fred Travis and Jonathan Shear, "Focused Attention, Open Monitoring and

Automatic Self-transcending," *Consciousness and Cognition,* Vol. 19, Issue (2010). See also Warren, *Head Trip,* 289.

3.   See Antoine Lutz, John D. Dunne, Richard J. Davidson, "Meditation and the Neuroscience of Consciousness" in *The Cambridge Handbook of Consciousness,* ed. Philip David Zalano, Morris Moscovich and Evan Thompson (New York: Cambridge University Press, 2007); Zoran Jospiovic, "Duality and Nonduality in Meditation Research," *Consciousness and Cognition,* Vol. 19, Issue 4 (2010); Jake H. Davis and Evan Thompson, "From the Five Aggregates to Phenomenal Consciousness: Towards a Cross-cultural Cognitive Science," in *Blackwell Companion to Buddhist Philosophy,* ed. Steven M. Emmanuel (Hoboken, NJ: Wiley-Blackwell, 2012).

4.   See Richard Shankman, *The Experience of Samadhi* (Boston: Shambhala, 2008), 79–83, 97–100; Shaila Catherine, *Focused and Fearless* (Somerville, MA: Wisdom, 2008), 153–59.

5.   See Ajahn Brahm, *Mindfulness, Bliss, and Beyond* (Somerville, MA: Wisdom, 2006), 21–23, 137–149.

6.   See Brahm, *Mindfulness,* 25–28; Leigh Brasington, "Sharpening Manjushri's Sword," www.leighb.com/jhana2a.htm.

7.   For other accounts, see Brahm, *Mindfulness,* 127–72; Catherine, *Focused and Fearless,* 121–51; Shankman, *Experience of Samadhi,* 32–48; Warren, *Head Trip,* 282–87.

8.   Quoted in Fields, *Swans,* 321.

Chapter 5

1.   See Goldstein, *One Dharma,* 157–83; Seager, *Buddhism in America,* 24.

2.   See Schmidt, *Dzogchen Primer;* Keith Dowman, ed., *Flight of the Garuda: The Dzogchen Tradition of Tibetan Buddhism* (Somerville, MA: Wisdom, 1994).

3.   Batchelor, *Awakening,* 207–9.

4.   See Francis Dojun Cook, *How to Raise an Ox* (Somerville, MA: Wisdom, 2001), 2–3; Kornfield, *After the Ecstasy,* 10–11; Goldstein, *One Dharma,* 173–75.

5.   Jeff Warren, "The Anxiety of the Long-Distance Meditator," *New York Times,* Dec. 17, 2012.

6.   Mahasi Sayadaw, "The Progress of Insight (Visuddhiñana-katha)," translated from Pali Nyanaponika Thera (Kandy, Sri Lanka: Buddhist Publication Society, 1994).

7.   For others' accounts of this particular path, see Ingram, *Mastering the Core Techniques of the Buddha;* Brahm, *Mindfulness, Bliss and Beyond;* Kornfield, *A Path With Heart.* For one account of the Tibetan three year-retreat, see

Ken McLeod, "The Three Year Retreat," in Morreale, *Complete Guide*, 229–34.

8. See Daniel Goleman, *The Meditative Mind* (New York: Putnam, 1988), 1–38; Daniel Ingram, *Mastering the Core Teachings of the Buddha* (London: Aeon Books, 2008); Goldstein, *One Dharma*, 161–67; Mahasi Sayadaw, *Practical Insight Meditation* (Kandy, Sri Lanka: Buddhist Publication Society, 1971); Brahm, *Mindfulness, Bliss, and Beyond*; Warren, *Head Trip*, 296–99.

9. Brahm, *Mindfulness, Bliss, and Beyond*, 211–230.

10. See Kornfield, *After the Ecstasy*, 110–12; Brahm, *Mindfulness, Bliss, and Beyond*, 231–54; Shankman, *The Experience of Samadhi*, 187-88.

11. See also Goldstein, *One Dharma*, 161–67; Brahm, *Mindfulness, Bliss, and Beyond*, 173–210.

12. Hakuin, the seventeenth-century Zen master mentioned above, stated that after his first *kensho*, "I was overcome by the Great Doubt." Quoted in Batchelor, *Awakening*, 207.

13. See Kornfield, *After the Ecstasy*, 113–17.

14. See Willoughby B. Britton, "The Dark Night Project," *Buddhist Geeks*, audio podcast, 26:31. www.buddhistgeeks.com/2011/09/bg-232-the-dark -night-project/; Shauna L. Shapiro, Roger Walsh, and Willoughby B. Britton, "An Analysis of Recent Meditation Research and Suggestions for Future Directions," *Journal for Meditation and Meditation Research* Vol. 3 (2003): 69–90. http://brittonlab.files.wordpress.com/2011/03/pdf4.pdf.

15. See Kornfield, *After the Ecstasy*, 61–106.

16. Brahm, *Mindfulness, Bliss, and Beyond*, 213.

17. Ibid., 214.

Chapter 7

1. David Loy, "Can Mindfulness Change a Corporation?" Turning Wheel Media, Feb. 19, 2013, www.buddhistpeacefellowship.org/can-mindfulness -change-a-corporation/.

2. Quoted in Seager, *Buddhism in America*, 245.

3. Quoted in Seager, *Buddhism in America*, 151.

4. Kornfield, *After the Ecstasy*, 161–71.

5. Kabat-Zinn, *Full Catastrophe Living*, 17.

6. See Kornfield, *After the Ecstasy*, 193–215.

7. On ways to stick with practice more effectively, see Kabat-Zinn, *Full Catastrophe Living*, 431–36.

8. Kabat-Zinn, *Full Catastrophe Living*, 33–40.

9. We Wu Wei, *Ask the Awakened* (Boulder, CO: Sentient, 2002), 23.

Chapter 8

1. On the BuJu phenomenon, see Seager, *Buddhism in America*, 225–31; Sutin, *All Is Change*, 277; Sylvia Boorstein, *That's Funny, You Don't Look Buddhist* (New York: HarperCollins, 1997); Brenda Shoshanna, *Jewish Dharma* (Philadelphia: Da Capo, 2008); Judith Linzer, *Torah and Dharma* (Northvale, NJ: J. Aronson, 1996).

2. See Seager, *Buddhism in America*, 221–25.

3. See Sutin, *All Is Change*, 277.

4. See Jay Michaelson, "Get Ready for Jewish iSpirituality," *Forward*, February 6, 2013.

5. See, e.g., Dzongsar Jamyang Khentse, *What Makes You Not a Buddhist* (Boston: Shambhala, 2007), 107.

6. See David Harvey, *The Condition of Postmodernity* (Malden, MA: Blackwell, 1990); Mark Siderits, Evan Thompson and Dan Zahavi, ed., *Self, No Self? Perspectives from Analytical, Phenomenological, and Indian Philosophical Traditions* (New York: Oxford University Press, 2010); Donald Lowe, *History of Bourgeois Perception* (Chicago: University of Chicago Press, 1982); Morris Berman, *The Reenchantment of the World* (Ithaca, NY: Cornell University Press, 1981); Charles Taylor, *Sources of the Self* (New York: Cambridge University Press, 1989). See also Jay Michaelson, "Nonduality, Neuroscience, and Postmodernism: The Dream of the Self," *Reality Sandwich*, April 11, 2011.

7. Susan Blackmore, *The Meme Machine* (New York: Oxford University Press, 1999); Susan Blackmore, "Waking from The Meme Dream," in Watson, Batchelor, and Claxton, eds., *Psychology of Awakening*, 112–22.

8. Dawkins coined the term "meme" in *The Selfish Gene*, in 1976.

9. See Richard Brodie, *Virus of the Mind* (New York: Hay House, 1996); Aaron Lynch, *Thought Contagion* (New York: Basic Books, 1996).

10. Daniel Dennett, *Consciousness Explained* (Boston: Little, Brown and Co., 1991), 210, 207.

11. See Blackmore, *Meme Machine*, 219–26.

12. Guy Claxton, "Neurotheology: Buddhism, Cognitive Science, and Mystical Experience," in Watson, Batchelor, and Claxton, eds., *Psychology of Awakening*, 90–111, 97.

13. See Blackmore, *Meme Machine*, 230.

14. Goldstein, *One Dharma*, 160–61.

15. Blackmore, "Waking," 119.

16. Fred Pfeil, "Subjects Without Selves: Contemporary Theory Accounts for the 'I'," in Watson, Batchelor and Claxton, eds., *Psychology of Awakening*, 40–54, 45.

17. Goldstein, *Insight Meditation* (Boston: Shambhala, 2003), 109–13.
18. Blackmore, "Waking," 120.
19. Quoted in Sutin, *All Is Change,* 117. Despite the phenomenological affinity, Hume apparently was not aware of Buddhist thought. Ibid, 114.
20. See Sutin, *All Is Change,* 330–331.
21. Winston Leyland, ed. *Queer Dharma: Voices of Gay Buddhists.* Volume 1. San Francisco: Gay Sunshine Press, 1997; Winston, Leyland, ed. *Queer Dharma: Voices of Gay Buddhists.* Volume 2. San Francisco: Gay Sunshine Press, 1999.
22. See, e.g., Roger Corless, "Coming Out in the Sangha: Queer Community in American Buddhism," in Prebish & Tanaka, eds, *Faces,* 253–65.
23. See Seager, *Buddhism in America,* 194–96.
24. Leonard Zwilling, "Homosexuality As Seen in Indian Buddhist Texts," in Cabezon, ed., *Buddhism, Sexuality, and Gender,* 203–14.
25. See Paul Gordon Schalow, "Kukai and the Tradition of Male Love in Japanese Buddhism," in Cabezon, ed., *Buddhism, Sexuality, and Gender,* 215–30; Ihara Saikaku, *The Great Mirror of Male Love* (Paul Schalow, trans.) (Stanford: Stanford University Press, 1991).
26. Gross, *Buddhism after Patriarchy,* 158.
27. Gross, *Buddhism after Patriarchy,* 165–67.

Chapter 9

1. See Christopher S. Queen, ed., *Engaged Buddhism in the West* (Somerville, MA: Wisdom, 2000); Donald Rothberg, "Responding to the Cries of the World: Socially Engaged Buddhism in North America," in Prebish and Tanaka, *Faces of Buddhism;* Seager, *Buddhism in America,* 201–13; Boucher, *Turning the Wheel,* 263–321; Batchelor, *Awakening,* 353–69; Prebish, *Luminous Passage,* 259–65.
2. See Helena Norberg-Hodge, "Compassion in the Age of the Global Economy," in Watson, Batchelor, and Claxton, eds., *Psychology of Awakening,* 55–67. Norberg-Hodge makes the astute observation that our globalized world of interdependence actually leads to less interdependence; instead of relying on our neighbors and communities, we participate in a global economy with invisible actors in conditions and places we never see.
3. Davidson, *Emotional Life,* at 222, citing Davidson (2007).
4. See Steve Taylor, *Back to Sanity* (Carlsbad, CA: Hay House, 2012); Steve Taylor, "Can Meditation Change the World?" *Out of the Darkness* (blog), *Psychology Today,* www.psychologytoday.com/blog/out-the-darkness/201212/can-meditation-change-the-world.
5. Jonathan Haidt, for example, has proposed five different moral values—harm and care, fairness, authority, in-group loyalty, and purity—and

observed that liberals simply don't have a high value of the third and fourth values, while conservatives weight them more than the first and second. See Jonathan Haidt, "The Moral Roots of Liberals and Conservatives," TED Talks. www.ted.com/talks/jonathan_haidt_on_the_moral_mind.html and http://yourmorals.org. Descriptively, Haidt's taxonomy is a useful one, and helps clarify how conservatives and liberals talk past one another. Normatively, however, surely there are value distinctions according to degree; while in-group loyalty and authority may have evolutionary or social value, an excess of them leads to ethnocentrism, totalitarianism, and even fascism. There are also temporal distinctions between values of use at times of distress, and those of use at times of relative safety; authority may be essential on a life-raft, but dangerous in a church. Thus, while I am intrigued by Haidt's model's descriptive capacity, it is not (and is perhaps not meant to be) a guide to moral reasoning.

6. See Stuart Smithers, "Occupy Buddhism: Or Why the Dalai Lama is a Marxist," *Tricycle,* June 12, 2012. This view, which owes itself to Eurocentric theorizing found in Nietzsche and other nineteenth-century philosophers, continues to be expressed today, e.g. by Marxist theoretician Slavoj Zizek, who describes Western Buddhism as a fetish which props up the status quo of capitalism.

7. Rothberg, "Responding," 275.

8. See Seager, *Buddhism in America,* 201–13; Batchelor, *Awakening,* 353–69; Donald Rothberg, "Responding," 266–86; Kornfield, *After the Ecstasy,* 269–80.

9. Coleman, *New Buddhism,* 117, n. 15.

10. Sutin, *All Is Change,* 334.

11. Seager, *Buddhism in America,* 204; Rothberg, "Responding," 268–73; Fields, *Swans,* 374–78; Sutin, *All Is Change,* 287–91.

12. Boucher, *Turning the Wheel,* 263–70; Seager, *Buddhism in America,* 203–7; Prebish, *Luminous Passage,* 209.

13. Sutin, *All Is Change,* 331–333. Rothberg, "Responding," 267.

14. Sweeping Zen Interview with Bernie Glassman, http://sweepingzen.com /bernie-glassman-interview/.

15. See Stuart Smithers, "Occupy Buddhism," *Tricycle.*

16. Boucher, *Turning the Wheel,* 276–326.

17. Boucher, *Turning the Wheel,* 271–76; Rothberg, "Responding," 266.

18. Gross, *Buddhism after Patriarchy,* 130–32, 167–70.

19. Gross, *Buddhism after Patriarchy,* 11–15, 102–14.

20. Boucher, *Turning the Wheel,* 210–56; Kornfield, *After the Ecstasy,* 139–57; Fields, *Swans,* 362–69; Seager, *Buddhism in America,* 186–87; Coleman, *New Buddhism,* 166–81. Interestingly, the first article in *Tricycle* magazine was about authority and exploitation in Buddhist communities. Seager, *Buddhism in America,* 187.

21. Boucher, *Turning the Wheel,* 210–56, 354–55.
22. See Boucher, *Turning the Wheel,* 214–20.
23. Then again, it may be more widespread than we think. Jack Kornfield conducted a poll of 54 Hindu, Buddhist, and Jain teachers in 1985; thirty-four reported having sex with their students, and half of the students in question felt badly about the affairs. Fields, *Swans,* 365.
24. See Fields, *Swans,* 365–66.
25. Boucher, *Turning the Wheel,* 214–20; Fields, *Swans,* 364.
26. Boucher, *Turning the Wheel,* 240–45.
27. Boucher, *Turning the Wheel,* 245–56; Fields, *Swans,* 362–63.
    28. See Mark Oppenheimer and Ian Lovett, "Zen Groups Distressed by Accusations Against Teacher," *New York Times,* Feb. 11, 2003. www.nytimes.com/2013/02/12/world/asia/zen-buddhists-roiled-by -accusations-against-teacher.html.
29. See Kornfield, *After the Ecstasy,* 148–50 (arguing that celibacy and similar norms do not include our "full humanity").
30. See Sutin, *All Is Change,* 305–17.
31. See Boucher, *Turning the Wheel,* 212. Fields notes that the duration of the power and authority is also problematic. In Japan, practitioners spend three or four years at a Zen center before "graduating" to a post elsewhere. In America, the time commitment is open-ended. Fields, *Swans,* 363.
32. Quoted in Fields, *Swans,* 364.
33. Rita M. Gross, "Helping the Iron Bird Fly: Western Buddhist Women and Issues of Authority in the Late 1990s," in Prebish & Tanaka, eds., the Faces of *Buddhism in America,* 238–52, 239–40.
34. Gross, "Helping," 241–42, 249–50.
35. Gross, "Helping," 241.
36. Lama Surya Das, *Awakening the Buddha Within,* 388–91.
37. See Kornfield, *After the Ecstasy,* 155–57.
38. See Abhisanda Sutta, Anguttara Nikaya, 10.176, Cunda Kammaraputta Sutta, Anguttara Nikaya, 8.39.
39. See Schwartz and Begley, *Mind and the Brain,* 21–53. Schwartz would no doubt strenuously object to this materialism. For the reasons discussed in Chapter Eight, though, I find it liberating rather than limiting.
40. See Doidge, *Brain That Changes Itself,* 112–21.
41. Seager, *Buddhism in America,* 217–21; Goldstein, *One Dharma,* 136–37.

INDEX

ACKNOWLEDGMENTS

Among the four "noble abidings" of Theravada Buddhism—lovingkindness, compassion, joy, and equanimity—gratitude is disappointingly absent. So I'd like to elevate it here, since I am deeply grateful to my teachers, collaborators, and fellow travelers on the path. First and most immediately, to those who agreed to be interviewed for this project: Stephen Batchelor, Sylvia Boorstein, Willoughby Britton, Adam Bucko, Richard Davidson, Kenneth Folk, Daniel Goleman, Vincent Horn, Daniel Ingram, Jon Kabat-Zinn, Susan Piver, Beth Resnick, Lama Surya Das, Anagarika Ñaniko (Oren Sofer), Joe Wielgosz, and Larry Yang. There are many more voices that could have been included here, but these provided so much breadth and insight, I am truly grateful. And to those who helped bring this book to fruition and have supported my work with generosity and care: Josh Baran, Ken Gordon and Daniel Pinchbeck at Evolver, Doug Reil and Emily Boyd and Nick Sanchez at North

Atlantic, Cryptik, James Shaheen at *Tricycle,* Judson Brewer, Daniel Ingram, Willoughby Britton, Harry Reis, Carlo Maria Ampil, Simon Abramson, Ben Rosenthal, Charles Halpern, Ed Hall, Brent Kideckel, and Ross Schwartz. To my dharma teachers past and present: Guy Armstrong, Rebecca Bradshaw, Sylvia Boorstein, Leigh Brasington, Seth Castleman, David Cooper, Shoshana Cooper, Keith Dowman, Steven Fulder, Joseph Goldstein, Ven. U Jagara, Ven. Pa Auk Sayadaw, Jeff Roth, Sharon Salzberg, Eliezer Sobel, Lama Surya Das, Christopher Titmuss, Ven. Vivekananda, and Sheila Peltz Weinberg. Finally, I would like to dedicate this book to my *kalyana mitta,* my noble friends, contemplative fellow travelers including but definitely not limited to my soul mate, Paul Dakin, Jacob Staub, Beth Resnick and Kenneth Folk, Bob Pileggi, Jill Hammer and Shoshana Jedwab, Oren Sofer, Joe Wielgosz, David Bauer, Eliezer Sobel, Shir Yaakov, David Ingber, Ari Weller, Roman Palitsky, Michael Kelly, John Stasio, and all those who have sat, chanted, studied, processed, breathed, debated, and striven alongside me for the happiness that does not depend upon conditions.

ABOUT THE AUTHOR

Photo by Kobi Sofer

Jay Michaelson is vice president of the Arcus Foundation, a leading funder of LGBT causes, as well as a writer and scholar of contemplative practice. He holds a PhD in Jewish Thought from Hebrew University of Jerusalem, a JD from Yale Law School, an MFA from Sarah Lawrence, and a BA from Columbia. His work on behalf of sexual minorities in religious communities has been featured in the *New York Times,* and on NPR and CNN. Michaelson has held teaching positions at Yale University, Boston University Law School, and City College, and has taught meditation at institutions from Kripalu to Burning Man. His writing appears regularly in the *Forward* newspaper, the Daily Beast, *Tricycle,* and the Huffington Post. In addition to founding four nonprofit organizations and one software company, Michaelson is the author of five books, most recently *God vs. Gay? The Religious Case for Equality,* a 2012 Lambda Literary Award finalist. He is qualified to teach in the Theravadan Buddhist tradition, Mahasi Sayadaw lineage.